Vampires and Fleas

A History of British Aircraft Preservation

Vampires
and Fleas

A History of British Aircraft Preservation

Alec Brew

The Crowood Press

First published in 2003 by
The Crowood Press Ltd
Ramsbury, Marlborough
Wiltshire SN8 2HR

www.crowood.com

British Library Cataloguing-in-Publication Data
A catalogue record for this book is available from the British Library.

ISBN 1 86126 631 6

Picture credits
A number of people have provided me with pictures for use in this
book. I have to thank Barry Abraham, Mark Ansell, Murray Flint, Nick
Forder, Steve Hague, Howard Heeley, Robert Rudhall, Graham
Sparkes, Steve Thompson and Julian Temple.

Frontispiece: A Flying Flea flying once again – the Aeroplane
Collection's Flea 'flying' into the Lower Byrom Street warehouse at
the Museum of Science and Industry, Manchester, to be used in a
design exhibition featuring ergonomics. Three MSIM staff look on
anxiously.

Typeset by Carreg Limited, Ross-on-Wye, Herefordshire
Reprographics by Black Cat Graphics, Bristol.
Printed and bound in Great Britain by Bookcraft, Midsomer Norton

Contents

Introduction

THE twentieth century was the century of the aeroplane. With its development, the world shrank, as people from different countries were brought together with increasing ease; at the same time, it totally altered the nature of war. On one level, the existence of aircraft-borne weapons made war too terrible even to contemplate; on another, it gave armed forces the capability to wage and win wars, as in Kosovo at the very end of the century, without significant losses of their own personnel and without ground or sea forces being involved.

If history starts when young men grow old and remember their youth, confirmation of this comes when interest in the history of a new technology begins to take hold. In the mid-1930s, a few rich young men began to take an interest in preserving old aircraft, but it was not until the 1960s that an aircraft preservation movement began to take shape in Britain. In 1967, the interests of a few individuals and a handful of disparate groups came together, and a new movement was born. In the last few decades, that movement has grown from a few scattered individuals and groups to an organization of a significant size. Under its umbrella, thousands of people are engaged in the preservation and restoration of old aircraft, working by themselves, or under the auspices of one of the hundreds of voluntary groups or official museums.

This is the story of a movement born out of enthusiasm, and as such *Vampires and Fleas* aims to concentrate on the amateur preservationists and the aircraft they saved. On the whole it is not the story of the people who own and fly old aircraft, whether for their own pleasure or, for good practical reasons, to feed the demands of the air-show industry or the film-makers. It is true that the best place to see a preserved aircraft is in the air, but the story of the vintage aircraft operator is a different one, although the demarcation lines are often blurred.

This is the story of a number of dedicated enthusiasts up and down the country, engaged in a labour of love. They have worked away (and continue to do so) week after week in freezing workshops, with few facilities and even less money, with the sole aim of restoring derelict old aircraft to their former glory.

CHAPTER 1

Beginnings

THE FIRST MUSEUM PIECE

THE Aeroplane for 4 June 1930 carried a short news item noting that the British government had been asked to consider acquiring Amy Johnson's Gipsy Moth, *Jason*, to secure it as a national treasure. The indomitable C.G. Grey, long-time editor of *The Aeroplane*, had something to say about the proposal in his editorial:

> What a silly question! Has anyone wanted to acquire as a national trophy Mr Hinkler's Avian which went to Australia in seven days' less time, or the Handley Page which first flew to India, or the Vickers Vimy which first flew to Australia? If we were to start on this sort of thing, we should want all London as a junk heap within a few years unless our racial habit of pioneering became atrophied. (C.G.G.)

Fortunately, despite Grey's opposition, Amy Johnson's Gipsy Moth was acquired for the nation and now forms part of the National Aeronautical Collection in London's Science Museum. Bert Hinkler's Avro Avian was preserved by Australia, the land of his birth, and now resides in Brisbane, but, tragically, the Handley Page that went to India and the Vimy that made it to Australia are no more. Instead, a replica of the Vimy was built to re-create the flight for its seventy-fifth anniversary.

Although C.G. Grey's 1930 editorial did not reflect it, aircraft preservation had already been a fact of life in Britain for a number of years. The first aircraft received by the Science Museum, the founder member of its National Aeronautical Collection, was the Cody biplane, which had been built after the Military Aircraft Competition in 1912. After a total flying time of only about $2^{1}/_{2}$ hours it was prepared for presentation to the Science Museum the following year, becoming the institution's first aircraft, and the first aircraft presented in this way to any British museum. In fact, the Science Museum had first become involved in the preservation of aeronautica as long ago as 1896, when Sir Hiram Maxim presented the steam engine and propeller from his giant aircraft, as well as a model of the machine.

A National War Museum

In 1917 the first official moves to create a national aircraft museum were made when Lord Rothermere, Secretary of State for Air, pushed through a decree in the Air Council. It stated that one example of every Royal Flying Corps and Royal Naval Air Service aircraft should be put aside for preservation, upon the type's retirement from military service. Discussions were held on the setting up of a national aircraft museum, and for a while an exhibition of many types was held in the National Agricultural Hall in Islington, north London.

However, in March 1917, the government had already decided that a national war museum should be set up, to commemorate for all time the effort and sacrifice of the Great War. With the support of the Dominion governments, the title Imperial War Museum was bestowed upon this institution. Most of the aircraft that had been displayed in Islington were passed on to the new museum, but perhaps the Royal Air Force, founded as recently as April 1918, was too young a service to worry about preserving its history. After the end of the war, its very survival was a matter of far greater urgency.

The Imperial War Museum was formally established in 1920, with a Board of Trustees, and on 2 July King George V declared the museum open in its temporary home in the Crystal Palace. It remained there until the end of 1923, but was then moved to the then Western Galleries of the Imperial Institute in South Kensington, south-west London, reopening on 11 November 1924. It remained on this site until 1935, when it was moved once again, this time to part of the former Bedlam Hospital in Lambeth, south London. The Duke of York, later King George VI, reopened the museum on 7 July 1936, and it has remained in the same location in Lambeth ever since.

Bedlam was probably an appropriate home for a museum about the Great War, but within its relatively small galleries there was not a great deal of room for aircraft, with all the other impediments of war. A handful of aircraft were displayed in the building, usually suspended above the other exhibits. These included the Short Type 184 seaplane, which flew at the Battle of Jutland, a Sopwith Camel, an RE.8, a BE.2C and a Bristol F.2B Fighter.

The museum suffered bomb damage during the Second World War, and the Short Type 184 was badly damaged. The building was closed to the public until 1946, by which time its remit had been extended to include the commemoration of the Second World War, and, subsequently, all the other wars of the twentieth century. A small number of Second World War aircraft found their way into the museum's crowded galleries, including a Spitfire, a Swordfish, a Lancaster nose, a Mosquito and, later on, a Meteor F.8.

The Science Museum

In 1928 the Science Museum's Aeronautical Collection, which by now had been augmented with several other significant aircraft, including A.V. Roe's first successful triplane, Alcock and Brown's Vickers Vimy and an Antoinette monoplane presented by Robert Blackburn, was enhanced with the most famous aircraft in the world. The first-ever aircraft, the Wright Brothers 1903 Flyer, was placed on loan, because the Wrights had fallen out with the Smithsonian Institute over their claims to pre-eminence.

The Flyer remained on display in London for twenty years, except during the war years, when it was stored in the London Underground for safety. The aircraft returned to the USA in 1948, and was thenceforth displayed in the Smithsonian Institute. It was replaced in London's Science Museum by an exact replica built by apprentices at de Havilland Aircraft.

The Science Museum's aircraft were displayed in the nearby Imperial Institute, in South Kensington, after the Imperial War Museum moved out, and remained there until the museum's new central building was built in the mid-1950s. A Flight Gallery was constructed on the top of that, and all the historic aircraft were displayed within this gallery, including many that had remained in store.

By then, the National Aeronautical Collection, as it had become known, included many other significant aircraft. Its JAP-Harding monoplane, Supermarine S.6B, Gloster E.28/39, Cierva Autogyro, SE.5A, Avro 504K, Fokker E.III, Hurricane, Spitfire, Me163B, V-1, Oka II Baka, Hill Pterodactyl and of course Amy Johnson's Gipsy Moth, were all on display, but there was a distinct lack of space. Some of the Science Museum's aircraft, such as the Handley Page HP.39 Gugnunc and Harry Dolman's Flying Flea, G-AEHM, presented to the collection in 1938, had to remain in store at Hayes in Middlesex, just outside London, until larger premises could be found.

RICHARD SHUTTLEWORTH AND HIS COLLECTION

Arguably, amateur aircraft preservation in Britain really began in Bedford, one day in 1935. At the end of a meeting to consider the construction of a Bedford Municipal Airport, local garage owner A.E. Grimmer had an interesting conversation with Richard Ormonde Shuttleworth from Old Warden. Grimmer knew that Shuttleworth was both a pilot and a collector of interesting vintage machinery, and offered to him free of charge his own two aircraft, a Bleriot monoplane and a Deperdussin monoplane.

Shuttleworth was a wealthy young man with ancestral links to the firm of Clayton and Shuttleworth, the Lincoln engineering company that had constructed several hundred aircraft during the First World War. The Shuttleworth family home at Old Warden was part of a considerable estate. Richard Shuttleworth was well known as a gentleman racing driver at Brooklands, with a healthy interest in old machinery. He bought a 1898 Panhard Levasseur car, for the princely sum of 25 shillings, and, after refurbishment, entered it in the

1929 London to Brighton run. He continued to seek out old vehicles, and his collection soon expanded to include motorbikes, cycles and horse-drawn vehicles. He refurbished them where necessary and returned them to running order, establishing the philosophy that continues in the Shuttleworth Trust to this day.

After Shuttleworth had learned to fly in 1932, he bought a four-year-old de Havilland DH.60X Moth, G-EBWD, and arranged the construction of a grass airfield with a small hangar for it on the family's land, alongside the Biggleswade Road. (Many years ago, this Moth set the record for one aircraft being based on the same airfield; with every year that passes, that record increases.) The Warden Engineering Company was set up to operate the airfield; it was based in the small hangar, with offices above.

His interest in aviation thoroughly aroused, Richard Shuttleworth went on to found the Warden Aviation Company, based at Heston, where he operated three Desoutter cabin monoplanes and a DH Dragon. For a short time, the Dragon was fitted out for aerial advertising flights, with an external light-bulb array. Shuttleworth also became a Director of Pobjoy Airmotor and Comper Aircraft, and flew a Comper Swift on a sales tour to India.

A.E. Grimmer had bought the first of his aircraft, the Bleriot Type XI, in 1912, after it had suffered a crash. He rebuilt it and flew it off and on until it was put into store at the outbreak of war. In 1914 he bought the Deperdussin monoplane, and also rebuilt and flew that for a while. After the war, Grimmer's aircraft were stored in Ampthill near Bedford, in his garage premises. At the meeting in Bedford in 1935, Grimmer offered the two aircraft to Richard Shuttleworth for free, provided only that they were looked after – and that some 300 empty oil drums were cleared away.

Richard Shuttleworth went to Ampthill the day after the meeting in Bedford, taking with him a friend and two lorries. He found that the two aircraft were little more than wrecks – indeed, an elder tree was growing through the Bleriot's tail, which was lying on a heap of scrap. The two aircraft were transported to Old Warden, and the process of rebuilding them to flying condition began. The rebuild took about eighteen months for each aircraft, but Shuttleworth was able to fly the Bleriot at the Royal Aeronautical Society Garden Party in 1937, 1938 and 1939. The Deperdussin also first flew again in 1937. The two aircraft continue to fly to this day – in very calm weather.

In 1936 Shuttleworth bought the remains of a Sopwith Dove, G-EBKY, the post-war civil conversion of the Sopwith Pup. He restored it to Pup configuration, with the spurious serial N5181. In the same year he bought another little First World War scout, a Hanriot HD.I. He restored this to flying condition as well, but in 1939 a wheel came off during a take-off and the aircraft was badly damaged when it landed. The wings of the Hanriot were lost in the war and the remains were stored until they were sold to a Californian in 1963. This particular aircraft was to return later to the RAF Museum.

To help restore his vintage aircraft Richard Shuttleworth bought a Blackburn Velos, a trainer version of the Blackburn Dart carrier-born torpedo plane. Unfortunately, he dismantled this to use the wood in its construction, rather than adding the aircraft to his collection in its entirety. However, having bought an 'instant collection', and added the Pup and the Hanriot, Shuttleworth went on to expand his fleet whenever possible. In 1937 he discovered and obtained the remains of a Blackburn 1912 Monoplane, largely hidden within a haystack. Its restoration to flying condition was not achieved until after the Second World War, but it is now the oldest flying British aircraft. In the same year he was given the remains of the ANEC II ultra-light monoplane G-EBJO. This aircraft has been stored ever since, and its restoration has only recently begun.

One other aircraft in Shuttleworth's collection, acquired before the Second World War, was the Desoutter G-AAPZ, operated at Heston, but later consigned to the collection at Old Warden, and totally rebuilt to flying condition in the 1990s.

At the outbreak of war, Richard Shuttleworth joined the RAF. The Old Warden airfield was used throughout the war for the refurbishment of light aircraft such as Proctors and Harvards, and during this time acquired a second hangar.

In 1940, Shuttleworth was killed test-flying a Fairey Battle bomber. After the war, his mother founded and endowed the Richard Ormonde Shuttleworth Remembrance Trust in his memory. The Trust's aims were in the area of education in aviation, forestry and agriculture; the themes of forestry and agriculture were catered for at the adjoining Shuttleworth Agricultural College. Old Warden airfield was operated by the Warden Engineering and Aviation Company – the two pre-war firms had been combined – and this became the de facto operating company for the Trust. It did not operate as a museum for many years, but was seen as a repository for the vintage aircraft that various companies found themselves renovating, for one reason or another, over the fifteen or so years after the war. These included the Bristol Fighter restored by the Bristol Aircraft Company in 1952, the SE.5A found at Armstrong-Whitworth and restored at Farnborough in 1959, the Wren restored at English Electric in 1957, and the Humming Bird restored by de Havilland in 1959.

It might seem that the Shuttleworth Trust was the perfect place for these aircraft to go; in fact, it was the only place, for there were no other suitable aircraft museums in Britain. The Trust had become a well-recognized national institution that was totally unique.

NASH AND HIS COLLECTION

Richard Shuttleworth was not the only gentleman racing driver who also took an interest in old aircraft, and began to build up a collection of them during

11

the 1930s. Like Shuttleworth, R.G.J. Nash raced at Brooklands and kept a workshop there. He began building up a collection of vintage vehicles and bicycles from 1929, calling it the International Horseless Carriage Corporation. In 1933 he increased the scope of his collection, beginning to acquire any First World War aircraft that he encountered.

In late 1935, a Sopwith Camel was bought by a Mr D.C. Mason of Hornchurch in Essex. In a letter published in *Popular Flying*, Mr Mason stated his intention to return the Camel to flying condition, even though it had been fitted with a 45hp Anzani engine by a previous owner, which rendered it rather underpowered. The basis of the Camel was F6314, a Boulton and Paul-built example, but it had undergone many restorations and rebuilds over the years, and contained parts of other aircraft, not least the engine. By April 1936, Nash had bought the Camel from Mr Mason and moved it to his store at Brooklands, where it was rebuilt and a Clerget rotary fitted. It was found to be riddled with dry rot, so, although it was taxied at the RAF Pageant at Hendon in June 1936, there was no chance of it being flown. Further restoration was undertaken after this appearance, but the Camel was destined to be consigned to storage with the other Nash aircraft at the outbreak of war.

One co-performer at the 1936 pageant was a Caudron G.III owned by Ken Waller, who had bought it in Belgium earlier that year, and flown it back to Great Britain via Ostend and Lympne. It was allocated the registration G-AETA, and was flown in the display, after which it was bought by Nash. In the same year, Nash also bought the Farman F.40, which was the prototype of the famous Maurice Farman biplane, and had logged 1,040 flying hours, carrying the serial F-FARB. This aircraft also appeared at the 1936 Hendon display, wearing the number '3'.

The oldest aircraft in Nash's collection were two Bleriot monoplanes, a Type XI and a Type XXVIII, the latter having been built for the 1914 Gordon-Bennett Race in the USA. It was overhauled at Brooklands in the years 1937-38. Nash also owned two Avro 504Ks – G-EBJE, which had been in use at Shoreham with Fred Miles until 1934, and E449, which had been converted to an Avro 548 with a 120hp Airdisco engine. The rarest aircraft in Nash's collection were a Fokker D.VII and a Sopwith Triplane, N5912, believed to be the last one built by Oakley & Co. at Ilford.

All of Nash's aircraft were stored, probably at Brooklands, during the war, and they did not re-emerge into public view until 1950, when several of them were refurbished and displayed at Farnborough. The following year they were displayed at Farnborough again, in the Royal Aero Club's 'Fifty Years of Flying' display. In December 1953 the eight aircraft were sold to the Royal Aeronautical Society, with the proviso that they would continue to be known as The Nash Collection, and would never be flown. They were an attractive basis for an aircraft museum, but were destined to remain in store for many years to come, with only brief public appearances.

CHAPTER 2

Skyfame

SUNDERLAND FLYING BOATS

LATE in 1959, Coastal Command attempted to bring back to Britain the last Short Sunderland flying boat from Singapore, where it had been withdrawn from service. The project was thwarted by red tape and the aircraft was not returned. Following the publicity associated with this failure, Welsh farmer Peter Thomas and his wife Gwladys set up a public appeal to raise £15,000 to obtain and transport one of the last Sunderlands operated by the New Zealand Air Force. Support was immediately forthcoming from such eminent figures as Lord Brabazon of Tara, Oswald Short, Sir Phillip Joubert and Sir Alan Cobham.

News came through that the French Navy was still operating three Sunderlands, and was about to retire them. An approach was made with a view to buying one, but, after correspondence between Sir Phillip Joubert and Admiral Suquet, one of the aircraft was offered as a gift. Arrangements were made to fly the aircraft to Pembroke Dock at Milford Haven, and on 24 March 1961 a huge crowd gathered to watch its arrival. The flying boat, ML824, swooped in with an escort of two Shackletons of No.201 Squadron, which had operated Sunderlands during the Second World War. The following day the Sunderland was formally handed over to Oswald Short, President of the newly formed Short Sunderland Trust. For a while, it was kept in a hangar of the old RAF base at Pembroke Dock, now operated by the Navy. Here, cleaning and re-painting could take place, but because of security considerations the aircraft was accessible to the public only on bank holidays.

The aircraft went on display at a new open site in Pembroke Dock, rented from the Admiralty, at Whitsuntide 1962. It was open to the public for just a shilling a head, and 11,000 people paid their bobs in the first year. The following summer a small building was erected for the shelter of the voluntary helpers, which included a replica of a Coastal Command Operations Room; during 1963 there were 12,000 visitors.

In 1964 the exterior of the Sunderland was re-painted, by hand, and the fabric control surfaces, which had rotted in the salt air, were replaced with metal covering. After the completion of the re-painting, Sqn Ldr F.E. Godfrey, Secretary of the Trust and a former flying-boat man, finally managed to equip the flying boat with guns and depth charges. In 1966 the 50,000th visitor toured the Sunderland, which was to continue to attract visitors in West Wales, until it was eventually moved to the Battle of Britain Museum at Hendon.

BIRTH OF A MUSEUM

In preserving the Sunderland, Peter and Gwladys Thomas had become aware of two issues. First, that there was no dedicated aircraft museum in Britain, although the Science Museum in London housed the National Aeronautical Collection on its top floor, and the Imperial War Museum in south London had a few aircraft on display. The Shuttleworth Trust included aircraft among its collection of vintage transport, mostly from pre-1939, but it was not open to the public on a regular basis until 1966. Second, the Thomases were amazed to realize that, just fifteen years after the end of the war, many of the most important British aircraft that had helped to win that war were fast disappearing. In fact, a number of types, such as the Albacore, Blenheim, Hampden, Whitley, Halifax and Barracuda, which existed in their thousands in 1945, were already believed to be extinct.

The Thomases decided to create a museum dedicated to the preservation of the war-winning aircraft that were in danger of disappearing. It would also be intended as a tribute to the many Commonwealth pilots who died in the war, including Peter Thomas's brother Desmond. The search began to track down aircraft and a suitable site. A target list of eight aircraft was drawn up: the collection should include a Mosquito, an Anson 1, an Oxford, a Firefly 1, a Beaufighter, a Blenheim, a Walrus and a Halifax. Of these, only a Mosquito had yet been preserved – the prototype, at the place of its birth, Salisbury Hall. The Thomases were determined that all the aircraft in the new museum would be typical service examples.

A limited company was set up and given the name Skyfame Ltd, and an appeal was made through the press for a suitable site for the museum. Almost at the same time the first aircraft was obtained, as No.3 Civilian Anti-Aircraft Co-operation Unit at Exeter began to retire the last few Mosquitos in service. In April 1963 Peter Thomas travelled to RAF Shawbury where the aircraft had been sent for disposal and bought TA719. Almost immediately he was approached by Film Aviation Services who wanted to use the aircraft, with some of the other ex-No.3 CAACU Mosquitos in the forthcoming Mirisch film production *633 Squadron*.

While the aircraft, with two reconditioned Merlins fitted, was starring in the film, which started shooting in June, an offer was received from the management of Gloucester/Cheltenham Airport at Staverton of a hangar to house the museum. With the Mosquito away, it was Avro Anson 1 N4877 that became the first aircraft to arrive at Staverton, on 31 August. The Mosquito followed on 16 October. (Peter Thomas had seen the Anson, G-AMDA, operated by Derby Aviation with its sister aircraft G-AIPA on radiation tests for fall-out over the Cardigan Bay area in 1962. It was the sight of these two aircraft careering about over West Wales at low altitude that alerted him to the fact that there were, in fact, any early Mark 1 Ansons left; and he made the purchase of one a priority.) These two aircraft were quickly followed by Christopher Storey's Henri Mignet Pou de Ciel (Flying Flea), and Guy Baker's C.30A, G-ACUU, both on indefinite loan from their owners. On 25 March the following year the third type on Peter Thomas's original list joined the collection when Airspeed Oxford V3388 flew into Staverton. This Oxford had been bought post-war by Boulton Paul Aircraft as their communications aircraft, based at Wolverhampton Airport as G-AHTW, and had not long retired from this role.

On the following day, 26 March, a flying demonstration was held at Staverton for the benefit of the press. Two days later, on the Saturday of the Easter weekend, the Skyfame Aircraft Museum was officially opened to the public, as the Desmond Commonwealth Flying Memorial, in commemoration of wartime Wellington pilot Desmond Thomas, Peter Thomas's brother.

Before the first of what were to become regular flying displays was held, on Whit Monday, a sixth aircraft joined the collection. The Fairey Firefly 1 was presented by its owners Svenska of Stockholm, which had been flying the naval fighter as a target tug. The aircraft flew from Sweden to Staverton on 5 May.

During the summer an accident to Mosquito TA719 rendered it no longer flyable, so the museum bought one of the other ex-Exeter stablemates, RS709. The TA719 was relegated to static display.

FULFILLING THE WISH LIST

During 1964 a Skyfame Supporters Society was formed, with an annual subscription of 1 guinea. Members were invited to assist with the maintenance and upkeep of the museum and received a quarterly magazine called *Skyfame Circuit*. Chairman of the Supporters Society was David Ogilvy and Secretary was Pauline Williams.

Having obtained four of the original list of eight aircraft types, Skyfame now purchased one type that was not on the list, an Avro York. G-AGNV was the last flying example and just about to be retired by Dan-Air. The aircraft made its last flight to Staverton on 9 October 1964, escorted by two Hastings of No.24 Squadron. The aircraft was re-painted as Winston Churchill's personal transport during the war, *Ascalon*.

In spring 1965, Skyfame was approached by Graham Johnson of the British Aircraft Corporation and some other enthusiasts from the Bristol area. They had located Miles Magister G-AFBS derelict at Bristol Airport and offered to restore the trainer if Skyfame would buy it. The Skyfame directors immediately agreed and the Magister was moved to Graham Johnson's house where it was restored and painted in RAF colours, before being transported to the museum on 16 October 1965.

Two weeks later the largest known surviving piece of a Halifax, another type on Peter Thomas's original list of eight, was transported to Staverton. It was delivered from the care of Graham Trant and Howard Levy, who had saved it after the cutting-up of the last surviving Halifax in Britain.

This was as far as Skyfame ever got towards obtaining the eight aircraft on its wish list. One or more examples of the other three, Blenheim, Beaufighter and Walrus, were tracked down to various parts of the world over the next few years, and progress made towards obtaining one of each, but for various reasons the deals never came to fruition.

Skyfame continued to obtain aircraft, but in a less structured manner. In February 1966 Percival Proctor G-ALCK arrived from the Royal Observer Corps at Tamworth, which had restored the derelict aircraft over many months, led by Chief Observer Thompson and Leading Observer David Peace. Later in 1966 the College of Aeronautics at Cranfield retired two aircraft from its 'Library of Aircraft' – the Saunders-Roe SR.A1 jet flying boat and the Hawker Tempest 2 – and these were passed into the tender care of Skyfame.

By 1967 the Skyfame Museum had twelve aircraft on display, as well as the Halifax nose, and was well established as the country's first museum dedicated solely to aircraft. More importantly, it had inspired many other people around Britain to become involved in aircraft preservation, making many realize that if action were not taken in the near future, for many aircraft it would be too late. Skyfame, more than any other organization, stopped the rot.

OPEN DAYS AT THE SHUTTLEWORTH TRUST

The Shuttleworth Trust, meanwhile, had made the change from vintage aircraft collection, which displayed its aircraft around the country but was not normally open to the public, to a working aircraft museum. Many of its aircraft had been maintained up to now by covenanted donations by major aircraft companies, but these funds were beginning to run out, and new sources of income were sought.

In June, July and August 1965 a number of open days were held, with a small number of aircraft being flown before crowds that numbered in the hundreds rather than the thousands. In addition the Shuttleworth Veteran Aeroplane Society was formed. At the time, it aimed for a purely passive membership, rather than one that would actively support the Trust in its restoration efforts, and run its new open days.

In 1966 the Trust opened its doors to the public every day, and soon a shop and restaurant were established. The airfield at this time was still quite small, and unsuitable for many aircraft types. During this time a permanent public enclosure was created on the airfield, with two grass runways running almost at right-angles, down each side of this enclosure. These runways were both lengthened so that slightly larger types could operate during flying displays. The layout was a marvellous one for displaying aircraft in the air as pilots could fly curved passes around the enclosure. The Shuttleworth Trust's flying displays, of which there were usually several every year, became a nostalgic and unmissable date in every aircraft enthusiast's diary. Annual trips to Old Warden and to Skyfame had become essential.

CHAPTER 3

Pioneers

EARLY SOCIETIES AND GROUPS

Northern Aircraft Preservation Society

IN January 1963 Britain's first purely enthusiast-based aircraft preservation and restoration organization was born. The Northern Aircraft Preservation Society (NAPS) proved to be the first of a host of such groups that began to proliferate shortly afterwards, inspired by its example. The importance of the creation of this group cannot be underestimated. Its members were demonstrating, for the first time, that obtaining vintage aircraft and restorating them to exhibition standards need not be left entirely to governmental or official organizations, or the very rich. By banding together, 'ordinary' people could also become involved. These were the first signs of the birth of a new nationwide movement.

NAPS was formed out of the Merseyside Society of Aviation Enthusiasts, one of many of the societies of aircraft enthusiasts that existed up and down Britain. The Merseyside group was one of the most influential of those societies, not least because of its publication in May 1961 of the first edition of *Wrecks and Relics*, the first attempted listing of all the non-flying aircraft in the country. *Wrecks and Relics*, now a biennial book from Midland Counties Publications, has become the bible of the aircraft preservation movement, which Merseyside members were to pioneer.

The Merseyside Society had acquired Avro Avian IIIA G-EBZM in 1960, just saving it from being burnt. Built at Avro's Newton Heath works in 1928, the aircraft had been flown by the well-known aviatrix Lady Heath, and subsequently used by the Liverpool and District Aero Club and then Giro Aviation, which flew pleasure flights from Southport Beach. After an accident it had been repaired by Martin Hearn at Hooton, but it was not ready to resume service when war broke out and ended up in storage. It did not fly again, becoming derelict after the war. Two employees of Eagle Aviation at Ringway Airport attempted to restore it to airworthy condition. but had to give up. It was about to be consigned to the flames when it was rescued by the Merseyside Society.

Its history made the Avian an ideal airframe to be preserved by a northern group, but, although their aims were laudable, its new owners were not really geared up to restoring aircraft. It remained in store until December 1962 when it was decided it would be passed on to a new group, which would be formed from those Merseyside members who were interested enough to become involved. The result was NAPS, which was formed with John Kenyon as its first Chairman. The group's immediate aim was to restore the Avian to exhibition standard, but the long-term aim was to collect further aircraft and artefacts, and, eventually, to create a northern aircraft museum.

The Merseyside Society still harboured ambitions to acquire an aircraft and during 1963 the Mosquito target tugs from CAACU Exeter were put up for sale, just in time to star in the film *633 Squadron*. An enquiry was made by MSAE via the local Conservative MP, but the price quoted proved to be well beyond their means. Some energetic lobbying of local councillors followed, and eventually the Liverpool Airport Committee agreed to buy one of the Mosquitos, TA634, with the intention of placing it on display at the main entrance to Speke Airport. This plan did not come to fruition, and, after the aircraft was delivered by air on 6 November 1963, it was kept in Speke's hangars for the next four years.

Meanwhile, NAPS acquired premises in Stockport for work on its Avian. The group members were faced with a bare hulk, without tail surfaces, with only one set of wings and no engine. The slow process of restoring the aircraft and tracking down the missing parts began. Later in the year, in December, the group also purchased Avro Avian IVM G-ABEE, from Selhurst Grammar School. This aircraft had also had a varied career, and somewhere along the way had acquired the fuselage of Avian IVM G-ACKE. As a metal-fuselage machine, G-ABEE was not entirely compatible with G-EBZM, but it did yield a number of spares for its older brother.

In the same month, NAPS also obtained a Slingsby Cadet TX.1 glider from the Avro Gliding Club at Woodford, together with a couple of odd wings. The Cadet TX.1 was a version of the pre-war T.7 Kirby Kadet, slightly modified and ordered in large numbers for the ATC. Later, with tapered wings, it became the Tutor, and the ATC version of this was the Cadet TX.2. NAPS made arrangements for the Cadet to be restored to ATC standards in a Bolton school.

Historic Aircraft Preservation Society

Another aviation society further north had almost pre-dated the entry of the Merseyside group into the world of aircraft preservation. On 17 March 1962 members of the Solway Group of Aviation Enthusiasts discovered the remains of a Hawker Hart trainer, K4972, at the Nelson-Tomlinson School at Wigton, Cumberland. They obtained the permission of the school authorities to examine and remove the Hart, which was in the loft of a building in the grounds. They found to their horror that the floor of the loft was rotten, which entailed some careful manoeuvres, especially as they only just had room to get the fuselage out and down the 10 feet to the ground.

The group made tentative progress towards restoring the remains, which were in extremely bad condition. The engine had been scrapped long ago, to prevent the floor of the loft from collapsing, and the engine bearers had been sawn off. Corrosion had taken its grip on the metal frame, and there was no undercarriage, wheels or propeller. The group decided that the restoration of the Hart was beyond their means and passed the remains on to the Royal Air Force on 16 October 1963, which placed it in storage at Henlow. The aircraft was eventually to be fully restored at RAF St Athan, was on display at Cosford and is now at Hendon.

At the opposite end of the country, in April 1963, the Air Britain, Air Relics Research Group, which had its beginnings in the early part of 1962, severed its connection with Air Britain, and changed its name to the Historic Aircraft Preservation Society. The instigators of this change were Malcolm D.N. Fisher, a young insurance broker, and Russell Snadden, a serving RAF officer, who wished to concentrate more on the preservation of aircraft and less on research. Fisher became Chairman of the new organization, and Snadden became Honorary Secretary. To begin with, the society was limited to twenty-five members for ease of administration, with Ian MacDonald producing a newsletter.

Its first aircraft was obtained only a month later. The Goodyear FG-1A Corsair, KD431, was surplus to requirements at the College of Aeronautics at Cranfield, and it was obtained by the society, which placed it on loan at RNAS Yeovilton. There, it was refurbished and put on display at open days.

Over the next eighteen months three more aircraft were obtained. On the group's own doorstep, at Biggin Hill, the local ATC had Seafire FR.47 VP441 in its 'care', but it had been badly damaged by vandals. The society obtained the Seafire and placed it on loan at RNAS Culdrose, where an extensive restoration was begun. The next aircraft obtained was a Supermarine Walrus, which was found derelict on Thame airfield, near Oxford, without wings or floats. HAPS obtained the aircraft when Russ Snadden handed over £25, and informed the curator of the Fleet Air Arm Museum. He arranged for the Walrus to be taken to RNAS Arbroath where the massive restoration task was undertaken by the RN Engineering School.

The Fleet Air Arm Museum

The Fleet Air Arm Museum itself was only just at the point of being formed. In the days before the A303 Ilchester bypass, the main route from the south to the south-west holiday region went right by RNAS Yeovilton. In an attempt to stop the road being blocked by passers-by stopping to watch the flying, a small display area was created at the instigation of the station C.O., Captain R.H.P. Carver, CBE, DSC. To add a little more interest, three historic aircraft – a Grumman Martlet, a Fairey Swordfish and a Supermarine Seafire – were parked alongside this area. There was such a good response to this small display that the Fleet Air Arm decided to create a permanent museum on the spot, utilizing one of the four hangars located in that part of the base. This helped overcome the maintenance problems of displaying the aircraft outdoors, and also coincided with the celebrations of the fiftieth anniversary of the creation of the Fleet Air Arm, which took place in May 1914.

The new Fleet Air Arm Museum was opened in May 1964 by HRH the Duke of Edinburgh, who was himself a matelot and an aviator. It was the first museum to be set up by any of the three services, and one of the first such museums anywhere in the world. The museum contained the HAPS Corsair, alongside other World War Two aircraft collected from other Fleet Air Arm Stations, including a Martlet (Wildcat), a Swordfish, an Avenger, a Seafire, and a Firefly that had been recently bought in Australia by the crew of HMS *Victorious*, and transported back aboard the carrier. In addition to these a representative collection of post-war Fleet Air Arm aircraft were gathered, including a Sea Hawk, a Sea Vampire, a Sea Fury, an Attacker, a Dragonfly, a Vampire T.22 and the locally built Wyvern. Outside the main door stood a Buccaneer S.1 prototype, which was to remain there for the next thirty-five years.

The Fleet Air Arm Museum became, with London's Science Museum and the Imperial War Museum, the third national museum displaying aircraft, alongside the two private collections at Shuttleworth and Skyfame.

Newark Air Museum
The Historic Aircraft Preservation Society was not the second voluntary society to enter the field, but the third. In 1963, in Nottinghamshire, another voluntary group had been born soon after NAPS, when Charles Waterfall and Neville Franklin banded together to create the group that became Newark Air Museum. Their first major acquisitions were Westland Wallace airframe parts secured from the undergrowth around RAF Cranwell.

DEVELOPING THE COLLECTIONS

In June 1964, NAPS acquired its first Henry Mignet HM.14 Pou de Ciel, the ubiquitous Flying Flea. This one had been built by S.O. Whiteley in Oldham in 1936 and, after only one attempt at flight, had been hung in the roof of his factory. The original Austin Seven engine disappeared but, after the Flying Flea had been acquired and restored by NAPS, a Scott A2S was installed. While being transported from Oldham to NAPS premises, the little aircraft made one last desperate attempt at becoming airborne, when the main wing tore free from the van on which it was being carried.

In February 1965, NAPS was given a BA Swallow, which had been deprived of its C of A at Carlisle because of glue failure. The aircraft was complete but for the engine; a replacement was soon obtained – ex-Mosscraft MA.1 G-AFMS, which had crashed at Yeadon. In the same month NAPS acquired Percival Proctor IV NP294. This sudden influx of larger aircraft – large, at least, for a group of under-funded amateurs – created a storage problem. It was solved by loaning the Proctor to the Lincolnshire Aircraft Preservation Society, which had recently formed in the Grimsby area.

On 13 May 1965 a magnificent event took place at the historic airfield of Biggin Hill. Avro Lancaster NX611 touched down after a 14,000-mile flight from Noumea in New Caledonia, where she had been serving with the Aeronavale. After being retired from active service she was acquired by the Historic Aircraft Preservation Society, which had raised the necessary £10,000 by donation and sponsorship, and via the generous assistance of many bodies, not least the Royal Australian Air Force, the Royal Air Force, Shell Petroleum and Hawker-Siddeley. The twenty-five members of HAPS organized the flight of the aircraft to Bankstown, New South Wales, in July 1964, while they found backers to return the aircraft to Britain. Their intention was to maintain the aircraft in flying condition, as a tribute to the sacrifices of Bomber Command during the Second World War.

Bringing the Lancaster back to Britain demanded a colossal effort by those concerned, which would not be equalled by any voluntary preservation group for many years. However, those who believed that the touchdown of NX611 on a British runway was the triumphant end to an interesting story were to be sadly mistaken; in fact, the Lancaster's arrival only marked the beginning of a saga of achievements and tragedies worthy of a Shakespeare play. Fortunately, the saga was to have a happy ending, but not for another quarter of a century.

Having already acquired two Avians, the Northern Aircraft Preservation Society bought its second Flying Flea in December 1965. It had been built by L.W. Taylor at Knutsford in 1937 and featured a moving rear wing, the modification that solved the Flea's fatal characteristic, which enabled it to enter a dive from which the pilot could not recover. This Flea had even been flown post-war in the Tenbury Wells area.

In January 1966, NAPS acquired a veritable fleet of gliders. E.W.T. Addyman of Harrogate had been the Secretary of the Harrogate Aero Club, designing and building a standard training glider (STG) for them in 1934. A second, slightly modified STG had been started in 1936 but had not been completed, as the club ceased flying in the same year. Mr Addyman then began the construction of an ultra-light aircraft powered by an Anzani engine, but this was not completed either. All three aircraft remained with the Addyman estate, which was sold to the local council in 1965; the council passed the aircraft on to NAPS in the following year.

In August 1965, the Italian Air Force presented a Sabre Mk.4 to the Historic Aircraft Preservation Society. The aircraft had been XB546, when it served with the Royal Air Force in the mid-1950s before being passed on to to the Italians. How should HAPS approach the problem of bringing the aircraft back from

Italy by road? In charge of transport on the ground were committee members Rodney Brown and Bernard Clarkson, and HAPS's pilot was Roy Perrin. For the first time a voluntary group was faced with dismantling an all-metal aircraft, and arranging its transportation by road over some distance. HAPS succeeded in the challenge, with the help of Manchester Tankers and sponsorship from J D Kay and Canadair.

At about the same time, the group obtained a Horsa glider fuselage and a Percival Proctor G-AOAR, which was painted up in military markings with the serial NP181.

FINDING A MUSEUM LOCATION

The problems of running a voluntary society with only twenty-five members were becoming acutely apparent in HAPS, especially with the increasing acquisition of such large aircraft. It was decided to increase membership, with the introduction of a new class of Associate Member. The subscription would be 21 shillings, or 1 guinea in old money, and there would be an extra incentive to join in that membership would also include social membership of the County Flying Club at Biggin Hill.

The society was also trying to find a base where it could open a museum. The favoured location was Biggin Hill, one of the most famous airfields in the country, and the place where several of the aircraft were based. However, planning permission and lack of funds were serious obstacles that needed to be overcome. Late in 1966, the waters were muddied by publicity given to a new organization calling itself the British Historic Aircraft Museum Biggin Hill. This group seemed to be linking its proposals with the HAPS aircraft, but HAPS Chairman Malcolm (Bill) Fisher was quick to refute this. In the mean time, HAPS was exploring the possibility of setting up a small museum at the Dart Valley Railway at Buckfastleigh in Devon, as an extra attraction for the railway, on a seasonal basis. Neither of these museum proposals ever came to fruition.

On 1 January 1967 HAPS took the significant step of becoming a non-profit-making company limited by guarantee, with the new name of Reflectaire Ltd. The move, encouraged by John Roast, should have led to a more substantial existence. It had the effect of limiting the members' liability, but it also took the running of the society out of the members' hands, and led to Biggin Hill giving the society notice to remove its aircraft as soon as possible.

CHAPTER 4

1967 – Coming of Age

CONTROL COLUMN

DURING 1967 there was a fundamental change in the nature of aircraft preservation in Britain. The movement had been characterized by a handful of disconnected groups struggling in isolation, often in ignorance of the existence of each other, let alone what they were all trying to do. In 1967, it became a national movement.

The catalyst for this dramatic change was the birth of *Control Column – The Aircraft Preservation Journal*, a magazine devoted entirely to recording the efforts of the various aircraft preservation and restoration groups. For the first time, members of the individual preservation groups, as well as others interested in their activities, could find out what was going on. This new exchange of information led directly later in the year to the formation of the British Aircraft Preservation Council (BAPC), a national body. Its aim was not to govern the groups but to help co-ordinate their activities, to disseminate information, and to set standards.

Control Column had begun life four years before as the newsletter of the Northern Aircraft Preservation Society, distributed free to its members as one of the benefits of membership. In March 1967 it was re-born as the house journal of three aircraft preservation societies – the Northern, the Lincolnshire and the Historic. It was still produced by NAPS and edited by Peter Schofield, but it contained news not just of the three societies with which it was associated, but also of the preservation movement as a whole.

Issues No. 1 and 2

The first issue of *Control Column* contained twelve pages within its blue-trimmed cover, and featured on the front a photograph of the Fleet Air Arm Museum's newly restored Walrus, on loan from HAPS. The plan was to bring out the first issue in January free to members of the three societies, and 1 shilling to others. However, because of delays and higher than expected costs, the magazine eventually went on general sale in March for 1s 6d, the new date being applied with a simple sticker over the old, with the cover price being altered by hand!

There were three standard columns: 'Newsdesk', with general preservation news; 'Around the Collections', with news from various aircraft collections around the country; and 'Society Column' with news specific to the three societies. The first issue also contained an article on the history of the Walrus and the restoration of L2301, the Fleet Air Arm Museum's example, and an amusing letter from the Italian Air Force concerning the movement of HAPS's Sabre, G-ATBF, from Novara to Colerne. There was also an appeal for some advertisements to help defray the costs of the new magazine.

Having circumnavigated numerous obstacles in the production of the first issue, notably a substantial discrepancy between the amount of copy the editor and the plate-makers thought they could accommodate, Peter Schofield was to be congratulated – both on producing such a good magazine, and on not throwing in the towel immediately. Something totally new, the first issue was grabbed eagerly by every enthusiast who came across it.

The second issue appeared on time, produced by a different printer, based in Littleborough, Lancashire. The NAPS HM.14 Pou de Ciel (Flying Flea) featured on the cover was the only aircraft on public display in the whole of the north of England (on loan at Capesthorne Hall). Shamefully, in an area of Britain that had such close associations with Avro, Blackburn Aircraft, English Electric, and others, had nothing to show for half a century of aviation history except a French home-built built by S.O. Whiteley in Rishworth in 1936. It was the official apathy that had brought about this shocking state of affairs – a situation that the preservation groups were trying desperately to improve.

Editorial Developments
With *Control Column* up and running, and each new issue eagerly awaited and avidly read by a growing number of enthusiasts, it was not long before new changes were on the way. Issue No. 5, in July, displayed a new name above the editorial: the Midland Aircraft Preservation Society. MAPS had been inaugurated at a meeting in Coventry on 24 May, with a steering committee of three appointed: Chairman Carl Butler, who was rebuilding a Mosscraft in his lounge, Treasurer Ron Randall, part owner of the BAC Drone G-AEKV, and Secretary Rodger Smith. The new society's first acquisition was a First World War four-blade propeller, probably from an RE.8. From July, *Control Column* was issued free to all members of MAPS.

A few dissenting voices were heard as new groups appeared, with some people fearing that the arena was becoming too crowded. This may seem extraordinary, considering the number of groups flourishing around the country thirty years later, but May's *Control Column* included a story showing why such fears were being expressed. The British Historic Aircraft Museum and the Lincolnshire APS had both apparently been negotiating with different members of the same family for Proctor 4, G-AOBW, which was located at Stanmore. LAPS had even announced in April's *Control Column* that it was theirs, only to find that it had suddenly been spirited away by Tony Osborne to Southend. Tony Osborne had created the British Historic Aircraft Museum originally associated with Biggin Hill, but now based at Southend, with the express intention of creating an aircraft museum there. Although it was officially Osborne's personal fiefdom, the BHAM was soon supported by a number of local enthusiasts.

In an era when new groups were desperate to acquire aircraft – any aircraft – the different societies saw themselves in competition with one another whenever a new example became available. Nevertheless new groups continued to establish themselves, often inspired by an awareness of what was being done elsewhere, which could be read about every month in *Control Column*.

Before the end of the year three more names were added to the list of *Control Column* supporters. In November both the Newark Air Museum and the South Wales Historic Aircraft Preservation Society, which had been formed in March in Cardiff, at the instigation of Malcolm Sketchley, were added to the masthead. SWHAPS was initially involved in two pursuits: the support of the restoration activities at RAF St Athan and the investigation of aircraft wreck sites in the mountains of South Wales.

In December, Skyfame Ltd joined the steadily growing list of organizations for whose members the magazine was becoming required reading.

BRITISH AIRCRAFT PRESERVATION COUNCIL

In August, within the pages of *Control Column*, NAPS Chairman John Kenyon formally proposed the setting up of a British Aircraft Preservation Council, with a three-point broad outline.

1. The council was to comprise representatives of all the aircraft preservation groups in Great Britain.
2. The council was to meet to discuss the overall national situation and formulate acceptable policies for furthering the improvement.
3. Meetings were to be held at a mutually agreed centre or centres, as frequently as considered practical.

Kenyon also suggested some of the functions that the council might fulfill:

- formulation of co-ordinated general policies;
- interchange of technical information, plans, spares lists and other data;
- institution of political lobbying and other forms of collective bargaining;
- arrangement of exchange of exhibits between organizations, on loan or otherwise;
- discussion of plans for obtaining and exhibiting specific aircraft, too large or too expensive to be handled by any individual group;
- presentation of its views in a national magazine;
- encouragement of financial support from all sources.

John Kenyon invited all groups interested in his proposals to contact him directly. Thereafter he circulated all known preservation groups with his proposals and this eventually resulted in a meeting on 28 October, held at the Rolls-Royce Social Centre at Derby.

On the appointed date, thirty-one delegates assembled, including Jack Bruce of the RAF Museum, Lt Cdr Cox, the Assistant Curator of the Fleet Air Arm Museum, Peter Thomas of Skyfame, B.E. Drinkwater of the British Historic Aircraft Museum, and representatives from Newark, NAPS, LAPS, HAPS, MAPS and SWHAPS. The Shuttleworth Trust were the only noteworthy absentees, but it was only illness and an imminent air display that prevented their participation.

John Kenyon opened the discussion with a forty-five-minute talk outlining his proposals. He spoke of the rapid growth of the movement and the necessity for co-operation and mutual assistance. He acknowledged the very different aims and structure of many of the organizations represented, but pointed out that they all had a common aim. He stressed that it would be better to present a united front to those who stood in the way of the preservation and restoration of historic aircraft, and of their public exhibition for the better education of the general public.

As the general discussions began, one thing became quickly apparent – everyone seemed to think that the British Aircraft Preservation Council already existed, and began to get carried away with talk about the way ahead. Kenyon brought the delegates back down to earth, formally proposing the formation of the BAPC. There were no dissenters to the proposal, or the name, and everyone agreed that the new organization should be advisory rather than managerial.

It was agreed that every member group could send two delegates, but would have only one vote. The first formal meeting of the new council would take place at the same venue on Saturday 9 December, a draft constitution would be approved, and the timetable for future meetings agreed. The meeting would also agree a rota for the Chairmanship, and would appoint a Secretary.

Areas for investigation included the encouragement of new groups in areas not served by existing ones, and the sponsoring of joint publicity. Ways of acquiring new aircraft were to be discussed with regard to the requirements of each group, with joint action on major projects where appropriate. In practical terms it was proposed to circulate lists of parts and information that were required or available.

The spirit of goodwill at the meeting was tangible. No miraculous pool of money had been created, and there had been no sudden exchange of aircraft or other exhibits, there had simply been a recognition of the fact that the individual groups were all a part of a larger movement, and that it would be better for all concerned if they co-operated towards their joint aims.

It was an historic meeting, with the thirty-one delegates creating a body of lasting importance and relevance in the world of aircraft preservation. Particular thanks were owed to Bill Harrison for arranging the meeting and to Reg Worthington who acted as Official Recorder, but above all it was John Kenyon who had had the dream and who had made it happen.

VOLUME 2

Shortly after that first meeting there was a slight hiccup in the forward march of the new movement, when Peter Schofield and the Northern APS gave up the publication of *Control Column*. Schofield had taken over the Chairmanship of NAPS from John Kenyon. After a three-month break, a new *Control Column* emerged, published by the Newark Air Museum, and edited by Neville Franklin. The first issue of Volume 2 came out in April 1968, in a slightly larger format, with a white cover. It still comprised twelve inside pages, but the price had gone up to 2 shillings. The same six organizations offered it free to their members. (Some, like the Midland APS, offered their members a cheaper membership without a free copy of *Control Column*.)

The content of the magazine was much as before, but there were two new regular features. Leslie Hunt was the contributor for 'Veteran and Vintage Vettings', virtually a monthly update of the newly published fourth edition of his book *Veteran and Vintage Aircraft*. There was also a modellers' page, which usually included a three-view drawing of the aircraft featured.

CHAPTER 5

Consolidation

BIRTH OF A NEW APS

A FTER the sudden expansion in the number of groups during 1967, and the creation of *Control Column* and the BAPC, 1968 saw a period of consolidation. For a while, no new names appeared on the masthead of the magazine. None the less, the publication of *Control Column* had led a number of enthusiasts to the realization that they could participate in the preservation and restoration of veteran aircraft, even in an amateur capacity. Many were inspired to join one of the new groups.

At the time it was said there was almost a standard route taken by new groups into the aircraft preservation movement. It would begin with one or two local enthusiasts – with more initiative than most – placing a small advert in the local paper, and a group of like-minded enthusiasts gathering in a suitable venue, usually a pub. Resolutions would be passed, plans made, dreams aired, and a new aircraft preservation society would spring into existence.

It would then become imperative to acquire an aircraft, for it is not possible to be an aircraft preservation society without an aircraft to preserve. A visit to the local airfield would usually result in the discovery of a derelict example parked in the long grass; it was often a Percival Proctor, but sometimes it could be a Miles Messenger, or even something slightly more exotic, like a Prentice. A certain amount of pleading with the owner, coupled with convincing arguments describing the restoration process to which the aircraft would be subjected, would usually result in the aircraft being acquired for little or nothing. The owner and, more importantly, the airfield operator would usually be glad to see the back of it.

Ecstatic at being the owner of a real aircraft, the infant APS would now be faced with the dual problems of transporting and storing its new acquisition. Aircraft that could be dismantled, such as the Proctor, were infinitely preferable to those such as the Messenger, which could only be dismantled with a saw. Cutting up an aircraft in order to save it caused a crisis of conscience in more than one group.

News of the acquisition of the new 'exhibit' would flash like wildfire round the aircraft enthusiasts in the locality, and a rumour of an aircraft hanging in the rafters of a local farmer's barn would inevitably surface. Excited members would set off to investigate, usually to discover that the aircraft was a Flying

Flea, in any number of stages of completion. Discussions with the farmer would reveal that the aircraft was started in 1936 by his father/uncle/brother/friend, and never finished because of the ban on flying Henri Mignet Pou de Ciels. Convinced it was a historic local aviation artefact, which ought to be preserved, and that the members of the infant APS were the only people who could be trusted to the task, the farmer would give them the remains (probably secretly glad to see the back of it).

The members of the new society would now be the proud owners of an aircraft *collection*. Having achieved this exalted ambition, the realization would soon dawn on them that the most important thing an aircraft collection needs is money. Suddenly, finding ways of raising money would become the most urgent item on the agenda.

It became standard procedure to exhibit at local air displays, selling aircraft kits, *Control Column* and other publications. The Flying Flea would be knocked together in a presentable state to become an exhibit. In those dim and distant days the presence of an aircraft preservation society, with something to put on show, was regarded by most air-display organizers as an added attraction, and they would assign free space.

For example, when MAPS exhibited at the air display at Halfpenny Green in 1968, the members borrowed a marquee in which to place their newly acquired Crossley Tom Thumb, a half-built pre-war wooden home-built aircraft, and their Flying Flea. Outside they towed over the local Air Scouts' Proctor and Anson to create an 'instant' aircraft museum, and charged an entry fee of sixpence. This, together with sales of kits, magazines, books, and Polaroid photos of people sitting in the Proctor, created a useful income. Some visitors complained about paying an extra fee after having already paid to come on to the airfield, but most realized it was for a good cause; since entry to the air display had cost them just half a crown, they had little cause for complaint compared with current prices. The sign over the marquee did cause some confusion, with several visitors asking where the maps were.

At displays such as this, more enthusiasts would be persuaded to part with subscription money to become members of the burgeoning organization, and would supply new leads to derelict aircraft and artefacts. At the Halfpenny Green display, for example, MAPS was pointed towards a garden in Shropshire that was using a number of Harvard canopies as cloches. The following weekend, the gardener was persuaded to part with one.

The collection would grow, usually with the acquisition from one of a number of various sources of a Vampire T.11. This would lead the society into the world of heavy metal, and present it with the urgent need to acquire its own premises in order to create the ultimate aim of most such groups – its own *aircraft museum*.

BUILDING COLLECTIONS

Many of the groups that were established in 1967 went through some variation of the above process. The Lincolnshire group had acquired its Proctor from NAPS in late 1966, and during the middle of 1967 had added to its collection by acquiring Gemini G-AKER, which had suffered a forced landing at Biggin Hill in 1965. Like many groups, they then took a turn into aviation archaeology, and investigated the wreck site of a Heinkel He 111 shot down on the beach at Chapel St Leonards, adding its Junkers Jumo 211 engines to the collection.

To begin its collection, the South Wales APS had purchased two gliders – a Grunau Baby and a Slingsby Tutor – from the Swansea Gliding Club. The aircraft were both largely complete but in need of extensive restoration work. The society had also been given a set of Tiger Moth wings, and one of its members, Peter Roberts, was building a Flying Flea in his garage, using some original parts and painting it as G-ADRY (although this was a registration that was never issued).

The Midland APS, with Bob Ogden (owner of BAC Drone, G-AEDB, and Flying Flea, G-AEOH) now installed as Chairman, had quickly gathered sundry exhibits from various sources. Beagle Aircraft had donated the rear fuselage of Auster Agricola VP-GAZ, an aircraft that had crashed in British Guiana, together with the static test frame fuselage of the Auster A.O.P.9. A Slingsby T.7 Cadet TX.1 glider was donated by the Cornish Gliding Club in January 1968, and this was followed by the Nyborg glider, a unique machine built in Worcester in 1936.

The expanding collection also soon boasted the remains of three ultra-light monoplanes. The battered fuselage of the Wheeler Slymph came on loan from the Shuttleworth Trust; the even more sparse remains of Parnall Pixie III, G-EBJG, were loaned to MAPS for a display at Coventry Airport, and then donated to the society; and finally Bob Ogden donated the wings of Flying Flea G-ARGV. The construction of a new fuselage was immediately instigated. A number of lock-up garages became the new homes for these varied items, which were joined later in the year by a Slingsby Tutor glider from Perranporth, a Grunau Baby glider, VT921, and the previously mentioned Crossley Tom Thumb.

Without definite aims at the beginning, and solid projects to work on from the start, interest in the societies would soon dwindle, as I discovered when I set up a West Midland branch of MAPS, based in Wolverhampton. With the approval of the committee, I placed an advert in the local paper and gathered together a number of local enthusiasts. A branch was formed and a number of meetings took place but, as an offshoot of the Coventry organization, our discussions were too full of 'ifs' and 'maybes' – 'If we get enough members,

31

maybe we can rent premises,' or 'If we get a member with the necessary expertise, maybe we can have one of MAPS's airframes to begin restoration work.'

In the circumstances, interest soon waned, as with other groups, both before and afterwards. This was why there were too few preservation groups to fully tap the potential that existed in many areas of the country.

RAF MUSEUM PROJECT

On 20 April 1968, following another very successful BAPC meeting at Capesthorne Hall in Cheshire, the first National Aircraft Preservation Dinner was held. It was actually NAPS's annual dinner, but the invitation to attend was extended to other delegates, with their partners, and many accepted. Peter Schofield, the new Chairman of NAPS, called on John Kenyon to outline the work done in the seven years of his tenure, and then Dr Tanner of the RAF Museum gave an interesting and amusing speech. The talking continued afterwards in the bar, and even when the bar closed there was a general reluctance to halt the discussions and go home to bed.

Many of the discussions centred on the creation of the forthcoming RAF Museum at Hendon, a project that had recently been boosted by the news that Hawker-Siddeley was preparing to donate its collection of vintage aircraft to the new venture. This largely flying collection included a Hawker Cygnet, a Hart, a Hurricane, a Sea Fury, a de Havilland Mosquito and a Blackburn B-2. Another collection earmarked for the new museum was the Nash Collection, owned by the Royal Aeronautical Society, which had offered its eight aircraft to various museums during the 1950s. They had finally been accepted by the RAF in 1964, on loan, and in 1967 the entire collection was moved into store at RAF Henlow, which was to become the museum's early storage facility.

The possibility of an RAF Museum had been mooted in the early 1960s by Dr John Tanner of Cranwell, who published a paper on the idea. (In fact, steps may have been taken to preserve examples of suitable RAF aircraft for such a museum as long ago as September 1944. In that month the Defiant N1671 was sent to No.52 M.U. at Cardiff for packing. All trace of it then disappeared until it was listed as part of the official Air Historical Branch Collection held at RAF Stanmore Park, in 1954. Also in 1944 No.52 M.U. had packed a number of aircraft marked 'For museum purposes'. These included the Spitfire Mk.IAs K9942 and X4590, both subsequently in the RAF Museum at Hendon; Spitfire IA P9444, later in the Science Museum's collection; R6915, later in the Imperial War Museum's collection; and Hurricanes P2617, later at Hendon, and L1592, later in the Science Museum. Clearly, someone was squirrelling away suitable airframes for preservation, but no trace of any official sanction or decision has ever been found.)

In the early 1960s, Dr Tanner's paper resulted in the Air Force Board forming a consultative committee chaired by Marshal of the Royal Air Force Sir Dermot Boyle. The committee recommended the creation of a museum and a board of trustees was created with Sir Dermot as Chairman and Dr Tanner as Director of the museum. Their first major decision involved a choice of site; it needed to have some historical connections and to be close to the main tourist trails. They settled on Hendon, one of the most historic airfields in Britain, with easy public transport access from central London. Two historic Belfast truss hangars were to be used as the core of the new museum, buried within the new building that would be created.

The Royal Air Force was in the process of gathering together examples of every one of its former aircraft for the Royal Review at Abingdon, celebrating its 50th anniversary. The process saved a number of aircraft that might otherwise have been scrapped, including the Sea Balliol WL732, which had just donated its engine to the Battle of Britain Memorial Flight, and would represent the Balliol T.2 in the line-up of RAF trainers. After Abingdon, many of the aircraft found their way to Hendon, or to the RAF Museum's reserve collections at Henlow and Cosford.

Further aircraft were held by the station museum at RAF Colerne in Wiltshire. There had been four historic aircraft held there for some time: Spitfire IIA P7350, Meteor F.4 VY229, a Me 262 and a Heinkel He 162. During 1966 a move was made to enlarge this collection, with two objects in mind: to increase the interest of the museum for station open days, and to provide a pool of preserved aircraft from which any prospective RAF museum could draw.

PUBLICATIONS AND REGISTERS

In 1968 the Merseyside Group of Aircraft Enthusiasts produced the third edition of its publication *Wrecks and Relics*, edited by S.G. Jones (after two editions edited by D.J. Stephens). It was becoming an essential biennial purchase for anyone interested in aircraft preservation, and at only 5 shillings per copy, plus sixpence for postage and packing, it represented excellent value for money. Les Hunt's *Veteran and Vintage Aircraft*, then a much larger hardback publication, was also essential reading.

The sixth meeting of the BAPC took place at Old Warden on 13 October 1968. There was much discussion about the number of airframes in the country that had no formal identity. These included aircraft that had not been completed, and therefore had never been registered, as well as replicas and full-scale models. The council felt that it would be worthwhile to create a register of these aircraft, and to assign them a BAPC serial number to help keep track of them.

Bob Ogden drew up the initial list and BAPC 1 was assigned to the Avro Triplane IV triplane owned by the Shuttleworth Trust, and built for the film *Those Magnificent Men in their Flying Machines*. The initial list in full read as follows:

Serial	Aircraft	Owner
BAPC 1	Avro Triplane IV replica	Shuttleworth
BAPC 2	Bristol Boxkite replica	Shuttleworth
BAPC 3	Bleriot XI	Shuttleworth
BAPC 4	Deperdussin monoplane	Shuttleworth
BAPC 5	Blackburn monoplane	Shuttleworth
BAPC 6	Avro Triplane 1 replica	Shuttleworth
BAPC 7	Southampton University man-powered a/c	Shuttleworth
BAPC 8	Dixon Ornithopter	Shuttleworth
BAPC 9	Bleriot XI replica	Shuttleworth
BAPC 10	Hafner Revoplane	Shuttleworth
BAPC 11	English Electric Wren	Shuttleworth
BAPC 12	Mignet Pou de Ciel	NAPS
BAPC 13	Mignet Pou de Ciel	P. Schofield
BAPC 14	Addyman standard training glider	NAPS
BAPC 15	Addyman STG	NAPS
BAPC 16	Addyman ultra-light	NAPS
BAPC 17	Woodhams Sprite	NAPS
BAPC 18	Killick man-powered helicopter	NAPS
BAPC 19	Bristol F.2B	NAPS
BAPC 20	Lee-Richards annular biplane replica	Newark
BAPC 21	Thruxton Jackaroo	Newark
BAPC 22	Mignet Pou de Ciel (G-AEOF)	Newark
BAPC 23	SE.5a (half-scale replica)	Newark
BAPC 24	Currie Wot (two-thirds-scale replica)	LAPS
BAPC 25	Nyborg glider	MAPS
BAPC 26	Auster AOP.9	MAPS
BAPC 27	Mignet Pou de Ciel	Bob Ogden
BAPC 28	Wright Flyer replica	Finningley Vintage Aircraft Club

All of the aircraft assigned BAPC numbers were owned by member groups or members of those groups. The Finningley Vintage Aircraft Club had built the Wright Flyer replica, and looked after a number of vintage RAF aircraft at the RAF station.

CHANGES AND DEVELOPMENTS IN THE GROUPS

During 1969 three preservation groups folded, including two of the most significant, although this was balanced by the creation of two more groups. Tony Osborne's British Historic Aircraft Museum venture at Southend collapsed, leaving a large and valuable collection of aircraft, including a Lincoln, a de Havilland Drover, a Mitchell, a Sea Fury, a Sea Hawk and a Proctor, in imminent danger of demise. The volunteers associated with BHAM were working hard to prepare the aircraft for exhibition up to the last, re-painting the B-25 Mitchell in RAF colours and fitting a mid-upper turret taken from a B-17.

The Historic Aircraft Preservation Society had been the one with the most successful groups, not least because of the return of the Lancaster from New Caledonia. During the year all the aircraft located at Biggin Hill were moved to Lavenham in Suffolk. Its Walrus, which had been on loan to the Fleet Air Arm Museum, was exchanged for a Seahawk, and the FAA also acquired the Corsair. HAPS by now had metamorphosed into the Reflectaire Preservation Group Ltd.

The new site at Lavenham was to prove less than ideal. The airfield itself, which was an old 8th Air Force bomber base, was in poor condition, and there were no hangars in which to undertake essential maintenance. On 7 February 1970 the Lancaster was flown to a new site, Hullavington in Wiltshire. One of the passengers on board was Richard Todd, who played Guy Gibson in the Dambusters film. The poor state of the aircraft after its long sojourn in the open was obvious to everyone, as sundry items, such as exhaust manifolds and a radio aerial, fell off during the flight. The Lancaster was housed inside a hangar at Hullavington, and was soon followed by the other Lavenham inmates, the Seafire and Sabre. Their stay at Hullavington was to be short-lived. On 26 June 1970 the Lancaster flew to Squires Gate Airport at Blackpool, followed again by the Seafire and Sabre. The plan was to set up a permanent aircraft museum, to attract summer-holiday visitors.

The Lincolnshire Aircraft Preservation Society, after its initial burst of enthusiasm and action, had run out of steam, without the necessary driving force and clarity of purpose needed by such voluntary organizations. Its collection was saved by a new Lincolnshire group which sprang up at the opposite end of the county. A group of enthusiasts in the Boston area, who had already co-operated in the investigation of a number of crash sites, held a meeting in a local college in January 1969 in Boston, and were very surprised when over sixty people turned up. The East Anglian Aviation Society was duly formed, primarily as a general aviation-interest society rather than a preservation group. The college Principal became Chairman for the first year, with Wing Commander C.A. Pike, OBE, AFC, as President and David Crow as Secretary.

The new society adopted the Barge Inn at Boston as its home base, and defined its objectives as follows:

1. To acquire and catologue items of aviation history and the preservation of old aircraft.

2. To encourage interest in old aviation history.
3. To form an aviation museum in the county.
4. To bring to the public eye items and events concerning aviation history.

At the October meeting they decided to change their name to the Lincolnshire Aviation Enthusiasts, to avoid any confusion with other groups. LAPS was now entirely defunct and its collection was offered to the new group. On 19 October, twenty of the new group's members travelled to Grimsby and fetched the collection, comprising aircraft, engines and artefacts.

Within a short time the society had leased a 2-acre piece of land in Tattershall in a disused railway goods yard, which included a small building. They obtained planning permission for the creation of an aircraft museum on the site, and set to work refurbishing it. Members wheeled wheelbarrows, erected fences, and painted anything that did not move. They were among the first to realize that running an aircraft museum involved cutting grass and painting doors as much as restoring aircraft. A man with a bulldozer came to their aid on one weekend, and they were able to fulfil their aim of opening Lincolnshire's first aircraft museum on 19 July 1970.

The museum was formally opened by Alderman G. Whitehead, the Deputy Mayor of Boston. The BAPC meeting had been held on the premises on the previous day to help publicize the new museum.

Another new group formed in 1969 was the Southern Aircraft Preservation Society. This remained a small, loose association of primarily Auster enthusiasts lead by M.D.N. 'Bill' Fisher of Peterborough, who had been instrumental in bringing the Historic Aircraft Preservation Society's Lancaster back from New Caledonia. Their main activity quickly became the restoration of Auster AOP.11 G-ASCC to airworthy standards.

The fruits of co-operation through BAPC became apparent when the Shuttleworth Trust loaned to NAPS its Avro Triplane I replica, now largely supplanted by its flying Avro Triplane IV replica. NAPS began the restoration of this aircraft, which is now on display at the Manchester Museum of Science and Industry.

The Newark Air Museum had in 1968 become the second of the volunteer groups, after HAPS, to turn itself into a limited company, with the full company title of Newark (Nottinghamshire and Lincolnshire) Air Museum Ltd. It later became a registered charity. In 1970 a 2-acre site was leased on Winthorpe Airfield near Newark and an 80 × 40ft building was erected in a 1-acre fenced area. Although the airfield was disused, its runway was still in existence and was to prove valuable space for the delivery of aircraft. Later, a gliding club began to operate next door to the infant museum, its flying and landing aircraft adding nicely to the atmosphere experienced by visitors.

CHAPTER 6

1970s – Heavy Metal

ACQUIRING JET AIRCRAFT

A PART from Skyfame, the voluntary groups had almost entirely put together collections of wooden light aircraft and gliders. This was a purely practical option, as small wooden aircraft were easy to transport and store, and, if the expertise were available, they were easier to restore than all-metal aircraft. There may also have been a certain lack of ambition, or at least a certain fear of taking on a large, complicated all-metal aircraft.

Two societies, Newark and Lincolnshire, took the lead in acquiring jet aircraft for the first time during 1970. Newark had been keeping an eye on Gloster Meteor FR.9 VZ608, which had been in use at Rolls-Royce as a test-bed for the RB.108 lift engine. Although it had been in use testing various engines at Hucknall since March 1951, delivered straight from the production line, it was believed to be the last Meteor FR.9. The RAF Museum was not interested in acquiring the aircraft so, when its testing days were over and it was purchased from the Ministry for use by Rolls-Royce's Fire Section, Newark approached the company. They were told they could have the Meteor if they could replace it with another aircraft with a sliding canopy.

After a countrywide search, Newark finally made a deal for the Civil Defence Meteor WH443, at Feltwell, which was already partly burnt. They bought it for scrap prices, and for the first time they undertook dismantling and transporting a jet fighter over 150 miles. Once WH443 had been erected at Hucknall, they then had to move VZ608 to Newark, and found that the fuselage had been strengthened so that the wings could not be removed at the transport joints. With just the outer wings off, the aircraft was over 20ft wide. With the co-operation of the authorities they planned an 80-mile route via the new M1 and the A1, four times longer than the direct route, and successfully moved the aircraft to their new base on Winthorpe airfield. This was the first Meteor ever preserved by a non-service unit in the UK.

On 19 December 1970 Vampire T.11 WZ549 was flown from RAF Shawbury to RAF Coningsby and placed on loan to the Lincolnshire Aircraft Enthusiasts. It was flown by Sq Ldr G.A. Talbot, and formally presented by RAF Coningsby Station Commander Group Capt C.R.G. Neville to the society's Chairman Mike Hodgson. The Vampire was then dismantled and transported to Tattershall, where it took pride of place inside the museum's main building.

Newark also acquired a Vampire T.11 in 1970, or, rather, the components of two Vampires, XK630 and WZ459, and decided to restore the latter as their second jet exhibit. Shortly afterwards they obtained the last Avro Anson XI, G-ALIH, which had been used by Echo Electronics; it was presented by them to the museum in a somewhat derelict condition. After hundreds of hours of work on the Anson, it was destroyed by fire, presumably started by vandals, but Newark were later able to replace it with another Anson. They added to their growing collection of metal aircraft when enthusiast Norman Pratlett loaned them Supermarine Swift WK277; the museum was later able to add an engine and mainwheels, which were missing when the Swift arrived.

STORIES OF RECOVERY

New groups were still being created, with two springing up in Cambridge and York. The new Cambridge Aircraft Preservation Society, with Steve Gotts as Secretary, soon acquired Miles Hawk Trainer G-AIUA, from Felthorpe, with the hope of maintaining it in flying condition.

The York Aircraft Preservation Group obtained temporary premises in Swinegate, York on 1 January and began renovating the building and moving in various artefacts and displays, so that it was able to open to the public on 31 May, with no more ceremony than the placing of a small sign on the door declaring 'Air Museum – York'. The displays were mainly concerned with various ex-crash site investigations, featuring a Mosquito, a Barracuda and a Halifax, and one complete floor of the building was taken up with a 1/72-scale airfield and railway layout. Open daily, the museum had an official opening on 21 August.

The saga of the Barracuda's discovery and recovery was one that was to be repeated at innumerable crash sites by innumerable groups over the next decade, but at the time was still an unusual way of obtaining a Second World War aircraft. The wreck was located on Whernside, Yorkshire's second-highest mountain; in May, the group had searched for hours before finding it. Markings inside the fin indicated that it was Boulton Paul-built, and it was eventually identified as DR314, which had been abandoned in the air in 1944. A full-scale expedition was mounted the following weekend to recover as much of the aircraft as possible. Society members Brian Rapier, Tony Agar and Eddie Franklin set off at 3am on the Saturday morning, in a Land Rover and a wartime Jeep towing a low loader, to drive the 80 miles to Whernside. Much of the first day was spent digging out first one vehicle then the other, and then rebuilding a stone wall that fell on one of them. A Simca van arrived with two fresh members, Freda and Riley Watson. Camp was made near a viaduct and more members arrived, bringing with them the unwelcome rain.

At 7am on the Sunday morning they set off up the 2-mile climb to the site, taking with them some shear legs, which Dave Broadley had just brought, to raise the engine. As the rain poured down and a thunderstorm lashed across the desolate hillsides, the engine was lifted out, followed by the front fuselage. Two intrepid reporters from the *Northern Echo* and the *Yorkshire Post* hung around, wondering what they were doing there.

The group added a wheel and tyre from a nearby dip, and, with the vehicles loaded up, returned to York. By 10pm the weary crew had unloaded all the relics into the museum and locked the door.

MORE COMMERCIAL MUSEUMS

Historic Aircraft Museum (Southend) Ltd

In May 1971 a new aircraft museum was launched at Southend, rising from the ashes of the debacle of the British Historic Aircraft Museum. Named the Historic Aircraft Museum (Southend) Ltd, it was part of a commercial project backed by the Budge Bros Group Ltd and Canterbury Group Management Co. Ltd. It was to be sited on Aviation Way, next to the airfield, and would also include a hotel, motel, petrol station and restaurant. The museum would have a new exhibition hangar for up to twenty aircraft, built on the opposite side of the road from the new airport hotel. All the surviving aircraft from the failed BHAM on the eastern boundary were towed across to become part of the new operation, and numerous new aircraft exhibits were to be purchased.

A professional advisory committee was formed, including two engineers from Aviation Traders, Bob Batt and Charlie Murrell. Leslie Hunt, who lived in Southend-on-Sea, would be the historical advisor.

Torbay Air Museum

Shortly afterwards, well-known broadcaster Keith Fordyce formed the Torbay Air Museum, based on buildings at Barton Pines, Higher Blagdon, in Devon, with a view to running the museum on commercial lines. It was set in a 4-acre site, 3 miles inland from the sea between Paignton and Totnes. Numerous indoor exhibits – artefacts, photographs, documents and other relics – were supplemented by a grassy outdoor aircraft park. There was a museum shop and a cafeteria, and admission was a modest 25p for adults and 15p for children.

The museum purchased a number of exhibits from various sources, including the prototype DH.110, Sea Venom, Sea Hawk and Miles Messenger. In a spirit of co-operation, the Shuttleworth Trust also loaned a number of aircraft, including the Desoutter, Skeeter, Provost and Primary Glider.

At about the same time, the Shuttleworth Trust loaned its Bleriot replica (BAPC.9) to the Midland APS. A team including Rodger Smith, Jim Titford and Rick Clarke went to fetch it, transporting it to a building in Stratford for renovation. They immediately began referring to it as a 'Humber monoplane replica', as Bleriots were built by Humber in Coventry under licence. To add credibility to the name change a Humber engine, which was itself a licence-built version of the Bleriot's Anzani, was borrowed from the Herbert Art Gallery and Museum in Coventry.

THE FEDERATION OF AVIATION SOCIETIES

Groups were finding that aircraft preservation meant more than just preserving aircraft. At Tattershall, the Lincolnshire Enthusiasts, having done considerable refurbishing work and landscaping on the site to get it ready to open as a museum the previous year, were now in the process of erecting a new 85 × 19ft building, which would serve as a workshop and additional display area. At Newark they were erecting their new building, while at the same time erecting the ex-Echo Electronics Anson, with refurbishing work being done to the Meteor FR.9.

The Historic APS had become Reflectaire Ltd, and had moved its collection to Squires Gate Airport, Blackpool; the Lancaster was its prize exhibit. Its intention was to create an aircraft museum, but a dispute with the local council had brought plans to a halt. By the time the seventeenth meeting of the BAPC was held there, on 21 August 1971, there was talk of moving the aircraft yet again. On 5 November the council gave the society 28 days' notice to move, but Reflectaire Ltd went into voluntary liquidation, leaving its Lancaster, Sabre, Mew Gull and Seafire in some peril.

At the same meeting the East Anglian Aviation Society reported that it hoped to have a museum open soon, and that the first aircraft was expected to be a Sea Vixen. The heavy metal being preserved was getting heavier.

Museums with greater financial backing, such as the project at Southend, were able to harbour even higher ambitions, and in October the largest exhibit in any aircraft museum in Britain, Blackburn Beverley XB261, flew in there for preservation. The museum had recently purchased a Provost and a Meteor T.7, and a Javelin, a Provost, a Tiger Moth and a Fiat G-46 would shortly follow, to fill the new exhibition hangar. The voluntary preservation groups could only watch with envy as those with thicker wallets snapped up aircraft in such numbers.

During the year the main aviation societies in the country, with a combined membership of over 4,000, joined together as the Federation of Aviation Societies. Their aim was to publicize themselves as responsible bodies, and to outlaw those enthusiasts who broke the law. There were nine initial members, several of whom had connections with the aircraft preservation movement:

- Air Circle International;
- Blackbushe Aviation Research Group;
- Central Scotland Aviation Society;
- Gatwick Aviation Society;

- LAAS International;
- Merseyside Society of Aviation Enthusiasts;
- Midland Counties Aviation Society;
- West London Aviation Society.

At the next BAPC Meeting, held at the RAF Museum at Hendon, which was still twelve months away from opening, the Merseyside Society applied to join. They had of course been instrumental in creating the Northern Aircraft Preservation Society as a splinter group, and now had aspirations of obtaining their own aircraft, giving them a foot in both camps.

Also applying to join were the Air Museum York and the new Torbay Aircraft Museum. On 22 October, at the end of a first successful season, the Torbay Museum was to hold a 'Donor's Day' as a thank you to the seventy enthusiasts who had assisted in its creation. The museum then closed down for the winter, during which it obtained a second Provost, supplementing that on loan from the Shuttleworth Trust, a Proctor from Brooklands, and a Hurricane mock-up on loan from Doug Bianchi.

The Hurricane was one of those built for the *Battle of Britain* film in 1969, a film that was to have an even greater beneficial effect on the aircraft preservation movement than *633 Squadron* a few years before. Not only did a number of the full-scale models made for the film survive the 'Luftwaffe' attacks (or, at least, the pyrotechnics of the special effects department), but also large numbers of Spitfires, in particular, were gathered in from gate guardian duties at many RAF stations, and refurbished. Many of these were put into the air to fly in the film, while others only took a static role on the film sets. Nevertheless, many of these have also been put back into the air in subsequent years, and a high proportion of the aircraft in the film never had to face a permanent life exposed to the elements again. It is fair to say that, if the *Battle of Britain* had not been made, many gate guardian Spitfires would probably have been scrapped and replaced by recently retired jets once the effects of the elements had taken their toll.

SUMMER VISITORS

It was announced that Torbay would re-open for business on 30 March, hopefully on a year-round basis, despite the heavy reliance placed on visitors who were holidaying in the Torquay area. This area was inevitably quieter in the winter, although many visitors to the not-too-distant Fleet Air Arm Museum made the effort to visit Torbay too.

Southend was another museum that would have to rely heavily on summer visitors, and it was officially opened on 26 May 1972, with the late inclusion of a CASA 2.111, a Stampe, a Miles Gemini, an Anson, a Sea Prince and a Sycamore, with a Fieseler Storch and a Harvard on the way. The museum was

41

opened by Air Marshal Sir Harry Burton KBE, CBE, Air Officer Commanding in Chief Air Support Command, who thirty-one years before had been the first RAF prisoner of war to escape from a German camp. He had used a table knife to undo the screws securing his cell bars at Stalag Luft 1, and had slipped away, escaping by ferry to Sweden. Others present included General Michael Donnet, the Belgian Military Attaché in London, who had flown from Southend, then RAF Rochford, as C.O. of No.64 Squadron. He announced his intention of arranging the donation of a Belgian Air Force F-84 to the museum to mark the service at Rochford of 349 and 350 (Belgian) Squadrons during the war. Also present was Air Commodore Alan Deere DSO, OBE, DFC, who represented No.54 Squadron, two of whose Phantoms flew over during the opening ceremony.

Awaiting restoration at the time of the opening at Southend was Europe's only de Havilland Drover, which would shortly appear in the colours of the Australian Flying Doctor service. Also in store were a Fairchild Argus and a Westland Dragonfly.

Control Column heaped praise on the new venture, which would surely be the envy of the many voluntary groups, but criticized the 'high' price of entry (50p!). This perhaps reflected the difference in thinking between a commercial enterprise, albeit one supported by enthusiastic volunteers, and the amateur organizations that were still widespread in the aircraft preservation movement, many of whom were almost embarrassed to charge visitors anything.

VISCOUNT PRESERVATION TRUST

The twentieth meeting of the BAPC was once more held in the Manchester area so that many members could attend the NAPS Annual Dinner the previous evening. Delegates were shown round the Peel Green workshops. NAPS had recently acquired a Wallis Autogyro on loan, and the single-seat Murray Helicopter of 1951 vintage. There was exciting news from just down the East Lancs Road – the oldest turboprop airliner in the world, Vickers Viscount G-ALWF, was to be preserved at Speke. Its operators, Cambrian Airways, had offered it for a nominal £2,500, and would fly it in, before replacing its engines with time-expired examples. The purchase price of the aircraft and its upkeep would be handled by a newly formed trust.

On 12 April 1972 Viscount G-ALWF made its last-ever flight, Cardiff–Heathrow–Speke, to be handed over to the Viscount Preservation Trust, which would look after it. As the second production Viscount it was the oldest turbine airliner in the world and the first complex post-war airliner to be preserved in Britain.

The trust was founded by Paul St John Turner, who had already written a history of the Viscount. He became its Chairman, and members also included Peter Schofield of NAPS, and a number of Merseyside Aviation Society members. Chairman of the advisory board was Mr C. Herring, Chairman and Managing Director of British Air Services Ltd, and other members of the advisory board included Sir Peter Masefield and Mr D.J. Davies, the Managing Director of Cambrian Airways.

The Trust quickly discovered what a huge task it had taken on. Just to clean and prepare G-ALWF for the opening ceremony involved over 1,000 man hours of work put in by over thirty Trust members. First, the entire aircraft was brushed and washed with clean water. Then the unpainted areas were scraped with perspex scrapers to remove all areas of corrosion, and a special metal polish was applied and rubbed off. Often up to three coats were needed until the required mirror-like finish was achieved. It was discovered that this really arduous work resulted in only about 2 square feet of skin being completed for every man hour. As soon as each small area was polished it was sprayed with car wax to seal off the skin from the salt-laden air blowing in off the Mersey Estuary. Cambrian Airways' fitters drained the fuel system and, after changing the engines, filled them with inhibiting fluid to help preserve them. They also isolated items in the electrical system which might be dangerous if inadvertently operated.

The official opening of the Viscount for public display was carried out on 5 December 1972 by Alderman Robert Meadows, Lord Mayor of Liverpool. It was hoped that the upkeep of the aircraft would be paid for by donations, subscriptions and a 10p entrance fee for guided tours given to the general public. Sadly, just a few months later, access to the Viscount had to be denied not only to the public but also to Trust members, because of fears over IRA and other terrorist activity.

The Viscount Preservation Trust was admitted to the BAPC at the next meeting, bringing the membership up to nineteen. It was noted at the time that there were still eight organizations in the country that were concerned with aircraft preservation, but were not yet members.

REFLECTAIRE SALE

Less than positive news came from Blackpool, with the announced auction of the aircraft owned by the defunct Reflectaire Ltd. The Fleet Air Arm Museum had already purchased the Corsair, and had the Walrus handed over, and Tom Storey had bought the remains of Mew Gull G-AEXF, to begin its return to flying condition. A dealer had bought the Seafire, and was expected to sell it on to the United States. The main item in the auction would of course be Lancaster NX611, although one other lot, the soggy cockpit section of a Mosquito, was to have long-standing consequences.

Auctions of historic aircraft and artefacts have become commonplace nowadays, with several taking place every year, but the Reflectaire sale was one of the first. The auctioneers were far from competent in aeronautical matters, and the whole affair became something of a farce. Those who drew up the catalogue clearly had only a cursory knowledge of aviation and many of the descriptions of the lots bore very little resemblance to the reality. The F.86E Sabre was described as an F-84 and sold for a paltry £380 to a Mr Bracewell, who intended it as a plaything for his children. He also paid £40 for two Lancaster-sized wheels and tyres. A 'Mosquito tailwheel' was bought by Newark and turned out to be some kind of Vickers oleo leg. 'Tiger Moth wing struts' were suspiciously long, and clearly from a Cadet glider. The Cadet glider on sale, which was heavily damaged, was bought by a Mr Roast for £20, after the bidding stuck at £2 for some time. It is not known whether it had any struts.

Eight vehicles raised a total of £800 but the rest of the aeronautica only raised less than £200 all told, including £20 from Keith Fordyce for Lancaster mid-upper turret glazing and £7 from Tony Agar for the Mosquito cockpit. The prize lot, Lancaster NX611, was withdrawn when the bidding stalled at £9,500. It was sold a few days later to Lord Lilford for £12,000. He was under the ilusion that it was in flying condition and hoped to fly it to his Garstang estate for display. He very quickly learned the truth!

The sorry story of what had started out so gloriously as the Historic Aircraft Preservation Society, with the Lancaster flying into Biggin Hill in May 1965, had come to a sad end. At least that was the end of Reflectaire and its Managing Director, neither of whom had brought much credit to the aircraft-preservation movement.

On a positive note, a number of good things were salvaged from the wreckage. The Mew Gull took to the air after a prolonged restoration, the pitiful Mosquito cockpit formed the basis for Tony Agar's epic rebuild of his Mosquito night-fighter, and the Lancaster was saved.

THE IMPORTANCE OF ESTABLISHING A MUSEUM

In the decade following the establishment of Skyfame, which, with the Shuttleworth Trust Collection, had doubled the number of full-time aircraft museums in the country to two, the aircraft-preservation movement had only now added to that number, with the opening of the Torbay Aircraft Museum and the Historic Aircraft Museum at Southend. It is true to say that the Fleet Air Arm Museum had opened in the interim, and the Mosquito Appeal Fund Museum, as it was currently known, had expanded from just exhibiting the Mosquito prototype at Salisbury Hall to a museum with further de Havilland exhibits.

There were also two part-time museums in existence, open only on Sundays: Newark Air Museum and the Lincolnshire Aviation Museum at Tattershall. A third part-time museum in York had opened and then closed, upping sticks and moving 200 miles to Kirby Misperton near the Flamingo Zoo

Park near Malton. The members abandoned and left behind in York formed a new group, the Yorkshire Aircraft Preservation Group, but had neither aircraft or premises.

The 'Grand Old Men' of the movement, the Northern APS, now had over twenty aircraft in their collection, but were still no nearer establishing a museum in the Manchester area. They were, however, well known for placing their aircraft on loan with museums all over the country. In 1972 their aircraft could be found on display in locations as far apart as Torbay, Southend, Bradford, Newcastle and Edinburgh, making their collection more national than northern! This policy, which continues to this day, was to the mutual benefit of all concerned. NAPS found places to locate its aircraft, while the receiving museums were able instantly to add to their collections. Taking aircraft on loan was quickly established as a way of adding variety to a collection, and a way of rotating exhibits in a small museum to give it a continuing freshness.

Without its own premises, the Northern APS was caught in the trap that other groups such as the Midland and South Wales APS were still experiencing. Exhibiting at air displays and other events, both to raise money and to raise public awareness of their existence, was a continuous drain on members' energies. Groups such as Newark, which had managed to create its own museum at Winthorpe, found that fund-raising could be concentrated there. Although money hardly flooded in, there was at least a continuous dribble of funds into the coffers; of course, this advantage had to be balanced against the overheads created.

The Newark society consolidated its position with the official opening of the museum on 14 April 1973, to coincide with the tenth anniversary of the formation of the group. The President of the museum was now Air Commodore David Bonham Carter CBE, DFC, whose thirty-one years in the RAF included a wartime spell at Waddington where he was a Lancaster pilot. Vice Presidents were Charles Waterfall and Leslie Hunt. The museum was opened by Air Chief Marshal the Honourable Sir Ralph Cochrane GBE, KCB, AFT, and there were a substantial number of visiting aircraft gracing Winthorpe's runway. The 24th BPAC meeting was held at Newark the following day.

SCOTLAND

In 1972 the aircraft-preservation movement spread north of the border with the creation of the Scottish Aircraft Preservation Group, centred on Glasgow. It quickly acquired Auster G-ALES from Perth, towing it behind a van for 40 miles to its new home in Bathgate Technical College.

Earlier, Scotland had had its own private warbird operator in the form of Sir Williams Roberts, who developed a collection at Strathallan. Before and during the 1960s, the ownership of flying World War Two combat aircraft had been almost exclusively the preserve of the military, with the odd notable

45

exception. For example, a Spitfire seen flying at any air show was usually John Fairey's two-seat MkVIII, G-AIDN. For a time, this pale blue aircraft was the only such 'warbird' to be seen in Britain, then Charles Masefield imported his red and white Mustang, seen as an almost unbelievable event by many enthusiasts at the time, but serving as the inspiration for a host of such imports since.

The Strathallan collection grew quickly. Most of the airframes were destined to be restored to airworthy condition and to appear at air shows, although their location north of the border made transits long and expensive.

On 11 August there was a last flight for the RAF Bristol Sycamore, when XG554 flew from Upavon to the Torbay Air Museum for preservation. It became the thirteenth complete aircraft on display at Torbay. One of the others, the British Aircraft Swallow G-AFGE, had formerly belonged to another private collection, that of Bertram Arden, who kept a number of light aircraft on his farm next to the Exeter bypass. During the 1950s and 60s he was well known for giving these aircraft the occasional clandestine flip, although they did not hold current certificates of airworthiness!

ACQUIRING HEAVY METAL

The Imperial War Museum in Lambeth had aircraft on display from its opening, first a small number of First World War types, including an RE.8, a Short seaplane, a BE.2C and Sopwith Camel, and a Bristol F.2B Fighter, and then some Second World War types, including a Spitfire, a Swordfish, a Mosquito, a Heinkel He 162, an Me 163 Komet, a Meteor F.8 and a Zero, as well as Typhoon and Lancaster cockpits. Space at Lambeth was limited, as the museum had been built as a hospital, but it had somehow to display the history of the First World War, and its remit was widened as more wars came and went. In 1972 the museum began to use the recently closed RAF Duxford, in itself a very historic airfield, as a store for further acquisitions.

This facility gave the museum the space to preserve large aircraft, and a runway on which to deliver them. The first seeds were sown for a development that would slowly become the most important aircraft preservation centre in Europe. On 22 August 1972 the Avro Shackleton MR.3/3 landed at Duxford as one of the first arrivals. The voluntary sector, in the shape of the East Anglian Aviation Society, had a part to play at Duxford from the start. Other interests included the hope to open in the near future an Eighth Air Force Exhibition in the Control Tower at Bassingbourn.

At about this time Hawker-Siddeley Aviation at Woodford had a number of Vampire T.11s in store, which they had bought back from their previous operators, hoping to sell them on. This now looked unlikely and so an offer was made through the BAPC to dispose of these aircraft for a nominal fee. A few groups had already tested the water with the acquisition of complex jet aircraft; now every voluntary group in the country suddenly had the chance to take on its own piece of heavy metal. It was almost as if a test hurdle had been placed in front of every aircraft preservation society; would they wish to jump over it?

CHAPTER 7

Rapid Expansion

HENDON AND DUXFORD

ON 15 November 1972 the RAF Museum at Hendon was formally opened by The Queen. Thirty-seven aircraft were initially on display in a purpose-built museum based around some historic World War One hangars. Instantly, a new benchmark for the static display of historic aircraft had been set. The surroundings and displays were pristine, as were the aircraft, at least externally. The Fleet Air Arm Museum had shown the way some years before, but Hendon set new standards in spaciousness and sheer size.

At the same time a rival with a slightly different philosophy was being created in Cambridgshire. The Imperial War Museum store at Duxford, which already contained a Shackleton, Sea Venom, Sea Vampire, Sea Vixen, Canberra, Gannet and Mustang, added a Beagle 206, Beagle Pup and Auster AOP.9. An Anson, Magister, Junkers Ju 52 and a Super Sabre were also expected in the near future, but it was another expected arrival that would set Duxford apart from Hendon. Ormond Haydon-Baillie's 'Royalist Air Force' of privately owned warbirds was expected to take up residence.

It was this combination of national museum, voluntary group (the East Anglian Aviation Society, later the Duxford Aviation Society) and private warbird operators that would eventually make Duxford such a special place. It became a collection of historic aircraft set on an active airfield, and including flying aircraft. The Shuttleworth Trust had already achieved this distinction, but Duxford was to be on a significantly larger scale. Additionally, the aircraft exhibited were to come from the entire spectrum, with the East Anglian Aviation Society taking the first steps towards what would become an impressive collection of civil airliners with the acquisition of Hunting's DC-3, G-ANAF, later in the year.

NEW BAPC MEMBERS

An aviation archaeology group, the Chiltern Historic Aircraft Preservation Group, was a notable new attendee at the first BAPC meeting of 1973. Formed by Peter Halliday of High Wycombe, it had already excavated a Hurricane crash site and would excavate a Wellington site later in the year. Early meetings were at High Wycombe College, and the group soon become a BAPC member, although there were a number of dissenting voices against the inclusion of such groups in the council.

Although some of the preservation groups had already done some of their own crash-site investigation, the growth of groups whose primary aim was the discovery, excavation and investigation of crash sites was a new phenomenon during the 1970s. The groups quickly came to represent a separate movement, inevitably with a finite lifetime, as all known crash sites were eventually investigated and all reasonable items of wreckage removed. The newly coined term for such activities was aviation archaeology.

At the same BAPC meeting the Lincolnshire Aviation Society, as it was now known, reported a new exhibit at its museum at Tattershall – de Havilland Dove G-AHRI. The aircraft was collected from Brooklands on 3 February and en route to Lincolnshire carefully negotiated a low bridge. The next low bridge was marked as being 11in higher than the last one, so the transport team drove confidently under it. There was a sickening jolt and crash, and after stopping they discovered that the top of the fin had been knocked off. It seems that such markings should never be trusted!

The speed of expansion of the aircraft-preservation movement during the mid-1970s was exemplified at the next BAPC meeting, when no less than six new members were voted in. As well as the Chiltern Group, these were the Strathallan Collection, the Historic Aircraft Preservation Group, the Solway Aviation Society (who, famously, had saved the Hawker Hart Trainer now exhibited at Hendon), the Science Museum, which contained within its National Aeronautical Collection on its top floor some of the most singularly historic aircraft in the country, the Norfolk and Suffolk Aviation Society and the Northern Aeroplane Workshops.

The Northern Aeroplane Workshops organization was different from most others in the movement in that its aim was not to create its own aircraft museum or even to preserve its own aircraft, but to preserve and pass on the skills of building early aircraft and to support the Shuttleworth Collection by the construction of exact flying replicas of significant World War One aircraft. Their first task quickly crystallized into the construction of a Sopwith Triplane from original drawings, for which Shuttleworth's supplied the Clerget engine. It was a daunting task, which was to take many years to come to fruition. Chairman was John Langham, and the actual construction was under the direction of Eric Barraclough, who had previously worked at Heston Aircraft and Auster's. A workshop was established initially in the Dewsbury area.

The Northern Aeroplane Workshops was not the first such group. The 49 Group in Bristol was still working on its Magister replica, which would eventually find its way to the Woodley Museum, but NAW was certainly to become the most remarkable organization of its kind.

MAPS EXPANDS

In the Midlands, MAPS was making rapid strides in a more traditional way. Following Newark and Tattershall, it had entered the world of jet aircraft acquisition in a big way. It acquired two of the earliest surviving jet fighters in the country, the Vampire F.1, VF301 from the gate at RAF Debden, and the Meteor F.4, EE531, from RAF Lasham. The latter proved an instant source of income for the society when it was placed on the forecourt of Meteor Ford, a car dealers in Moseley, Birmingham! As well as these two jets, MAPS also took delivery of its first Vampire T.11, XE872, which was moved for display to the Blue Lias pub at Stockton, near Rugby. The two Vampires, the F.1 and the T.11, brought the total of de Havilland aircraft owned by MAPS to four, along with the fuselage of the Fox Moth, G-ACCB, and the Rapide, G-AJBJ.

The rapid pace of acquisitions meant that the society had little or no time for long-term restoration, although the Flying Flea G-AEGV had just emerged from an extensive re-fit and re-paint, and it was hoped that the University of Aston Gliding Club would rebuild the Slingsby Cadet. With so much time being spent dismantling, moving and re-erecting new exhibits, there was little left over for serious restoration work, even if suitable premises and facilities had been available. As a result, there were some calls to halt the rate of acquisition.

One long-term benefit of the acquisitions being made by MAPS, and by many other societies at about this time, was that aircraft that otherwise would probably have been burned or scrapped, such as the Fox Moth and Rapide, were tucked away safely. Although MAPS members, for example, were never able to do anything with the aircraft themselves, those aircraft would re-emerge years later to be sold to individuals with the wherewithal to put them back in the air. Later in the year, MAPS also acquired Percival Q-6 G-AFFO, from Redhill, minus outer wings. Again, the society itself could do little with the Percival, other than place it in store, but years later it was destined to be sold to someone prepared to restore it to flying condition.

In common with most groups, MAPS still tended to acquire every aircraft that came along, with no kind of formal collecting policy, but this magpie instinct certainly saved a significant number of aircraft that would otherwise have disappeared.

RAF MUSEUM ACQUISITIONS

The RAF Museum now entered the field of aviation archaeology in a big way. Conscious that there were no Handley Page Halifaxes left in the world, it sent a combined team, from the RAF British sub-aqua club and the Norwegians, to raise Halifax 'S for Sugar' W1048 from the depths of Lake Hoklingen in Norway, where she had crash-landed on the ice in 1942 after attacking the

Tirpitz. The extraordinary operation brought probably the most complete and original World War Two heavy bomber in existence back for eventual display in the RAF Museum, albeit in an un-restored state. Although a small start was made, the costs of restoration were soon discovered to be massive, and there were strong arguments for leaving the aircraft as she was found. Restoration would have meant literally throwing away much of the structure and skin of the aircraft and replacing it with new metal. The result would have been a part-replica, and the real historic value of the aircraft as it was, completely original, displaying the battle damage it received and showing the effects of its crash-landing and its thirty-year immersion in the lake, would have been lost for ever.

At about the same time the RAF acquired another World War Two heavy bomber, the ex-HAPS/Reflectaire Lancaster NX611, which had been bought at the Blackpool sale by Lord Lilford. When Lord Lilford discovered that what he had bought was far from being in flying condition, he put the aircraft up for sale, but no offers matched his asking price. Conscious that Blackpool Council was charging him £5 per day parking fee, and that the aircraft was continuing to suffer in the salt-laden Blackpool air, he handed the aircraft over to the RAF in a ceremony on 2 August 1972, with Group Captain Richard Lockyer accepting the generous gift.

Warrant Officer Peter H. Higgins MBE took charge of the dismantling and removal of the Lancaster, with a team of ten airmen, all of whom were volunteers giving up part of their leave for the task. They began their work in appalling conditions of driving rain, intense cold and winds gusting up to 50 knots, but in less than a week the aircraft was at Scampton, ready to be refurbished, and eventually to be placed on the gate, where an even more famous Lancaster, R5868, had once stood. Warrant Officer Higgins, who had worked on Manchesters, Lancasters and Lincolns during his time, and his team, were then able to return to the slightly more comfortable maintenance of the RAF's Vulcan bombers.

More New Members and Some Bad News

At the next meeting of the BAPC, at Southend, disquiet was already being expressed about the future of the Historic Aircraft Museum. Full-time staff had been laid off, but assurances were given that there was no fear of closure. The number of members of the BAPC increased yet again, to thirty-two, with the inclusion of the Airborne Forces Museum and the Battle of Britain Museum, another aircraft archaeology group. Its Chairman Mike Llewellyn sought to assure the doubters, who believed that some of the 'wreck-hunters' had brought disrepute to the whole movement, that his group was in fact a competent and responsible organization. Indeed, it had investigated dozens of crash sites and placed many of the finds on display at Chilham Castle in Kent.

At the same meeting the Norfolk and Suffolk Society, by now a traditional voluntary aircraft-preservation group, was able to announce that it had acquired an Anson from Norwich Airport and had moved it to Bungay, close to the Norfolk/Suffolk border. In this way, the seeds had been sown for what would become in time a large museum.

One piece of bad news was announced in the last edition of *Control Column* for 1973: the cover price, which had remained at 12.5p for three years, would have to be increased to a massive 15p from January 1974.

Further bad news for the preservation movement came early in 1974. The advisory committee to the Historic Aircraft Museum at Southend disbanded, with effect from 8 February. The fate of the country's first purpose-built aircraft museum seemed to depend on the Southend Council elections on 1 April. The first attempt at an aircraft museum as a commercial venture, Southend had struggled from the outset, and yet even as it teetered on the brink, rare new exhibits (at least for Britain) continued to arrive. A Fairchild Cornell was delivered via Felixstowe docks and the official handing-over ceremony of the Belgian Air Force Thunderstreak took place on 15 March.

The museum at Southend was also one beneficiary of the dispersal of a batch of Vampire T.11s from Hawker-Siddeley at Woodford, via the BAPC. The acquisition of these aircraft was vitally important to many of the voluntary groups, initiating many of them into the world of preserving jet aircraft, and even kick-starting a number of museum projects. The disposal of the thirteen Vampires had been completed by the beginning of 1974, and the lucky recipients were as follows:

1.   The Imperial War Museum took WZ590, and placed it in its store at Duxford.
2.   Lincolnshire Air Museum acquired XD447, its second Vampire T.11.
3.   The Merseyside Aviation Society cemented its move into aircraft preservation with the acquisition of WZ553, which went into store at Speke.
4.   The Midland Aircraft Preservation Society acquired XE872 and put it on display at the Blue Lias Inn at Stockton.
5.   Newark Air Museum obtained XD593.
6.   The Northern Aircraft Preservation Society added two of the Vampires, XD435 and XD535, to its large collection; with the usual storage problems, it passed them into the care of Harpurhey ATC and the Royal Umpire Museum at Croston, respectively.
7.   Skyfame Museum obtained WZ515.
8.   The Solway Aviation Society was the first group to obtain one of these Vampires, WZ507, which was placed on display at Carlisle Airport.
9.   Southend Air Museum obtained XK625.

10.   The South Wales Historic Aircraft Preservation Society acquired WZ425, the twenty-first production aircraft, and the oldest of the batch. It moved it to Rhoose Airport, where it became the society's first resident there.

11.   The Strathallan Collection took XD403 to add to its growing museum.

12.   Torbay Air Museum obtained XE995.

13.   The Yorkshire Aircraft Preservation Society made WZ557 their first complete aircraft.

Today, eleven of these thirteen Vampires are still preserved, although only two of them, those at Newark and Duxford, are still owned by the same organization. Five of the others were disposed of when groups or museums folded. Vampires were becoming the common currency of aircraft preservation – every museum seemed to have one, and some had more than one.

AROUND THE STATIONS

The twenty-seventh meeting of the BAPC was held at RAF Colerne. This station had always had one of the better-organized station museums, which now had a new, rather unwieldy name – 'The Strike Command Historic Aircraft Regional Collection Centre'. The museum had recently acquired the Handley Page H.P.115 and Hastings TG536, and was expecting a Catalina from Denmark. Later in the year a B-24 would also fly in, a gift from the Indian Air Force. This would make a total of thirty-one aircraft on display, creating one of the largest and finest aircraft museums in the world. Unfortunately, however, it was not open regularly to the public, offering only the occasional open day and appointments by special prior permission.

Colerne was not the only RAF station to hold its own substantial aircraft collection. There were others at St Athan, Finningley and Cosford, apart from the RAF Museum store at Henlow. Cosford was the first of the four to open on a regular basis, as the Aerospace Museum, initially on the first Sunday of the month during the summer only. With the eventual closure of both Colerne and Finningly, Cosford was destined to expand dramatically, with the acquisition of most of their aircraft; it became one of the world's major museums in its own right.

The Royal Air Force also had three other collections of old airframes, usually recently retired from service. There were the ground instructional aircraft, mostly at Halton and Cosford, but also to be found elsewhere, which were largely well looked after, apart from those subject to battle-damage repair training. There were two other types of collection across Britain: the 'gate guardians' and the Air Training Corps airframes. The condition of these depended largely on the RAF station or the ATC squadron concerned, as they were all usually kept out of doors. Most were treated well and, where there were particularly enthusiastic personnel involved, some were kept with exceptional care; a few fared less well.

These aircraft – sometimes, in the case of ATC units, they were no more than cockpits – were often retired not just from active service, but also from ground instructional use for RAF training. They therefore tended to be quite old, and some were already truly historic, representing a national resource that the aircraft-preservation movement could tap into in the future. Indeed, there were still Spitfires and even Hurricanes to be found on gate guardian duty. Very often, their existence reflected a particular interest of the station concerned in 'its' airframe, and a desire to keep it and look after it.

DEVELOPMENTS IN THE SOCIETIES

At about this time there was another change of name when the Northern Aircraft Preservation Society followed the example of Newark and became a limited company, with the new title of the Aeroplane Collection Ltd. At almost the same time a new society was born in the same area with the formation of the Stockport Aircraft Preservation Society, chaired by M. Eastman, reflecting a divergence of opinion within NAPS as to where the society was going, and what its aims should be. For the time being, Stockport's application to join the BAPC was put on hold. Two groups in the same area was seen as a result of conflict, and a potential source of further conflict. Nevertheless the delay in accepting Stockport's application only lasted until the next BAPC meeting, by which time the group was working on a Vampire T.11, WZ518, and several Miles Gemini sections, from at least six aircraft, from which it hoped to build three complete machines. The group had adopted premises at the old 61 M.U. site at Handworth, Cheshire, and another immediate addition was Auster J.1N G-AGXT.

Other collections were able to announce at the meeting a tidal wave of new additions. The Lincolnshire Air Museum had acquired two aircraft – Auster AOP.9 XK417 and Westland Dragonfly WH991 – on loan from a local scrap dealer, an almost unheard-of piece of largesse from a profession reputed throughout the preservation movement for knowing the price per pound of everything and the value of nothing.

The East Anglian Aviation Society was able to announce that its Dan-Air Comet 4 G-APDB would be flown in to Duxford (once again showing the huge advantage of having an active runway), where it would join the society's Magister, Dove and DC-3. At the same time the EAAS was restoring Shuttleworth's Spitfire, AR501, in one of the hangars at Duxford, which were slowly becoming a restoration centre for many projects and organizations. Also in storage at Duxford were Shuttleworth's Anson and MAPS' Percival Q-6.

The first ever open day at Duxford was held on 23 June 1974. Although no flying display was scheduled, visiting aircraft were allowed a couple of passes down the crowd line, and things were enlivened by the landing of a British Airways Boeing 737 and a USAF Hercules. Haydon-Baillie's three flyable aircraft were a centre of attraction as was the EAAS's Comet 4, for which there was a long queue to file through at 20p a time. Also on display was the Consolidated B-24, which was at Duxford for a prolonged stay before moving on to Yesterday's Air Force at Chino. A second open day was planned for October with the first flying display for July 1975.

In a version of the EAAS/Imperial War Museum relationship, the Aircraft Preservation Society of Scotland was admitted to membership of BAPC, and would act in support of the growing collection of the Royal Scottish Museum held at East Fortune airfield, which would soon include the BAC.221, WG774. They had NAPS's Rapide G-ADAH and B.A. Swallow G-AEVZ on loan, and the Weir W.2 autogyro on loan from the Science Museum. East Fortune was a government-funded operation, effectively the National Aircraft Museum of Scotland.

The Chiltern HAPG confounded those who had believed its members to be merely 'wreck-hunters' by acquiring Venom NF.3 WX788, from Flint Technical College, and then a Provost, XF898, from Southall College of Aeronautics. The group was based in the High Wycombe area, although the Secretary, R. Barfoot, lived in Maidenhead. The Venom and the Provost were stored on a farm for some time, but were eventually turfed out; the Provost went to a private owner and the Venom went to the Wales Aircraft Museum at Rhoose.

The north-east of Britain was one area of the country that had remained something of a black hole as far as aircraft preservation was concerned. In 1974 Tony Blenkinsop helped form the North East Vintage and Veteran Aircraft Association, based on Usworth Airfield, Sunderland. The Sunderland Aero Club lent its briefing room for society meetings, and various visits and expeditions were planned until the day when the new group could obtain its first aircraft. When its first acquisition was made possible, it was not just one aircraft but a fleet. One local man donated a number of relics, all of which had been built by his father in a small miner's cottage. The first was a Luton Minor, built between 1937 and 1944 from plans that appeared in *Practical Mechanics*. The other surviving aircraft acquired by the society were a home-built helicopter and a Bensen gyro-glider. To this fleet the group quickly added a Westland Dragonfly HAR.3, WG724, from a scrapyard, a Gloster Meteor F.8, WL181, derelict at RAF Acklington, the fuselage of Jet Provost Mk.5, XW331, and Vampire T.11 VW518.

There was another name change at Salisbury Hall, where the museum was re-titled the Mosquito Aircraft Museum. The new name harked back to the days when the Mosquito prototype was the only aircraft there, and the number of aircraft on the site doubled, with the donation by Liverpool Council of Mosquito Mk.35 TA634. When the Mosquito was moved, most of the pipework and control runs were severed, as it was believed it would never fly again; for the time being, it had to be displayed outside, which, although it appealed to photographers, was not good for its wooden structure. Many de Havilland aircraft were wooden, or at least had a large proportion of wood in their structure, like the early jets, so a large new hangar was a matter of priority. However, much of the takings went to the RAF Benevolent Fund, making funding a new building difficult.

The museum was rapidly becoming the premier collection of de Havilland aircraft as a whole. A Vampire FB.6, J-1008, arrived in April. A gift of the Swiss Air Force, the aircraft was flown to Hatfield and officially handed over to Mr W. Lambert, Director of Hawker-Siddeley Aviation and museum committee member by Captain Buergisser, the Swiss Assistant Defence Attaché. Another acquisition was the Hornet Moth G-ADOT, and a Sea Vixen was expected in the near future.

As the Swiss Air Force retired its immaculate Venoms, a number found their way to Britain, with J-1172 going to Colerne for the Royal Air Force Museum's reserve collection. A rather more spectacular last flight was made on 15 August by ex-51 RAF Squadron Comet 2 XK655, which flew to retirement from Wyton to the Strathallan collection. Unusually for a jet transport, the intention was to land the aircraft on Strathallan's short grass runway. After a long wait for a suitable headwind, the pilot made five approaches before he was satisfied; on touchdown, the starboard undercarriage was wiped off. The Comet came to rest on one wing-tip without too much damage, and it was soon resting on its wheels once more.

Already at Strathallan there were five Avro Ansons Mk.21s, four of which were for sale, a de Havilland DH.82 Dragon, and a Miles Magister, with a Lancaster expected from Canada, and a Firefly from Australia. Another of 51 Squadron's Comet 2s, XK696, was delivered to the Imperial War Museum at Duxford, this one landing somewhat less dramatically.

THE MIDLAND AIR MUSEUM

On 18 January 1975 the Midland Aircraft Preservation Society, still lacking suitable premises of its own, hosted the thirty-first BAPC meeting at the National Agricultural Centre at Stoneleigh, in Warwickshire. The increasingly urgent need for premises was highlighted by Chairman John Berkeley, who was able to announce MAPS's acquisition of its twenty-first aircraft, the Fairey ultra-light helicopter from Cranfield. Two more member groups were elected to the council. The Surrey Aircraft Preservation Society, based at the Parish Church Hall in Leatherhead and run by President Neville Duke, was apparently already the proud owner of three donated aircraft – a Vampire, a Proctor and a Tiger Moth. The second new member was the North Eastern Vintage and Veteran

Aircraft Association, based in Newcastle with an expanding collection, and hoping to set up a museum in a safari park.

Relief for MAPS' accommodation problems was at hand. On 9 June the Libraries, Arts and Leisure Committee of Coventry Council gave the go-ahead for the society to set up the Midland Air Museum at Baginton Airport. An area of land next to the airport's approach road was allocated, and the first priority for the new museum was the acquisition and erection of some security fencing, to fence in 3,000sq yds, and the erection of a small building to house minor exhibits. Like Newark and Tattershall before them, MAPS members were discovering that opening and running an aircraft museum meant building work rather than aircraft work; at the same time, they had to find the resources and the time to move their latest acquisitions, the fuselage of a Gnat F.1 from Lucas Aerospace, Wolverhampton, and the Boulton Paul P.111A, on indefinite loan from the College of Aeronautics at Cranfield.

Interestingly, Dowty Boulton Paul Ltd had been offered the P.111A when it became surplus to requirements at Cranfield, and made initial plans to mount it on top of their gatehouse. They soon discovered, however, that it could not be dismantled, because the delta wing and fuselage was a single integrated structure; indeed, this should not have come as a complete surprise, since it was they who had built the aircraft only twenty-five years before! They concluded that transport from Cranfield would prove too difficult and too expensive, so they gave up the idea of acquiring it.

The volunteers at MAPS managed to solve the transport problems, and arranged for the little delta to be moved to Coventry as one of the first residents of the new museum. Their first idea of getting a USAF helicopter to airlift it were scuppered by the fuel restriction in force at the time, so they enlisted the help of the Ford Motor Car Co., which provided a truck courtesy of C.H. Soan's and Sons Ltd, of Leamington. With a 25-ft wide load, the truck moved out of Cranfield at 4am on Sunday 13 July, and with a police escort moved up the almost deserted M1 and A45 to its new home.

The first seeds of a definite theme for the new museum – early jet aircraft – were sown when MAPS acquired a Whittle engine from a Coventry scrapyard, and arranged for it to be overhauled by Rover apprentices. Frank Whittle had developed his first engine just down the road at Lutterworth, and the society already possessed several early jets, including the Vampire F.1 and the Meteor F.4 (currently on display at Sandvik Ltd, Bentham, Gloucestershire, the factory where it was made).

AROUND THE COUNTRY

Another more commercial collection of historic aircraft was being gathered at an old flooded gravel pit next to the Staines to Chertsey road in Surrey. A new division of the Ready Mix Concrete Group, Leisure Sport Ltd, was developing a theme park on the site, and was collecting aircraft with a naval theme, beginning with Sea Hawk WV798, Whirlwind XM655 and Sea Vixen XP919. These were to be augmented by a series of replicas, the first of which was to be a taxiable Supermarine S.5.

Large new museum exhibits around the country were the Lancaster G-BCOH, ex-KB976, which had flown in to Strathallan, and would shortly be followed by its younger brother, Shackleton T.4 VP293, and also an ex-Monarch Airlines Bristol Britannia, G-AOVT, and a Convair VT-29B-CO, 0-17899, both new arrivals at Duxford. These had been preceded by the arrival of a Varsity earlier in the year, and would be joined shortly by a Boeing B-17 from France. The Flight Line at Duxford was already becoming one of the most impressive collections of large aircraft in the world, with another new addition expected from Speke.

The Viscount Preservation Trust's Viscount G-ALWF had languished at Speke Airport almost since its arrival there, out of the public domain because of security problems. For a while it remained in its hangar, and donated its outer wings to Cambrian Airways Viscount 701s that were still operating. Time-expired wings were exchanged but not fitted because of the space needed in the hangar, which eventually caused G-ALWF to be pushed outside. After an approach, it was offered to Duxford, to join a rapidly growing collection of airliners, and a team from the Duxford Aviation Society began the long trek to Liverpool every weekend for two months to dismantle the aircraft.

Team numbers varied, and they were aided in their endeavours by some members of the Merseyside Aviation Society. Work was delayed mainly by the wing spar bolts, which had seized in their holes. There were thirty to remove and the rate was only four per weekend! They were further hampered by the increasingly wintry weather. Airfields are never the most comfortable place to work outdoors in winter, and Speke is more exposed to the weather than most.

The last visit of the year was on 6 December, and then there was a break until 10 January, when work on dismantling the tailplane continued. By 14 February the various aircraft parts were being loaded on trailers, provided by Crane Fruehauf Trailers of Dereham, and on Friday 20 February a 'dummy' removal was staged for the benefit of the BBC *Look North* cameras. The fuselage finally left for real the following day, pulled by trucks provided by Crewe Haulage, to make its 200-mile trip to Duxford, with the wings following a week later. Now, 'all' that remained was to re-assemble the aircraft in time for the first Duxford open day of the year, in June.

BAPC DEVELOPMENTS

Control Column reported in September 1975 that the BAPC had elected three

Vice-Chairmen, Donald Storer of the Royal Scottish Museum, David Ogilvy of the Shuttleworth Trust, and John Langham of the Northern Aeroplane Workshops. The BAPC administrative workload was increasing by the month; four new members had been added at the last meeting of 1976, held at the Torbay Air Museum. Among them, the Humberside Aircraft Preservation Society (Secretary Mrs D.L. Diamond), based at Immingham, already owned the frame of Auster J.1N G-AIJI, and Messenger fuselage G-AKBM. The near-by South Yorkshire Aviation Society (Chairman Mike Cook), of Doncaster, already owned a Meteor NF.14 and a Bristol Sycamore. The latter group had started in the usual way with a meeting of local enthusiasts, including Mike Cook, Ray Dixon and Wendy Mills, who later on became Manager of Netherthorpe Airfield.

At the other end of the country, the Cornwall Aeronautical Park Ltd had been formed by ex- and serving Fleet Air Arm members to display aircraft in an enclosure next to RNAS Culdrose. Their first exhibits were two Sea Hawks, two Whirlwinds and a Sycamore. Finally, Doug Bianchi's Personal Plane Services also joined BAPC.

Reginald Mitchell Museum

Perhaps the most famous aircraft designer Britain had produced, other than those who gave their names to the companies they founded, was Reginald Mitchell. As the fortieth anniversary of the first flight of his Spitfire approached, the people of Southampton made plans to create a permanent memorial to the man who, though born in Staffordshire, had brought such prestige to the town during the course of his career.

The council had been presented with his Supermarine S.6A in 1948, and had displayed it for many years at the Mayflower Park end of the Royal Pier, where the sea air had caused considerable damage. In 1967 it was removed to South Marston to be refurbished by Vickers-Supermarine, and it had languished in storage ever since. Over these years, many people in Southampton, particularly the Junior Chamber of Commerce, had worked towards the creation of a Mitchell Memorial Museum, but in mid-1975 the struggle had been abandoned.

On 1 September 1976, after vigorous lobbying, Southampton City Council agreed not to demolish the old Marlands Dance Hall in the city centre, but to hand it over to a new R.J. Mitchell Committee, which planned to refurbish and rebuild to house the S.6A and the Spitfire XXIV, PK683. (The latter had also been returned to the town of its construction, from RAF Changi in Singapore.) President of the Committee was Wing Commander Don Bennett, who presided over an appeal for £3,000 to set up the museum, with a target date for opening of March 1976.

INTERESTING PROJECTS

The January 1976 edition of *Control Column* described, for the first time in any detail, the remarkable project being undertaken by Tony Agar and friends in Yorkshire. Many years before, it had reported Agar's acquisition of a Mosquito cockpit at the Reflectaire sale at Blackpool, for the princely sum of £7.00, and had mentioned from time to time his continued search across the length and breadth of the country for Mosquito parts. In January 1976, it printed a photograph of Agar wheeling the complete fuselage of a Mosquito out of his garage. Painted in the markings of No.169 Squadron and with the serial HJ711, it had finally outgrown the garage, and was on the way to larger premises, at Elvington airfield near York. Tony Agar was a good example of an aircraft-preservation group member of the York Air Museum who had latched on to his own project with a single-mindedness that carried it steadily forward even when the group itself was falling by the wayside; progress continues slowly today, over thirty years later, and completion is now in sight.

Later in the year another report in *Control Column* contained the first grains of a preservation saga that is also still progressing slowly today. Climbing Mount Tsatsa in Northern Sweden, two Swedish mountain climbers came upon the wreckage of Handley Page Hampden AE436. It had been one of sixteen Hampdens that left Sumburgh in the Shetlands on 4 September 1942, en route to Murmansk, from where they were intended to operate against German naval forces in northern waters. Nine of the aircraft failed to reach their destination and AE436 was one of these. It had hit Tsatsa on a stony plateau just west of the peak (which stood at an altitude of over 6,000ft). The aircraft broke up on impact and burst into flames, but two of the five crew members, the pilot and the wireless operator, survived. The wireless operator was able to walk free, as the tail boom had broken off just behind his position, and the two men struggled for five days across the mountains until they came to a village. No attempt was made to reach the three dead crew members in the wreck, which was soon covered by winter snows.

After the three climbers reported their find, Norwegian Air Force personnel flew to the site by helicopter, and the remains of the dead crew men were removed, and buried in a war cemetery at Gothenburg. The RAF Museum took an immediate interest in the wreckage, as there was no surviving Hampden in Britain, and plans were made to bring the wreckage down off the mountain. Ultimately, in fact, the RAF Museum relinquished the aircraft, when they obtained a rather more undamaged Hampden wreck from Russia. AE436 eventually ended up in a shed on East Kirkby aerodrome, part of the Lincolnshire Aviation Heritage Centre, and became the subject of a painstaking restoration by Brian Nicholls and a tiny band of helpers. When Brian Nicholls died in 1996, at the tragically early age of 34, his widow Janet, along with the helpers, continued the work as the Brian Nicholls Hampden Project. The project continues today, and ranks as the metal equivalent of Tony Agar's wooden wonder.

TWO SUNDERLANDS

In 1977, Short Sunderland ML824, the preservation of which had kick-started the whole aircraft-preservation movement in Britain, made its first appearance at its new home, the RAF Museum Hendon. It was displayed outside next to the Beverley for a while, before going into store in the Grahame-White hangar to await the appearance of its permanent home in the Battle of Britain Museum. This was the aircraft that had brought Peter Thomas on to the scene and prompted his formation of the Skyfame Aircraft Museum.

Despite the tremendous success of actually preserving the flying boat in a climate of indifference towards aircraft preservation, Pembroke Dock had never been a suitable place for its long-term survival. Although it had been built for a sea-going life, nearly twenty years of standing in the salt-laden air had inevitably taken their toll. Movement to external display at Hendon was no guarantee of survival; indeed, the Sunderland's temporary outdoor companion, the Blackburn Beverley, was subsequently scrapped. It was some time before something more than surface restoration of the Sunderland began, and by then there was another Sunderland in the country. The Imperial War Museum acquired ML796 from La Baule in France, and another epic dismantling and moving job was undertaken.

Transporting the two Sunderlands was a difficult job, but was necessary for all of Hendon's exhibits, even landplanes in flying condition, because of the lack of a runway. The Imperial War Museum at Duxford had been able to fly in large landplanes to its active runways, but was also now having trouble on that score. Plans for the M11 would cut 1,000ft from the length of the main runway, as well as severing the taxiway. Those 1,000ft were vital if the pre-production Concorde 01, expected soon, was to be flown. Plans were hastily made to get the aircraft there before the construction crews arrived.

The British Concorde prototype 002, owned by the Science Museum, was to go on display at Yeovilton, a slightly incongrous location, but as near to its birthplace in Bristol as could be found. From the opposite end of the chronological spectrum, the cockpit of the Short 184, which had flown at the Battle of Jutland, was also coming from the Imperial War Museum, to go in the Fleet Air Arm Museum's new extension.

MORE BAPC MEMBERS

The Duxford Aviation Society had been born out of the East Anglian Aviation Society, to support the Imperial War Museum's plans for Duxford airfield, which now included the complete restoration of all the airfield buildings, some of which dated back to the First World War. They were valuable as historic exhibits themselves, as well as providing a home for the growing collection, which now numbered over fifty aircraft. The East Anglian Aviation Society continued in support of other projects in the region and became a limited company, and both groups became BAPC members.

Other new BAPC members were the R.J. Mitchell Hall, the 501 Bristol Aircraft Preservation Group, which already owned Chipmunk, WG362, and the British Rotor-craft Collection. A new aircraft museum was also in the offing, just as an old one was faced with closure. The Lincolnshire Aviation Society's lease on the site at Tattershall was to expire in June 1976, and they were faced with finding a new home; at the same time the South Wales group had finally acquired a site for a museum at Rhoose Airport. They already had a Vampire T.11, Gannet, Proctor and Sea Venom in position, and had been promised a Viscount 800.

Another aircraft soon to arrive at Rhoose was a Vickers Varsity, a type just being retired from the RAF. Several examples were to find their way immediately into museums. As well as the one flying down to South Wales, one went to a MAPS member at Coventry, and one each to Waddington, Newark and Duxford.

In the 1976 New Year's Honours List Leslie Hunt was honoured with the award of the MBE, not for his services towards the aircraft preservation movement, but for his fund-raising activities for the Trueloves School for physically handicapped boys at Ingatestone, Essex. In fact, his two interests were closely linked. Each edition of his book *Veteran and Vintage Aircraft*, which had become the 'bible' of the aircraft-preservation movement, even before *Wrecks and Relics*, had been produced in order to raise funds for the Trueloves School. The first paperback edition had appeared in 1965 and had raised £660 for the school. The third and fourth editions were commercially produced in hardback. With the book, and by other means through the Southend Branch of the RAFA, Leslie Hunt had helped raise tens of thousands of pounds for the School and for Muscular Dystrophy Research, and at the same time had raised awareness of the Aircraft Preservation Movement.

In the mid-1970s, Hunt was giving up production of his book, but the publication *Wrecks and Relics*, now edited by Ken Ellis, was already taking up the mantle of *Veteran and Vintage Aircraft*. At the same time, *Control Column* was changing, with an increase in the cover price from 16p to 25p, and a decrease in the number of editions per year from twelve to eight.

ANOTHER GENEROUS DISTRIBUTION

In 1976 the aircraft-preservation movement was about to get the most amazing distribution of 'free' aircraft, eclipsing even the earlier dispersal of Vampire T.11s from Hawker-Siddeley at Woodford. A large number of French Air Force jet aircraft, paid for by the American Military Aid Programme, and the Offshore Procurement Program, in effect Lend-Lease, were coming to the end of their lease periods. They consisted of North-American F-100 Super Sabres, Dassault Mystere IVA jet fighters and Lockheed T-33 jet trainers. The aircraft were flown to USAF Sculthorpe in Norfolk for disposal. A few were recycled and passed on to the Turkish and Greek Air Forces, but most were unwanted, especially the Mysteres, which were an unknown quantity to the USAF.

Group Captain T. Stafford (retired), Chairman of the Newark Air Museum at the time, approached a friend in the US 3rd Air Force, and suggested some of the airframes should be preserved at Winthorpe. In the ensuing discussions, the USAF became aware of the extent of the British preservation movement, and decided as a public relations exercise to offer many of the aircraft as a gift to any group that could care for them. Unfortunately, Customs and Excise then announced that they would charge VAT and import duty on any aircraft allocated to a preservation group, which immediately put the acquisition of the aircraft out of the reach of most groups.

After discussions with customs, the deal was changed, and the aircraft were offered on indefinite loan to any suitable aircraft-preservation group that could provide an adequate home. Customs agreed to waive any tax or duty, as the aircraft would not be permanent imports, at least not on paper. Over the next few years a large number of groups and museums took advantage of this offer, and the bounty was distributed all over Britain (see list below). Many of the organizations concerned acquired their aircraft right away, but others were not even yet in existence. The French aircraft were later augmented by ex-Belgian and Turkish aircraft of the same types. Many were also put on display at other USAF bases.

Aerospace Museum, Cosford
   T-33A, 17473
Bomber County Aviation Museum
   Mystere IVA 101
City of Norwich Aviation Museum
   Mystere IVA 121; T-33A 16718
Dumfries and Galloway Aviation Museum
   Mystere IVA 318; Super Sabre 42163; T-33A FT-36
Imperial War Museum, Duxford
   Mystere IVA 57; Super Sabre 42165; T-33A 14286
Lashenden Air Warfare Museum
   Mystere IVA 84; Super Sabre 63938
Loughborough and Leicester Air Museum
   Mystere IVA 85; Super Sabre 42239 (later returned to USAF)
Midland Air Museum, Coventry
   Mystere IVA 70; Super Sabre 42174; T-33A 14419

Newark Air Museum
        Mystere IVA 83; Super Sabre 42223; T-33A 19036
Norfolk and Suffolk Aviation Museum, Flixton
        Mystere IVA 79; Super Sabre 42196; T-33A 54433
North Eastern Aircraft Museum
        Mystere IVA 146; Super Sabre 42157; T-33A 54439
Rebel Air Museum, Andrewsfield
        Mystere IVA 319
Wales Aircraft Museum, Rhoose
        Mystere IVA 59; Super Sabre 42160; T-33A 29963
Wealden Aircraft Group
        T-33A 19252

De Havilland Moth G-EBWD at Old Warden. The founder member of the Shuttleworth Collection, although it was a modern light aircraft when Richard Shuttleworth first bought it, this Moth has been based on the same airfield longer than any aircraft, anywhere.

The 1912 Blackburn Monoplane at Old Warden in 1968. The oldest flyable British aircraft, it was one of the earliest members of Shuttleworth's fleet.

One of the first of Richard Shuttleworth's vintage aircraft, the Pup that was converted from a Sopwith Dove.

The Cierva C.30A, G-ACUU, one of the non-scheduled arrivals at Skyfame, and now preserved as HM580 at Duxford.

The wings of the Avian G-EBZM being examined by a Northern Aircraft Preservation Society member at Ringway in around 1961.

The Northern Aircraft Preservation Society's Flea, in and on the Chairman's Ford Cortina!

THE

AIRCRAFT

PRESERVATION

JOURNAL

1/6

CONTROL

COLUMN

MARCH 1967

The cover of the first Control Column, *featuring the Fleet Air Arm Museum's Walrus.*

Ray Ingham helping to unload the Northern Aircraft Preservation Society's Swallow in 1965, in front of young onlookers.

The Historic Aircraft Preservation Society's Sabre, 19607, at Biggin Hill after its arrival from Italy.

Fleas abounding. In various stages of construction, G-AEGV and G-AEOH of the Midland Aircraft Preservation Society, and G-AEBB of the Shuttleworth Trust at Old Warden in 1969.

The Halfpenny Green Air Show in 1969, with an 'instant aircraft museum' in the foreground. Outside the Midland Aircraft Preservation Society's marquee, the local Air Scouts' Anson and Proctor add variety. MAPS later owned the Anson, now with the Jet Age Collection.

The remains of the unique Parnall Pixie, assembled outside one of the lock-up garages that provided the Midland Aircraft Preservation Society with its first premises; around 1969.

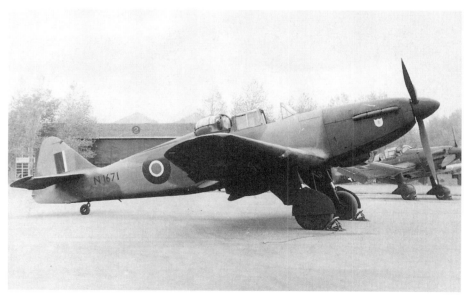

The world's last complete Defiant, N1671, at RAF St Athan in 1963, wearing an entirely spurious colour scheme, with one of its former adversaries, the Junkers Ju 87, behind.

The Boulton Paul Sea Balliol, WL732, at the RAF's 50th Anniversary review at Abingdon, a display which might have saved the type from extinction.

Vampire T.11 WZ458, of the British Historic Aircraft Museum, at Southend in 1970. Behind are other aircraft awaiting their fate – Sea Hawk, Anson and Mitchell.

The official opening of the Tattershall Air Museum in 1970.

The College of Aeronautics, Cranwell's 'Library of Flight', with the Boulton Paul P.111A in front of the unfinished Hawker P.1121, and Sabre, Supermarine 545 and Tempest II behind.

John Constable Reeve applying TLC to Vampire T.11 XK624, at Flixton in 1982.

The Meteor FR.9, VZ608, on display at Newark – the first of their 'heavy metal'.

CHAPTER 8

Warbirds

PRIVATE OWNERS

ORMOND Haydon-Baillie was the first British pilot to put together a collection of flying Second World War and post-war combat aircraft, what would later be called warbirds. Born in Britain during the Second World War, he moved to Canada in 1962 and joined the Royal Canadian Air Force in 1964. He was a serving officer for ten years, flying mostly fighters. Before leaving the RCAF, in spring 1973, he acquired his own air force, consisting of Lockheed Silver Stars CF-EHB and CF-IHB, painted in flamboyant silver and black colour schemes, and named 'Silver Knight' and 'Black Knight' respectively. He also purchased Hawker Sea Fury CF-CHB, which was painted in RAF camouflage colours with his own initials as code letters. To back up these three flyers, Haydon-Baillie also bought the derelict airframes of two Bristol Blenheims as well as twenty-three Mercury engines, and tons of spares for all the aircraft.

During 1973, Haydon-Baillie moved his entire collection, known as the 'Royalist Air Force' in something of a British homage to the 'Confederate Air Force', back to England. The two Silver Stars and the Sea Fury were flown to their new home at Southend, while the rest were shipped into Harwich. Britain was witnessing the arrival of a new phenomenon – a private owner with a fleet of his own warbirds.

'Warbirds' was an American expression, used to denote ex-military combat aircraft that were in private hands. In Britain there had always been the odd ex-fighter owned privately, from the First World War SE.5As and Camels, which were flown between the wars, to a few Spitfires and Hurricanes flown in the late 1940s and early 1950s. However, the breed had largely died out as the cost of keeping them in the air rose steadily.

One exception was the Spitfire Tr VIII, G-AIDN, owned by Viv Bellamy and then by John Fairey; for a while, it was the only Spitfire to be seen at air shows around Britain. In 1961 a Mustang appeared on the British Civil Register for the first time, when G-ARKD was imported by Ron Flockhart for an attempt on the England to Australia record. The attempt ended abruptly at Athens, where the aircraft burnt out. This was followed in 1962 by a second aircraft, registered G-ARUK, which crashed in Australia while on a test flight.

The country was Mustang-less then until 1967 when Mike Keegan imported red and white Mustang N6356T, though it was still more of a piece of self-indulgence than an attempt to place a new and exciting aircraft on the air-show circuit. Charles Masefield was its usual pilot in the air races in which it was entered. The aircraft was sold for use in a film in 1970 and then went back to the United States.

GROWTH OF THE AIR-SHOW INDUSTRY

One development was to have a significant impact on the import of warbirds and lead to a Mustang return once more – the growth during the late 1970s and 80s of the air-show industry. In the earlier years, air shows had been RAF or Fleet Air Arm affairs, with the military providing the aircraft. Alternatively, they were small displays put on by local flying clubs, featuring a mix of RAF aircraft in exchange for large donations to the RAFA Benevolent Fund, alongside light aircraft from the flying clubs themselves, residents of the airfield concerned, and also, typically, the aircraft of the Tiger Club.

By the 1970s, the days when every RAF airfield was open around Battle of Britain Day, usually for free, were long gone. In 1975, only Biggin Hill, St Athan, Leuchars and Finningley were open, three on 14 September and one on the 21st.

The Battle of Britain Historic Aircraft Flight, with Spitfires, Hurricane and Lancaster PA474, and the Fleet Air Arm Historic Flight, with Swordfish, Firefly and Sea Fury, would always fly the military historic aircraft flag, but, as air-show entrance prices increased, as the world became more and more commercial, 'punters' began to demand increasingly unusual aircraft in the skies. Warbird operators began to be in great demand, to service that need. Suddenly, there was a potential financial return for the acquisition of exotic aircraft from around the world, and their restoration to flying condition. In addition, their appreciating value, helped by their increasing scarcity, meant that old aircraft were becoming financial assets rather than depreciating toys.

THE HAYDON-BAILLIE AIRCRAFT AND NAVAL COLLECTION

When Ormond Haydon-Baillie moved his collection to Duxford, he became the pioneering warbird operator at this airfield, which has now become world-renowned for such operators. Haydon-Baillie's collection was increased when he added the Canadair CF.100, 18393, from the College of Aeronautics at Cranfield, and Chipmunk WG307. Later on he added a Sabre and a Meteor F.8 and undertook the purchase of some Spitfires from India. In 1977 he purchased a P.51D Mustang from the United States, and shortly afterwards flew it to West Germany for an air display at Mainz-Finthen. Taking off after the display the Mustang crashed, tragically killing Haydon-Baillie and a local glider pilot in the second seat fitted to the aircraft. The world of aviation had lost a flamboyant and skilful pilot, who had lived life to the full.

The Haydon-Baillie Aircraft and Naval Collection, as it was known, continued to function under the direction of Ormond's brother, Wensley. He supervised the return of the eight Spitfires from India, as well as the collection and transportation to England of a host of aeronatica that Ormond had purchased in West Germany, including five Sabres, a Sea Fury, numerous engines, and a mountain of spare parts for Sabre, T-33 and Sea Fury. The collection also included two Vosper-Thorneycroft high-speed patrol boats. Eventually, the flying of aircraft in the collection ceased, and most of the aircraft were moved from Duxford and eventually sold off.

Military Aircraft Owners' Association and PPS

The warbirds' movement, if it could be considered as such, was formalized in 1975, with the establishment of the Military Aircraft Owners' Association. The organization was formed to assist and promote the certification, ownership and operation of ex-military and historic aircraft that for various reasons could not qualify for a Certificate of Airworthiness. A special Permit to Fly was to be devised in conjunction with the Civil Aviation Authority, to allow the reasonable operation of warbirds, and the organization limited its membership to the operators of such aircraft.

Doug Bianchi of Personal Plane Services at Booker was a prime mover in the formation of the Military Aircraft Owners' Association. He had wide experience of the restoration and operation of a number of aircraft, having served an apprenticeship before the war with Robert Kronfield's British Aircraft Company at Hanworth, and also serving with the engineering arms of several civil companies. During the war he had been in charge of the Air Transport Auxiliary's AFTS. Founded in 1947, Personal Plane Services was initially based at Blackbushe in Hampshire, but moved to White Waltham two years later. In 1965 the company moved to Booker when that airfield was relinquished by the RAF.

The rebuild and refurbishment of privately owned historic aircraft was always a large part of the PPS business, with work on aircraft such as Alex Henshaw's Mew Gull G-AEXF and Patrick Lindsay's SE.5a, but its basic business was the routine maintenance of ordinary light aircraft, and the conversion of ex-RAF aircraft, such as Tiger Moths, Proctors and Magisters, for civil owners. Via its offshoot company Bianchi Aviation Film Services, PPS also became involved in supplying aircraft for film and television dramas, often being asked to construct flying replicas. The popular film *Those Magnificent Men in their Flying Machines* featured a number of PPS replicas, including the Vickers 22 and no less than three Demoiselles. The company has also built a large number of First World War replicas, including a Pfalz D.III, Fokker E.III, Morane-Saulnier N monoplane, and Sopwith Triplane.

With the growth of the warbird movement PPS found itself involved in the intricate rebuild to flying condition of a series of Second World War combat aircraft. One of the first was a Lysander, with Spitfires, YAK.11 and Dewoitine D-26 being among other notable projects.

One of PPS's regular customers over the years was Patrick Lindsay, Senior Picture Director of Christie's auction house, who was an avid collector of vintage vehicles and aircraft. As well as his SE.5a, PPS looked after the build and maintenance of his Fiat G-46, Morane MS.230, Hawker Fury replica, Stampe SV.4C and the Spitfire IA in which he would often arrive to officiate at Christie's growing number of aircraft auctions. This Spitfire, G-AIST, was often a far more valuable aircraft than any of the lots being sold in such auctions.

In December 1977 Doug Bianchi died, but the business was carried on by his widow Edna and son Tony, with twenty employees, including sixteen on the engineering side.

MORE WARBIRDS

One of the star features of subsequent British air shows arrived in the country on 15 March 1975, when Ted White's Euroworld Ltd imported the ex-French Boeing B-17 N17TE. After a rebuild to Second World War standard, this aircraft was named *Sally B*, and, with Don Bullock as the early pilot, quickly became a star of the air-show scene. In 1980 the Sally B Supporters Club was formed, the first time an aircraft in this country had ever had its own fan club. It went on to become a film star many times, most notably in the ITV series *We'll Meet Again* and in the feature film *Memphis Belle*.

During the winter of 1980/81 the aircraft received a huge overhaul at Duxford, being kitted out with a full set of turrets for the first time. Eurowold also bought a Douglas A-26 Invader, N3710G, to fly on the air-show circuit. Tragically, in 1980, this aircraft, while being flown by Don Bullock, failed to pull out of a manoeuvre at the Biggin Hill Air Show and crashed, killing all on board.

Another warbird collector with a growing collection at the beginning of the 1980s was Spencer Flack. He owned two Sea Furies and was restoring a Hunter to fly, all in his own personal all-red Flackair paint scheme. In January 1979 he became the proud owner of Spitfire FR XIV G-FIRE, from the Strathallan Collection. All that remained was an extensive restoration, so that G-FIRE could join his other aircraft in the air.

Flack was of the opinion that whoever paid the bills could paint his aircraft in whatever colour he liked, and he consistently resisted all calls to use some sort of military scheme. His all-red aircraft were certainly a distinctive feature of the warbird scene in the early 1980s and the Spitfire and the Hunter in particular looked wonderful in their all-red coats. Today, any owner of one of these aircraft, which may have been re-painted in a camouflage scheme, has the choice of re-painting it in a *genuine* all-red colour scheme, as worn when Spencer Flack owned it.

Having suffered injuries during a crash at the controls of one of his own Sea Furies, Flack began operating the P-51D Mustang NL-1051S *Sunny VIII*, an aircraft that was not painted in his all-red scheme. It was a step towards the norm of displaying aircraft in an authentic colour scheme, but he would still choose the aircraft concerned because they were particularly colourful or attractive examples of the type.

CHAPTER 9

1977 – Ten Years After

IN 1977 the British Aircraft Preservation Council celebrated its tenth anniversary, and the number of its members passed the half-century mark. From small beginnings it had grown enormously, and now had a wide variety of organizations under its umbrella. Its members ranged from huge national museums, such as Hendon and Duxford, to tiny voluntary groups with a handful of enthusiastic members working away on their own small projects. Some members had come and gone, for others the writing was already on the wall, as an early rush of enthusiasm and activity had been dampened by a dose of realism. In the case of others there had been name changes, or different goals.

The picture of BAPC membership in 1977 was as follows.

BAPC MEMBERS 1977

The Aeroplane Collection
The first in the list was, under its original name of the Northern Aircraft Preservation Society, the first of all voluntary groups, and the instigator of both *Control Column* and the BAPC. With twenty-five aircraft on its books, it was still looking for a museum site of its own, and many of the airframes were on loan far and wide. An Air and Space Museum in Manchester was just around the corner, however.

Airborne Forces Museum
Concerned mainly with the history of those soldiers trained to jump out of perfectly serviceable aircraft, its BAPC membership reflected the Horsa and Hotspur glider cockpits and the Dakota exhibited at its museum at Aldershot.

Aircraft Preservation Society of Scotland
Formed in 1974, this society filled a gap for the amateur aviation archaeologist and aircraft restorers of Scotland. Banding together was the best way of repelling waves of wreck-hunters from south of the border. The society also worked in support of the Royal Scottish Museum's new facility at East Fortune airfield.

Aircraft Radio Museum

Largely the sole preserve of John Coggins, who had been BAPC's first public relations officer, this impressive collection of specialized equipment was based at Coventry Airport. It was in the process of acquiring Jet Provost XR654.

Museum of Army Flying

This museum, established in a redundant cinema at Middle Wallop, was concerned with the history of those soldiers who preferred not to jump out of perfectly serviceable aircraft. Like their colleagues at Aldershot, they exhibited a Horsa glider fuselage, and also possessed an Auster AOP.9 and a Saro Skeeter Mk.12.

Battle of Britain Museum

Having started life as an aviation archaeologists' collection, displayed at Chilham Castle in Kent, it now owned a number of Battle of Britain film mock-up aircraft, as well as a Vampire and a Sea Fury.

British Rotorcraft Museum

This specialist collection had its origins in 1963, and was largely the inspiration of one man, Elfan ap Rees. A substantial collection of British helicopters had already been built up, with a Saro Skeeter, a Bristol Sycamore, a Westland Whirlwind and Dragonfly, a Bristol Belvedere, a Thruxton Gadfly and a Campbell Cougar. A museum site at Weston-super-Mare airfield was in the offing with four open days planned for later in the year.

Chiltern Historical Aircraft Preservation Group

This aviation archaeology group, based at High Wycombe, had recently added a Venom and a Provost to its collection.

Cornwall Aircraft Park (Helston) Ltd

An outdoor display of aircraft, largely of a naval nature, bordering RNAS Culdrose, with a small indoor display.

Dan-Air Preservation Group

A dedicated group working on the restoration of former Dan-Air airliners residing at Lasham, an Airspeed Ambassador and the Avro York used for many years as a bunkhouse by the Air Scouts. A DC-3 was also imminent.

Dumfries and Galloway Aviation Group

This group had long been investigating crash sites in southern Scotland and had now acquired a site at the former RAF airfield of Tinwald Downs, where members hoped to open a museum in 1978 featuring their newly acquired Vampire T.11.

Durney Aeronautical Collection
The strictly private collection of David Johnson, the main item of which was the fuselage of Rapide G-ALAX.

Duxford Aviation Society
Born out of the East Anglian Aviation Society, DAS worked in close conjunction with the Imperial War Museum at Duxford, but also possessed its own magnificent and growing collection of civil airliners, in which Concorde G-AXDN was undoubtedly the star.

East Anglian Aviation Society
Alphabetically close to its sibling at Duxford, EAAS continued a wide range of activities, largely centred on the former airfield at Bassingbourn.

Fenland Aircraft Preservation Society
Largely restricted its activities to investigating crash sites in East Anglia, and in particular the soft ground of the fens. It was hoping to open a museum at Christchurch, Cambridge, but Wisbech was to prove a more likely home.

501 Bristol Aircraft Preservation Grouop
Hoping to concentrate on Bristol-built aircraft, this infant group's sole aircraft was a Chipmunk.

Fleet Air Arm Museum
The first national aircraft museum to open, this growing collection at Yeovilton was still directly associated with the Royal Navy Historic Flight, and so was one of the few aircraft museums in Britain to fly some of its aircraft. Fund-raising for further extensions was always a priority, and the second hangar of a four-phase development plan was due to open later in 1977.

Historic Aircraft Museum
The only completely purpose-built aircraft museum in Britain, this commercial undertaking at Southend housed thirty-two aircraft, some on loan. Disquiet was still being expressed about its future, justifiably as it turned out.

Humberside Aircraft Preservation Society
A recent group but including members from previous societies that had folded. This group was busily collecting exhibits at its premises at Elsham Hall Gardens, which had just opened as a museum, on a limited basis. Its Gemini and Messenger had been joined by a number of Auster airframes and a Westland Dragonfly helicopter.

Imperial War Museum
Although a small number of aircraft were still on display at the museum itself, in Lambeth, south London, the vast majority of its collection of over thirty military aircraft was on display and open to the public at Duxford airfield, in itself a historic monument. Also displayed here were the private collections of Russavia, Robs Lamplough and Ormond Haydon-Baillie.

Lincolnshire Aviation Museum
This was one of the first voluntary groups to open its own museum, at Tattershall. Although the lease was due to expire, throwing an air of uncertainty over the venture, a new building was soon to be erected – an old Nissen hut, gifted by Edna Bianchi, widow of Doug Bianchi.

Merseyside Aviation Society
The father of the Northern Aircraft Preservation Society, MAS had maintained its own intermittent connections with hardware preservation, and was currently working on a Fa.330 gyro-glider and a Vampire T.11.

Midland Aircraft Preservation Society
Also celebrating its tenth anniversary in 1977, MAPS was in the throes of setting up its own museum at Coventry Airport, and moving in its growing collection of airframes.

R.J. Mitchell Hall
Just a year old, this small museum in Southampton, celebrating the life and career of Reginald Mitchell, had been a great success, and would have an even brighter future.

Mosquito Aircraft Museum
Having begun life as a way of preserving the Mosquito prototype at the place of its birth, the museum had now become Britain's first museum devoted to the products of one aircraft manufacturer, and was seeking ways of providing cover for its growing collection of de Havilland aircraft.

Newark Air Museum
Rivalling NAPS for title of first voluntary group, Newark had made more rapid progress than its Lancashire counterpart, with a secure home at Winthorpe, and a large and growing collection open to the public.They were just about to start the huge task of moving Shackleton WR977, on ten trucks, and reassembling it at Winthorpe.

Norfolk and Suffolk Aviation Museum

Now fully established at Flixton, members of this group were both practising wreckologists and aircraft collectors. Their museum was open on a regular basis for free.

North East Vintage and Veteran Aircraft Association

This group was making rapid progress towards its dream of an aircraft museum at Sunderland Airport, which seemed an entirely appropriate location. Little did they know that one day it would become the back gate of a Japanese car plant!

Northern Aeroplane Workshops

An entirely unique group, which was trying to preserve skills rather than aircraft. The Shuttleworth Trust were to become the beneficiaries of the hardware those skills would produce, with the Sopwith Triplane well on the way.

Personal Plane Services Ltd

Doug Bianchi's company, based at High Wycombe, was well known for the restoration of old aircraft and the production of reproductions and replicas for film and television roles.

Royal Air Force Museum

About three dozen aircraft were on show in the new RAF Museum at Hendon, barely a quarter of those held by the museum. The rest were in the reserve collections at Cosford and St Athan, and in the storage and workshop facility at Cardington.

RAF Cosford Aerospace Museum

Regularly open as a museum in its own right, the Aerospace Museum was already showing signs of specializing in research and development aircraft and Axis aircraft. The first airliners that would form the British Airways Collection had already arrived, looking a little out of place on an RAF station.

RAF St Athan Historic Aircraft Museum

This was more of a store than a museum as it was not generally open to the public. As Hendon expanded the St Athan collection grew smaller, but it remained an important centre for restoration.

Royal Scottish Museum

A 'Duxford north of the border' was being established at East Fortune, with a Museum of Flight, which was not yet open on a regular basis.

Science Museum

The National Aeronautical Collection on the top floor of the Science Museum in South Kensington, London, housed about two dozen aircraft, many of them truly historic in every respect.

Shuttleworth Trust

A transport museum, rather than just an aircraft museum, although the aircraft have always been the greatest attraction. Already by 1977 the Trust was the grandfather of the aircraft preservation movement.

Skyfame Aircraft Museum

Having already filled its solitary hanger, by 1977 Skyfame's new acquisitions had dwindled to nothing. With the growth of the warbird movement the writing was probably already on the wall for this pioneer collection, unless radical changes were made to its operations.

Solway Aviation Society

This society had recently added a Meteor 14 to its Vampire T.11, which was already on display at Carlisle Airport, and was hoping to create a museum in England's far north.

South Wales Aircraft Preservation Society

Also celebrating its tenth anniversary in 1977, this society had finally managed to set up the Wales Aircraft Museum at Rhoose Airport, although it was having to operate from inside a Viscount fuselage. Despite having gathered a large collection of all-metal aircraft at the airport, it was still intending to display engines and other items at Swansea Technical College.

South Yorkshire Aviation Society

This society had managed to open a small aircraft museum at Nostell Priory near Wakefield in 1976. Centred on its Meteor 14 and Sycamore, it was open most weekends.

Southern Aircraft Research Associates

A small group of technically qualified enthusiasts with an interest in preserving aircraft and compiling production records with a view to future publications.

Strathallan Aircraft Collection

Starting in 1976 with the purchase of the Hurricane and two Spitfires, Sir William Roberts had added aircraft at an astonishing rate, and had put them back into the air. A new museum hangar had just been finished; the only possible drawback for this delightfully sited collection was its relatively remote location.

Surrey and Sussex Aviation Society
Beginning life in 1974 as the Surrey Aircraft Preservation Society, the society had annexed Sussex. Despite efforts to acquire its own complete aircraft, most of the activities lay in the field of aircraft archaeology.

Torbay Aircraft Museum
Opened in 1971, Torbay had grown quickly to begin with but, like Skyfame, it had reached a certain critical mass. It was now beginning to stagnate and was relying heavily on summer holidaymakers to the area.

Ulster Folk and Transport Museum
A wide-ranging museum that owned a small number of aircraft including a Spitfire and a Miles Whitney Straight. The only BAPC member in Northern Ireland.

Viscount Preservation Trust
Formed to preserve Viscount G-ALWF at Speke Airport, the trust had lost its *raison d'être* now that the Viscount had moved to Duxford.

Yorkshire Aircraft Preservation Society
The society had acquired the control tower at the former airfield of Acaster Malbis and was proceeding with plans to open a small museum there.

ASSOCIATE MEMBERS

There were also a number of Associate Members of BAPC, who did not have voting rights.

Aeroplane Monthly
The Moth Club of the Antique Airplane Association (USA)
Aviation News
The Brooklands Society
Control Column
Derby Industrial Museum (became a full member later in 1977)
Irish Aviation Museum
Loughborough Leicester Air Museum Preservation Society (full member later in 1977)
Model and Allied Publications Ltd
Second World War Aircraft Preservation Society (full member later in 1977)
Society of Licensed Aircraft Engineers and Technologists

FLIGHT HERITAGE 1977

To celebrate its first ten years, BAPC decided it was an opportune moment to hold its first aircraft restoration and preservation symposium, entitled 'Flight Heritage 1977'. A special organizing committee was formed under John Berkeley, Chairman of the Midland Air Museum. The symposium was held on 8/9 October at the National Agricultural Centre, Stoneleigh, Warwickshire, not far from Coventry Airport.

A small number of exhibits were gathered in the buildings at Stoneleigh, including the Humber Monoplane replica (BAPC.9) from the Midland Air Museum, Jet Provost T.4 fuselage from the Aircraft Radio Museum, Fa.330 gyroglider from Merseyside, Sea Hawk XE340 from the Fleet Air Arm Museum and Fi.103 from the Aerospace Museum, Cosford.

Speakers gave talks about specific projects, including the Lilienthal glider, DH.88 Comet, Ferguson Monoplane, Bristol Belvedere and Concorde 002. The next session was a series of talks on various types of aircraft museum, and the speakers included Keith Fordyce of the Torbay Air Museum, J. Donald Storer of the Museum of Flight, East Fortune, Peter Schofield of the Aeroplane Collection, and Peter Green of Newark.

The final session of the first day concerned some of the important questions to be asked by the preservation movement. David Ogilvy posed the question 'What and where to fly?' Ivor Jenkins asked, 'What should we preserve and how?'

Sunday's session opened with talks by Vernon Hillier of Torbay on 'Display and Layout' and by John Berkeley on 'External Display Techniques' – a subject of great interest to most cash-starved voluntary groups. John Langham of Northern Aeroplane Workshops also gave a talk.

After a display of vintage radios by John Coggins, the talking continued in an informal but no less intense manner. The symposium was considered a great success, and plans were immediately made to hold another one in two years' time.

CHAPTER 10

Contraction and New Expansion

SKYFAME CLOSES

AFTER the celebrations of 1977, the news that Skyfame was to close came as a shock in the following year. It had enjoyed bright beginnings fourteen years before and had garnered much goodwill throughout the movement over the years, but an eight-fold rent increase on its hangar, imposed by the local council, meant that it was no longer economically viable. Peter Thomas decided to transfer the bulk of the collection to the Imperial War Museum at Duxford, so that they would at least be preserved in a suitable environment.

The museum finally closed to the public on 2 January 1978, and plans were initiated to move the aircraft to Duxford by 31 March. On 25 January the aircraft were moved from the hangar and lined up on the airfield; by 8.30am they were ready for the press and television to view them together for the last time. At the same time a crane moved into the hangar and began to load all the engines, the hovercraft lift fan and the Halifax nose on to the first of many trailers that were to make the 130-mile journey to Cambridgeshire. Also going on the first day of the move was the Bristol Sycamore helicopter.

On Friday 27 January the Cierva C.30 Autogyro and Percival Proctor were on their way, and the following day Ron Gourlay arrived from the Royal Navy Historical Flight at Yeovilton to supervise the dismantling of the Firefly, working in pouring rain and strong winds. By Sunday the Miles Magister and Short Sherpa had departed. On 31 January, a larger crane arrived and loaded the Firefly fuselage on to a trailer. Obviously this aircraft did not want to leave, because as the truck began to move it dived off the back and crashed on to its belly. Re-loaded more securely, it finally left the site.

The Duxford Aviation Society members, and the Skyfame team, for whom it must have been a dreadfully sad task, continued steadily to dismantle the aircraft, all of them in the approved manner, and never resorting to the hacksaw. They were each fitted to specially made trestles, constructed by a local joiner, before being loaded on trailers. The Hastings was the last aircraft to go, and, being the largest, it took the longest to dismantle. At the same time, all the myriad small items – the models, pictures and small artefacts – were also being packed.

Finally the hangar was empty, and it was all hands to the broom to sweep it out, before closing the doors for the last time, and walking away. It was a sad day for all concerned, but a better end to a museum's existence than was to prove the case on other occasions.

One aircraft that fared less well was an Auster AOP.9 XK418, which, on completion of her Army career, was allocated for gate guardian duties. This was not at all a suitable role for a fabric-covered aircraft, and the 'solution' was to replace the fabric with aluminium sheeting, rivetted to the frame! In addition, the windscreen was painted black on the inside, to hide the fact that the pilot's seat and instrumentation were missing. A change of plan then followed and XK418 was pushed aside, scheduled for disposal. Having had these gross indignities thrust upon it the little Auster took matters into its own hands and made a bid for freedom, aided by a gale-force wind. It flew about 400 yards and landed upside down, causing considerable damage, particularly to its tail.

The aircraft was then bought by Major Somerton-Rayner, as static support to his own flying Austers at Thruxton, but in 1978 were placed on loan with the Second World War Aircraft Preservation Society (despite being a post-war aircraft). Seven society members descended on Thruxton and dismantled the aircraft, transporting it to their Basingstoke base on a trailer pulled, appropriately, by a Second World War jeep. As a typical example of how a small preservation group acquired an aircraft, this story was one that was being repeated up and down the country. In some cases, the career of an aircraft after retirement was more interesting than its career while it was flying.

SWWAPS, like many other groups that had grown out of aviation archaeology, soon took to acquiring aircraft before they had crashed. They eventually settled at Lasham and acquired the Sea Prince WF137, which displayed a further degree of compromise in their ambitions, given their title.

PENNINE AVIATION MUSEUM

At around this time, the aircraft-archaeology movement was mushrooming even more quickly than the aircraft-preservation movement, though they were just two disciplines of the same thing. The Aviation Archaeologists Association (AAA) had been formed in the latter half of 1973, and by 1978 it had over 200 members.

In the summer of 1975 the association negotiated with the local council and took over a derelict building and about half an acre of land at Moorlands Park, Bacup, on top of the Pennines, with the intention of creating the Pennine Aviation Museum. The location was not as strange as it may seem, as many of the wrecks investigated by the groups were actually in the immediate area. Their first tasks, as with so many other museum projects, were strictly building work – re-roofing the building, putting in a concrete floor, re-wiring it and knocking down internal partitions – as well as fencing in the land.

Exhibits arrived from AAA members all over the country, but the new museum was not to restrict itself to ex-crash-site items. In 1977 it acquired its first complete aircraft, in the shape of the ubiquitous Vampire T.11; this one, XK627, came from Hazel Grove Secondary School, Cheshire.

The Pennine Aviation Museum was duly elected to BAPC at the forty-fourth meeting at Duxford on 22 April 1978, just one of ten newly elected groups. The others were the International Auster Pilot Club, the Russavia Collection (based at Duxford with seventeen vintage aircraft, mostly gliders), the Vintage Aircraft Club (with 200 members owning 150 aircraft between them), Essex Aviation Group, Wessex Aviation Group (based at Wimborne, Dorset, with a Sea Venom, WM571, and a Harvard, FX442), Wealden Aviation Archaeology Group, Air Historical Group, 390 Memorial Air Museum, and Scotland West Aircraft Investigation Group.

In 1977 another aircraft-archaeology group opened a museum featuring the items recovered from its various digs. The Warplane Wreck Investigation Group Museum was sited within the thick walls of Fort Perch Rock, New Brighton. Built between 1827 and 1831 to protect the Mersey Estuary, the fort was in the sea at the end of a 100-yard causeway. The only major exhibit which was not an ex-crash-site item was the pod of a Vampire night fighter, recovered from a farm near Wrexham.

BATTLE OF BRITAIN MUSEUM

In Hendon, the RAF Museum was undertaking a significant expansion – on a new site near to the main museum, the Battle of Britain Museum was taking shape. This was a £2-million 420 × 120ft building dedicated to preserving the history of the Royal Air Force's most famous battle. It was officially opened by Queen Elizabeth the Queen Mother on 28 November 1978. She was greeted by Admiral Sir Charles Madden, Vice-Lieutenant of Greater London, and Fred Mulley, the Minister of Defence, and was then escorted round the new museum by Sir Denis Spotswood, Chairman of the Museum's Trustees, Sir Michael Beetham, Chief of Air Staff and Dr John Tanner, Museum Director.

The museum featured most of the combatants that took part in the Battle of Britain, facing one another on opposite sides of the museum. On the RAF side were Spitfire, Hurricane, Defiant, Blenheim and Gladiator. On the Axis side were Bf 109, Bf 110, HE 111, Ju 87, Ju 88, and Fiat CR.42. Separate displays illustrated all aspects of the battle, from the No.11 Group Operations Room to a NAAFI van in a section of 'bombed-out street'. In a separate section of the new museum, Peter Thomas's Short Sunderland, ex-Pembroke Dock, was finally put on display indoors, alongside a Walrus and a Lysander.

With several of the exhibits moving from the main museum, space was created for new exhibits from the RAF Museum's reserve collection, and these included a Bleriot Monoplane, Hanriot HD.I, Fokker D.VII, Vampire F.3 and Meteor F.8.

Members of BAPC were able to view these splendid new developments when the forty-seventh meeting was held at Hendon on 20 January 1979, where for the first time discussions were held regarding the preservation of buildings associated with aviation. Hendon was an entirely appropriate place for such discussions as the original museum was built around some First World War Belfast truss hangars, buried beneath a typical 1960s concrete structure. Within sight of the RAF Museum's front door was an even more historic hangar, that of the Grahame-White Company; its preservation would occupy many minds for the next twenty years.

Listing buildings associated with aviation was a novel concept, because they were of course all of twentieth-century origin. Although the century was already well into its last quarter, the idea that such architecture was worthy of preservation was not supported by many people.

MUSEUM DEVELOPMENTS

Significant moves in the creation of aircraft museums were announced by different groups. At Usworth, the currently named Northumbrian Aeronautical Collection had fenced off the area assigned to it and members were working on the restoration of a newly acquired Vickers Valetta. At Rhoose Airport, a further 5 acres had been added to the Wales Aircraft Museum, and a large building was being erected, and the Cornwall Aeronautical Park at Culdrose had also acquired further land for new exhibits. Finally, the Loughborough Leicester Air Museum had now been established at the East Midlands Airport, with its Super Sabre and ex-Merseyside Vampire T.11 moving in quite quickly.

A brief mention in the May/June issue of *Control Column* was made of a Wellington discovered by an Edinburgh University team making a sonar survey of Loch Ness. Royal Navy divers had investigated the wreck and had found it in excellent condition. Many finds were mentioned in this way in the pages of *Control Column* over the years, but this one was to have extensive consequences and was to inflict a not inconsiderable amount of hard work on an unsuspecting group of people in the Weybridge area.

Two issues of *Control Column* later, there was an article about a proposal to create a Brooklands Aviation Museum. In 1977 Weybridge Museum had held a small but interesting exhibition entitled 'Wings over Brooklands', which had been attended by over 6,500 people, many of whom wondered why it was not a permanent display at Brooklands itself. Many of the items in the exhibition had been loaned by the Vintage Aircraft and Flying Association, and, on its completion, were donated to Elmbridge Borough Council. The council accepted them on behalf of the museum and began the search for a suitable place to display them on a permanent basis.

By a lucky coincidence the Brooklands Airfield control tower/clubhouse had become vacant, and the existing owners had no immediate use for it. The council entered into negotiations to acquire the buildings, which dated from the 1930s, when it had been one of the finest such facilities in the country. The building, which was listed, offered 5,000sq ft and was more than adequate to house the 'Wings over Brooklands' material, and much more. An appeal was set up to raise £50,000 to refurbish the building and to create a Brooklands Aviation Museum.

Few branches of the Royal Aeronautical Society had ever indulged in hands-on aircraft restoration, but in 1978 the Medway Branch of the Society set itself the task of restoring RAF Manston's Spitfire LF XVI TB752 in fifteen months, with completion by 15 September 1979, Battle of Britain Day. After 8,000 man hours of work they succeeded, with just three days to spare. The aircraft, a real warrior that had shot down three German aircraft during the last months of the war, was restored to pristine condition, after languishing outdoors since arriving at Manston in 1945. It became a credit to the efforts of the society members, and an immediate appeal was launched to raise £25,000 for a building in which to house it.

Looking for another aircraft to work on, the Medway Branch found and purchased Meteor F.8 WK914, which had been lying on Manston's fire dump. They began its restoration, which, with a search for parts that was to take them all over the country, involved two and a half years of work.

AIR TRANSPORT COLLECTIONS

The airline Dan-Air was proving a great friend of the aircraft-preservation movement. The company operated airliners that had been retired by most other airlines, and often ended up as the last operators of particular types. When these types were finally retired, having had the last few airframe hours wrung out of them, they were ripe for preservation, and Dan-Air was amenable to allocating at least one example for posterity. At its base at Lasham, it already had an Airspeed Ambassador, an Avro York and a DC-3.

In 1980 Dan-Air retired the last Comet 4B in service, G-APYD, and it was acquired by the Science Museum National Aeronautical Collection's new Air Transport Collection, based at Wroughton in Wiltshire. The aircraft had flown for the first time twenty years before, on 3 May 1960. Initially destined for BEA, it actually went to the Greek airline Olympic Airways, as SX-DAL. It rejoined BEA in 1969 and was leased to Channel Airways, before joining Dan-Air in 1972. During its career it had flown 32,728 hours and made 18,586 landings.

A Dan-Air crew captained by Joe Wright flew the aircraft to Wroughton, where it was handed over to John Bagley, who was in charge of the new Air Transport Collection. The collection had started with the purchase of a Douglas DC-3 the previous year, and would soon be added to with the arrival of BEA Trident 1E G-AVYE, and an ex-BEA AEC Regal one-and-a-half-decker bus, which used to operate between the London Air Terminal and Heathrow.

The Comet was soon joined in a corner of the hangar by a far less publicized aircraft, a remnant of a venture that had begun twelve years earlier in Bristol, with a pair of Magister wings and a pile of fuselage metalwork. The 49 Group had sprung into existence in 1968 with the avowed intention of rebuilding the Magister to full static-display standards. Over the next three years this was largely achieved, although, as was often the case, the initial group of about ten enthusiasts had slowly waned in number. In 1974 the project came to a sad halt when vandals set fire to the aircraft, and the remains were entrusted to Graham Johnson and Ken Alderman. When the landowner wanted the remains to be cleared from the buildings where they were stored, John Bagley offered quarters at Wroughton, and the little Bristol project came to an end. Happily, the Magister was made of sterner stuff and achieved a new lease of life in its later years with the establishment of the museum at Woodley.

Wroughton had became the third major repository of airliners in the United Kingdom, after Duxford and the growing British Airways Collection at the Aerospace Museum at Cosford, which had recently added VC-10 G-ARVM, and was shortly to include a Boeing 707, both these aircraft being landed on Cosford's short runway.

The shortness of the runway would preclude the arrival of even larger airliners as they were retired from British Airways service. Their size would make dismantling and road transport an expensive proposition. In some eyes this made Cosford a strange choice for the location of the British Airways Collection.

A MUSEUM IN MANCHESTER

Cosford was expanding rapidly as an out-station of the RAF Museum. New exhibits were appearing almost weekly, and included, at the beginning of 1980, a Hawker Fury full-scale model, made in the Black Country, the Britten-Norman BN.1F G-ALZE, a Provost T.1, WW397, and noses from an Anson and a Venom FB.4.

Expansion had taken place at Hendon, and the Cosford facility in the Midlands was proving a great success, with as many as a thousand visitors a day, even on weekdays. Dr John Tanner and the trustees now began actively looking for a site for a new museum north of the Trent. Manchester seemed the obvious place and the City Council was approached. The council was enthusiastic and happened to have in its possession a building that was almost ideal for the purpose. The magnificent cast-iron structure of the City Hall had been built in 1880, and used for many years as a site for various exhibitions, and also for an annual Christmas circus.

The City Hall had closed in 1977 and was in need of extensive repairs and refurbishment, but the council agreed to undertake this, at a total cost of about £1.2 million. The RAF Museum agreed to supply the aircraft exhibits from its extensive collection, choosing any that had a particular Manchester connection, like those of Avro. The initial plan was to include thirteen aircraft, with an Avro Lincoln as the centrepiece (presumably RF398 from Cosford), together with an Avro 504, Anson and Avro 707. Further British aircraft would include a Bristol Belvedere, Hunter, Miles Hawk Major, Sycamore, and three Axis aircraft Fw 190, Mitsubishi 'Dinah' and Me 163.

No provision was made in the original scheme for the aircraft of the Aeroplane Collection, an organization that had been striving to create an aircraft museum in the Manchester area for over twenty years. In the event, only five of the originally suggested list of aircraft were to go on display at the new museum, and the Aeroplane Collection was to become involved in a pivotal role, with several of its aircraft being put on display. Some were restored by the Aeroplane Collection's members actually within the museum, in a refreshing 'hands-on' approach.

The building proved an excellent venue for an aircraft museum, with good natural lighting, and a gallery running all around, giving an aerial view of the exhibits. In the end, the centrepiece, dominating the middle of the hall, was an Avro Shackleton AEW.2, WR960, not the Lincoln.

The new museum became part of a huge new complex in the regenerated Deansgate area of the city, including the oldest passenger railway station in the country and other transported-related features. As a partnership between a national body, the RAF Museum, a city council and a voluntary preservation group, the Aeroplane Collection, the venture could not be faulted.

NORTH EAST AIRCRAFT MUSEUM

The North East Aircraft Museum, established at Sunderland Airport at Usworth in 1976/7, was also making rapid progress. It was now concerned with the construction of a workshop and a museum building, which the seventy members hoped to have ready for an opening to the public late in 1980.

On site, alongside the museum's ex-Sculthorpe bounty of T-33 and F-100 and ex-Woodford/via BAPC Vampire T.11, were its Dragonfly helicopter, Meteor F.8, Vickers Valetta and Avro Anson C.19 TX213. In store were the Brown Aircraft Collection of Luton Minor, Bensen gyro-glider and home-built helicopter. A new acquisition was Hawker Hunter F.51 E-419, formerly of the Royal Danish Air Force.

Following its earlier disposal of Vampire T.11s through the auspices of BAPC, British Aerospace was to prove an important benefactor of the various aircraft-preservation organizations for a second time when it began to dispose of a number of ex-Danish Air Force Hawker Hunter F.51s. The Hunters had been returned to Dunsfold for possible refurbishment and re-sale, but the process had not come to fruition. Apart from the North East Aircraft Museum, one of the earliest recipients of one of these aircraft was the new Wealden

Aviation Group, which acquired E-404, to put on display with its newly acquired ex-Sculthorpe Lockheed T-33A, 51-9252. Another beneficiary of British Aerospace's goodwill was the Midland Air Museum, which acquired Hunter E-425.

EAST ANGLIA

A similar venture to that taking place at Sunderland was under way in the depths of rural Suffolk, where the Norfolk and Suffolk Aviation Museum was being established at Flixton, near Bungay. Its collection was largely in the open behind the Flixton Buck public house, and, as well as the American bounty of a T-33, F-100 and Mystere, also included its first aircraft, Anson G-AWSA, a Meteor F.8, Spitfire replica, Provost WV605, on loan from Shuttleworth's, and its latest acquisition, Sea Vixen XJ482. Not far away, the Eastern Counties Aviation Association had adopted the title City of Norwich Aviation Museum for its location at Norwich Airport, where its Mystere and T-33 had been joined by a Vickers Valetta and a number of airport vehicles.

Having two aircraft museums in such close proximity did seem an unnecessary duplication of effort, especially as they had also been established at about the same time, but it did serve to show how 'local' a voluntary group had to be. To expect a sufficient number of working members to attend regularly, a long commute could not be part of the equation.

BRINGING A B-29 TO BRITAIN

If the establishment of new aircraft museums at widely different locations all over Britain had once seemed impractical to anyone but the most enthusiastic of aircraft enthusiasts, the developments at Duxford in March 1980 would have seemed like an impossible dream. Just half a dozen years before, anyone who had thought up a scheme to acquire a derelict Boeing B-29, restore it to flying condition, and fly it to Britain would have been dismissed as a dreamer; sometimes, it seems, dreams do come true.

The Imperial War Museum, seeking a B-29, was given 44-61748 on permanent loan. It was one of several B-29s residing at the USN target facility at China Lake, California. It had been placed at the desert site in 1956, but Aero Services Inc. of Tucson, Arizona had already revived two of the China Lake B-29s. It was they who in early 1979 returned to China Lake to use their expertise to put 44-61748 back into the air. Enough work was done on the airframe to get the R-3350 engines turning again, and to get the old bomber back into the air for the 100-mile flight to Aero Services' base at Tucson. There, a far more extensive restoration could be undertaken, to ready the B-29 for the long ferry flight to England.

The cost of this and the ferry flight itself was put at £40,000, one-third of the cost of dismantling the aircraft, shipping it and then reassembling it. The aircraft was routed via Flint, Michigan, Loring AFB in Maine, where it 'acquired' some Strategic Air Command badges, Gander, Greenland, and Keflavik, Iceland, before arriving in England at Mildenhall AFB, registered as G-BDHK. It made its final flight to Duxford on Sunday 2 March 1980. It would serve as a permanent memorial to the SAC crews that were based in Britain during the post-war years, as well as the RAF crews who operated Boeing Washingtons in the 1950s.

After the arrival of the B-29 the Imperial War Museum opened a permanent exhibition about the United States Eighth Air Force, in conjunction with the Eighth Air Force Memorial Museum Foundation. As Duxford had been the base for Eighth Air Force fighters from 1943 to 1945, it was an entirely appropriate location. Fifteen years later, these first seeds have grown into one of the most spectacular themed museum buildings in Europe, the American Air Museum.

If bringing a B-29 to Britain was a remarkable achievement, so too, in its own way, was the first flight of Vampire T.11 WZ507, put back into the air by the Solway Aviation Society. After extensive restoration work by the society's members, in particular Tom Stoddart and David Hutchinson, John Turnbull took the Vampire aloft from Carlisle for its first flight since 1969, on 17 February 1980. Turnbull was one of the aircraft's joint owners, with S. Topen and J. Chillingworth, who had taken the decision to put the aircraft back in the air despite it having resided in the open at Carlisle for eight years.

With B-29s being flown back over the Atlantic and voluntary societies putting jet aircraft into the air, the aircraft-preservation movement was showing that it could achieve almost anything.

CHAPTER 11

Arguments

QUESTIONING THE BAPC

DURING 1980 the pages of *Control Column* hosted an extraordinary debate about the workings and even the relevance of the British Aircraft Preservation Council. Jack Smallwood of the Northern Aeroplane Workshops had agreed to take over from Jean Davidson as BAPC Secretary. After attending his first BAPC meeting, at Sutton Bank, where a vintage glider meeting was taking place, and being introduced as the new secretary (although this was not ratified, since there were not enough members present), Smallwood wrote an article for *Control Column* called 'Let's Make BAPC Live'. The gist of his argument was that BAPC had become a bureaucratic organization largely irrelevant to the actual nuts and bolts of aircraft preservation.

Mike Russell of the Russavia Collection had welcomed the delegates to Sutton Bank with the observation that they were in a workshop, with the smell of spruce shavings, dope and oil in the air; in his view, it was exactly the sort of place where an aircraft-preservation organization should be meeting. Jack Smallwood sat listening to the toing and froing of the meeting, all the time yearning to be outside watching the vintage gliders taking to the air. He tried to reconcile what was going on in the meeting with the needs of the aircraft-preservation movement and found it difficult. He expressed his doubts in his article in *Control Column*: 'Some admin there must be, but admin alone will not restore aeroplanes, whilst aeroplanes can certainly be restored without admin!' He claimed that BAPC was doing 'virtually nothing towards the actual business of preserving aeroplanes'. He wished to see a greater technical involvement on the part of BAPC, and dismissed the 1977 restoration symposium as 'poorly supported'.

Smallwood proposed restricting the bureaucracy by limiting admin at meetings to the period before tea, and leaving the period after tea for more practical discussions. He also suggested printing BAPC minutes in *Control Column* so that group reports could be dispensed with at meetings.

The response to Smallwood's article appeared in the following issue of *Control Column*, when Brian R. Robinson, BAPC Information Officer, wrote an article entitled 'Let's Go Forward Together!' He refuted Smallwood's claim that BAPC was 'having very little impact on the aircraft-preservation community'. He argued that BAPC officers such as Jack Bruce of the RAF Museum, Donald Storer of the Royal Scottish Museum, David Ogilvy of the Shuttleworth

Collection and John Langham of Jack Smallwood's own group, the Northern Aeroplane Workshops (who had tragically died recently), would not be involved so closely with an organization that was having no impact.

Robinson went on to point out that BAPC was never intended to become actively involved in aircraft preservation itself, but was a disseminator of information, an organization that was designed to bring people together and to connect information with people in need of it. He also refuted the claim that the BAPC restoration symposium in 1977 had been a failure, and reminded readers that plans were in hand for further such gatherings.

In support of Jack Smallwood there was a letter from Paul Hare, the new Secretary of the Lincolnshire Aviation Society, who saw BAPC meetings as being in danger of becoming 'little more than a series of self-perpetuating admin'. He likened it to his own experience at Tattershall, where his time was taken up with administration and acting as a museum attendant, with no time left for hands-on restoration.

HANDS-ON PROJECTS

In the same issue of *Control Column* Jack Smallwood highlighted his own practical contribution to aircraft preservation, with an article entitled 'Back to the Drawing Board'. Looking for a project to follow their construction of an exact Sopwith Triplane replica for the Shuttleworth Trust, the Northern Aeroplane Workshops had acquired drawings of both the Sopwith Camel and the Bristol M.1C monoplane. There were insufficient Bristol drawings to consider the construction of a replica, unless a draughstman could be enlisted to fill the gaps. Despite a career as a structural engineer, working on rather heavier constructions than aircraft, Smallwood decided to return to the drawing board after a gap of twenty-five years to see what he could do. In March 1979 he moved a drawing board from John Langham's garage, where it had been secreted some years before, and set to work.

Following contacts they had already made, NAW eventually discovered that the Bristol Aeroplane Company, in its British Aerospace incarnation, had sixty-three more drawings of the monoplane, which they copied and sent on. These were followed by thirty-one further drawings that were unearthed at Old Warden, making a total of about 120. It seemed that Jack Smallwood would be able to fill in the gaps that remained, and this would be more than enough to enable the group to make an exact replica of the monoplane as its next project.

The Sopwith Triplane project had begun in an unheated Dewsbury workshop, with members working every Tuesday evening carefully making fittings. For a while they were able to use the metalwork workshop at Hough Side High School, Pudsey, which was nicely heated and quite well equipped; the disadvantage was that all work had to be cleared away at the end of every meeting. They moved to another unheated workshop, between Dewsbury and Halifax, where there was enough room for the Triplane fuselage jig, and for the wings to be constructed.

The death of John Langham in 1980 brought Ralph Thompson to the Chairmanship of NAW. He was the Clerget engine guru, who had carefully taken two grease-caked Clerget 9Bs received from Shuttleworth, and was turning them into one airworthy engine. Membership of NAW had risen from an initial twenty-five to around sixty and the co-ordination of all the members' efforts was an important factor, as many worked away from the workshop, making parts at home.

THE ARGUMENT CONTINUES

Jack Smallwood responded to Brian Robinson's article in *Control Column* with a second piece, entitled 'Laminar Flow for BAPC – By that Vortex Generator, Jack Smallwood'. He started by pointing out that, because of John Langham's unfortunate death, his own involvement in the activities of the Northern Aeroplane Workshops had increased to such a degree that he would not be able to spare the time to take up the post of BAPC Secretary.

He then proposed, as a leaving present, a different organization for BAPC meetings. Officers of the council would meet separately to undertake the boring admin matters while the other delegates mingled in a more social location, preferably with refreshments available, where they could make contacts and learn what each other was doing. The meeting would then be concluded with a short full session, in which essential items could be decided in short order.

The next issue of *Control Column*, in January 1981, contained a much shorter response from Brian Robinson, basically asserting that much of what Jack advocated was already being achieved. In his view, the 100-plus member/associate member groups of BAPC had made a success of the council and would continue to do so.

Control Column chose to highlight the spread of the aircraft-preservation movement by printing a map of the UK showing the location of every one of the seventy-six full UK members of BAPC. This had the effect of highlighting the fact that, despite the good number of groups involved in aircraft preservation, there were none north of Strathallan, near Perth, and even more remarkably only one in Wales (at Rhoose Airport, Cardiff).

DISPOSAL OF THE STRATHALLAN COLLECTION

The news from the BAPC's most northerly outpost was not encouraging. Owing to vastly increased rates imposed by the local council, the Strathallan Collection and airfield had closed down, and the exhibits were to be auctioned by Christie's on Monday 13 July 1981. The prospect of this impressive collection being sold and possibly exported across the Atlantic – or back across the Atlantic in some cases – was slightly eased when it emerged that Sir William Roberts did not intend to sell all of the aircraft. Nevertheless, the Hurricane would be the prime lot in the auction, followed closely by the Hudson and the Mosquito.

The fears of the preservation movement were proved to be ill founded on the day of the auction, as only one of Strathallan's aircraft crossed the Atlantic – the Mosquito was sold to Kermit Weeks of Florida, for £100,000. The prime lot, the Hurricane IIC G-AWLW was sold for £260,000 to the Davies Trust, which turned out to be one of Sir William Roberts' family trusts, so that the aircraft remained at Auchterader. Also remaining were the Lysander and the BA Swallow, which were withdrawn from the auction in the week before the sale. Not included in the sale and intended for future restoration were the Lancaster, Swordfish and Battle; also being retained were the Comet, Shackleton, Magister and Fokker Instructor.

Other aircraft were saved for Scotland by the Royal Scottish Museum, which bought five of the aircraft for the Museum of Flight at East Fortune: the de Havilland Dragon (£7,000), Bolingbroke IV (£18,000), Provost (£16,000), Puss Moth (£7,500) and G.A.L. Cygnet (£7,000). Two aircraft, the Hornet Moth (£6,000) and Miles M-18 (£3,500), were bought by the Scottish Aircraft Collection Trust of Scone, where they would be joined by the Desford (£5,500), which had been bought by Pace Petroleum.

The RAF Museum bought the Hudson for £16,000 and a threadbare Anson for £650. The bare frame of the Short Scion was sold to the Ulster Museum for an amazing £10,000, and they also bought the Miles Messenger for £1,300. Sir William Roberts' private Aero Commander 200D, which had only 300 hours logged, went for only £7,500. Colt Cars paid £20,000 for the Harvard, with the parts of a 75 per cent complete second example going for £450. Further lots were sold as follows:

Tiger Moth G-ANFV	£19,000
Tiger Moth G-APGL (dismantled)	£2,600
Prentice G-AOUL	£1,200
Moth Minor G-AFPN	£17,000
Grumman Avenger G-BTBM	£7,800
Miles Monarch G-AFLW	£2,600
Miles Monarch G-AFJU	£50
Dragon Rapide G-ALXT	£8,000
Merlin 76	£7,500
Merlin propeller	£1,400
Daimler-Benz DB605	£7,500
Merlin 225	£4,500

Merlin 225	£3,500
Napier Sea Lion	£2,600
Twin Wasp R-1830	£500
Merlin Meteor tank engine	£30

The debate continued in the April/May 1981 issue of *Control Column*, when Jack Smallwood's replacement as BAPC Secretary, Peter Kirk of Russavia, put his point of view. He made it clear that BAPC was what the membership made of it. The technical library, which had been built up over the thirteen years of its existence, was little used, the BAPC Secretary and the Editor of *Control Column* received little in the way of news and progress reports from any of the groups.

He dismissed the idea of disseminating news and requests for information during a social gathering of delegates as nonsense. Anyone attending would be unlikely to talk to any more than a fraction of the other delegates, mostly those they knew already, and groups that did not attend would not be involved either way. The only way to spread news was in a formal manner, whether through the published minutes, or the magazine.

The situation was to change in May/June 1981, when *Control Column* faced for the first time a very significant competitor. The first edition of *FlyPast*, edited by Mike Twite, was a fully commercial venture with sixty-eight pages, including four in full colour. It was a historic-aircraft magazine with a very significant emphasis on preservation, restoration and wreckology. A significant scoop in its first issue was a detailed article about the plan to raise the Loch Ness Wellington, and an article on the Pima County Aircraft Museum in Arizona. Bob Ogden, one-time Chairman of the Midland Aircraft Preservation Society, was soon to have a regular column describing the aircraft museums of the world. These articles provided a basis for his many excellent books on the subject.

In addition, there were sections on preservation news and aviation archaeology. In the early issues, they were tucked near the back of the magazine, but later on they expanded greatly and found their way to the very front. Most ominously for *Control Column*, the new magazine was on the shelves at every W.H. Smith and John Menzies, with snappy colourful covers that attracted a quickly growing readership.

CHAPTER 12

The 1980s

BOUNTY AT FAILSWORTH

FOR many years the Unimetals scrapyard in Failsworth, near Manchester, had been a Mecca for aircraft enthusiasts. The yard was abandoned, but held a huge variety of airframes, slowly deteriorating at the hands of vandals and the weather. John Stellings, Honorary Museum Manager of the North East Aircraft Museum, paid a passing visit to the yard in May 1981. He was amazed to discover a hive of activity, with airframes being cut up and carried away. An attempt had already been made to chop up with axes the two most historic airframes in the yard – the fuselage of the last surviving Bristol Brigand, RH746, and Mike Lithgow's Swift WK198, which had held the world air speed record for a short while. The workmen were just waiting for oxyacetylene torches to be brought, to make a better job of the desecration.

A hasty conference with the yard's owner, and telephone calls back to Sunderland, ascertained that the museum had enough money to buy some of the airframes, including the Brigand and the Swift, or enough money to transport them to the north-east, but not both. In the end an agreement was made with the owner, whereby two trailer loads of remains would be placed on a five-year loan with the museum. Eventually, two articulated trailers were loaded up with the Brigand and Swift fuselages, two sections of Firefly AS.5, the nose of WD889 and the rear fuselage of VT409, and the cockpit of Boulton Paul Balliol T.2 WN516, a Blackburn-built example. These parts had been cut up years before when the aircraft were originally brought to the yard (in the Balliol's case in 1957), and the engines had already moved on to another scrapyard in Halifax.

Two more of the Balliol cockpits, WN149 and WN534, were acquired by Kew Chemicals, and then passed on to the Pennine Aircraft Museum, which placed them into store at Charnock Richard until restoration of one could be started, using the other as a source of spare parts. The rest of the Failsworth yard was completely cleared to make way for a country park.

Having saved some of the aircraft from the yard, the North East Museum was faced with a decision: what to do with them. The pieces were in need of extensive restoration, but the museum was reluctant to put in the time and money required for aircraft it did not own, especially when there were so many other tasks to undertake on setting up the museum, and restoring other aircraft.

NEW MUSEUM ACQUISITIONS

At RAF Manston the Spitfire Memorial Building was officially opened on 16 June 1981 to display the Spitfire XVI TB752, which had been refurbished by the Medway Branch of the Royal Aeronautical Society. This group was rapidly acquiring a reputation for superlative restoration work, in many cases for other people, and they were to be trusted with the restoration of a number of RAF Museum aircraft in the future.

At Coventry the Midland Air Museum took delivery of a trio of aircraft that represented a bit of a departure from its theme of the development of the jet engine. The trio comprised two helicopters – a battered Whirlwind HAS.7, XK907, and Kaman Huskie HH-43B 624535, an unusual sight in Britain – as well as de Havilland Beaver 58-2062, of the United States Army. The Beaver had served as a VIP transport in Berlin, and was flown to Coventry inside a Chinook helicopter. Its presence at Coventry reflected the growing relationship between MAM and the United States Forces, which was to prove beneficial in the future.

The museum also acquired a Gloster Javelin FAW.8, XA699, which had been an instructional airframe at Cosford. This one did fit in well with the museum's growing collection of 1940s and 50s jets. It had been one of two Javelins at Cosford put up for tender; the Newark Air Museum was successful in its bid for the other one, XH992.

Moving a large aircraft such as a Javelin was a substantial task for a voluntary group, but Newark and MAM were becoming experienced in such tasks. Newark's approach was to visit Cosford to assess the problem and to study the relevant air publications and then to return with a complete plan, and with all the necessary equipment, two trailers and a crane all lined up. The outer wings and tail were removed over one weekend, and then the following weekend the fuselage, complete with inner wing and undercarriage, was loaded on a trailer. The inner wings were removed and loaded on the other trailer. The two loads then followed a route prescribed by the police, all the way to Newark, where the even more difficult task of putting it all back together could take place. This in turn was followed by the real work – the refurbishment of the new exhibit.

Shortly after the Javelin, Newark acquired an even bigger aircraft – the de Havilland Heron G-ANXB – and then a Meteor NF.12 from Cranwell. Moving large aircraft was becoming almost routine for them.

ROLLS-ROYCE HERITAGE TRUST AND BOMBER COMMAND MUSEUM

British Aerospace and its constituent parts had always been a great friend of the aircraft-preservation movement, with historic aircraft such as the Hawker Collection finding their way into museums, and then the Vampire T.11s from

Woodford and the Danish Hunters from Dunsfold being disposed of on very satisfactory terms. Rolls-Royce, which by now made up the entire British aero-engine industry, was soon to follow suit by supporting a venture to preserve history and traditions.

In 1981, with Rolls-Royce celebrating its seventy-fifth year, the Rolls-Royce Heritage Trust was set up to record and preserve the company's long engineering history, and to publish books on the company traditions and background. Branches were established in all the companies that made up the modern-day company: Rolls-Royce, Bristol, Armstrong-Siddeley, de Havilland Aero-Engines, Napier and Blackburn. The trust was independent of the company, although it operated with the company's full co-operation and encouragement. Interested people from outside could become involved, although inevitably it was retired employees that would form the backbone of the membership. These members would also be keen on the actual restoration of vintage engines, sooner rather than later; the Derby Industrial Museum, at The Silk Mill in Derby, already displayed a large collection of Rolls-Royce engines on loan from the company. Each branch of the trust was to build up its own collection of engines, with those at Bristol, Derby and Coventry (Armstrong-Siddeley) being the largest.

On 27 November 1981, a press conference was held at RAF Hendon to announce the next phase of the museum's development. A new Bomber Command Museum would be built alongside the original Belfast Truss hangars, covering 54,000sq ft, and costing £2.5 million. It would serve as a memorial to the 55,000 Bomber Command aircrew, together with the 65,000 USAF 8th and 9th Air Force aircrew who lost their lives during the Second World War.

It was anticipated that the Lancaster, Wellington and Vimy replica would move from the existing museum, to be displayed alongside the Halifax lifted from a Norwegian lake, a Vulcan, a Valiant, a DH.9 acquired from Poland, from the museum at Cracow, a BE.2C then under reconstruction at Cardington, and possibly the Avro 504K. In addition was hoped to acquire a B-17 and a B-25 to represent the two USAF air forces.

MOVEMENTS AROUND THE MUSEUMS

The various museums around Britain were making good progress, as their 1982 acquisitions show. The Norfolk and Suffolk Aviation Museum at Bungay received its seventeenth aircraft, Whirlwind HAS.7 XN304; Newark Air Museum took delivery of its twenty-fifth, Saab Safir 91B 56321, flown in from the Norwegian Air Force; the Second World War Aircraft Preservation Society at Lasham its tenth, Sea Hawk WV798, from Leisure Sport (incidentally, none of their ten aircraft were of Second World War vintage); and the Manchester Air and Space Museum its first, Magister T9707, ex-G-AKKR, which had been displayed at Hendon. The Magister was refurbished at RAF Abingdon and was erected in the new Manchester museum on 17 July, while John Laing Construction was still renovating the building around it. With the museum due to open at Easter 1983, other aircraft would be following the Maggie at regular intervals, with a Meteor NF.14, an ex-Swiss Air Force Venom and English Electric P.1A WG763 all coming in August.

Many of the exhibits for Manchester were taken from the Aerospace Museum at Cosford, but a replacement quickly arrived from the Royal Netherlands Naval Air Service in the shape of a Lockheed Neptune, and other new arrivals were to follow. In the same way the main RAF Museum at Hendon was to lose some of its exhibits to the new Bomber Command Museum, making way for the arrival of new exhibits, one of which was very controversial. The space formerly occupied by the Lancaster was taken by a Dornier Do 24 flying boat, donated by the Spanish Air Force. Although it was a very interesting and rare exhibit, few could see its relevance to a Royal Air Force Museum. The argument in favour was that, if its novelty drew visitors through the doors, then their entrance money would make a contribution towards those aircraft that were relevant. After a decent period of time, in deference to the sensibilities of the Spanish, and having allowed all who wished to see such a rare aircraft to do so, the Dornier would be moving on.

A similar degree of expansion was shortly to take place at Duxford, where the 'SuperHangar' was about to be built. Although in some cases this merely allowed certain aircraft such as the B-29 to come in out of the weather, it did free up space in the other hangars for yet more exhibits in Duxford's various collections.

In a much smaller way the Shuttleworth Trust was also expanding with the construction of its new de Havilland hangar, which would house the many de Havilland light aircraft in the collection. It was formally opened on 29 August 1982 by Group Captain John Cunningham, former de Havilland Chief Test Pilot. Not far away, at London Colney, another museum building dedicated to de Havilland aircraft was also under way. The Mosquito Aircraft Museum at Salisbury Hall was finally getting its new display hangar, which would be opened by the Queen Mother on 4 May 1984.

In Southampton the small R.J. Mitchell Memorial Museum was also expanding, into a new, much larger, building, due to open at Easter 1984. The original museum, in an old dance hall, had housed the Supermarine S.6A and Spitfire XXIV in a very successful display, but the new museum, to be built by the City Council, would allow many more aircraft to be displayed, reflecting the many aircraft manufacturers in the Solent area.

The largest exhibit was to become the Short Sandringham 'Southern Cross', which had been purchased by the Science Museum in 1981, and was currently beached at Lee-on-Solent, with restoration work under way at the hands of the Sandringham Flying Boat Society. Another future exhibit was being constructed a little way along the south coast by the Wessex Aviation Society, mainly in the hands of John May. This was a replica of the Wight Type 1 quadruplane, a four-wing First World War fighter prototype, built on the Isle of Wight.

Yet another collection was also taking shape at Sywell in Northamptonshire, where the Nene Valley Aviation Society was gathering some airframes, including two Whirlwinds, HAR.10 XJ726 and HAS.7 XL840, as well as Vampire T.11 XE935 and a Javelin cockpit. They also took on loan the Luton Minor, BPAC.97, from the North East Aircraft Museum, and began its restoration in a small workshop.

A new aviation museum opened at Tangmere, although it did not have any complete aircraft on display in its early days. Many of the artefacts were from the aviation-archaeology movement; they included the complete collection of the short-lived London Air Museum. The prime movers in this new museum were Jim Beedle, George Wilson and Andy Saunders, who, with a small team of helpers, had converted a derelict hut on the historic airfield into an impressive museum with a promising future.

One of the largest items on display was the rear fuselage of Boulton Paul Defiant N3378, which had crashed on Bleaklow Moor in 1941, and had been brought down by a small group of enthusiasts from Macclesfield. They carried a wheel up to the crash site, hoping to install it in the surviving tailwheel fork, and then to wheelbarrow the fuselage down off the hill. Unhappily for them, this plan did not work, and they ended up not only bodily carrying the fuselage, but the wheel as well! The Bleaklow site was a well-known one, and pieces of the Defiant had been spirited away all over the country. It would be some time before anyone came up with the idea of gathering them back together again. The Wealden Aviation group would shortly join forces with Tangmere, bringing with them their T-33.

The Museum of Army Flying at Middle Wallop was also expanding quite rapidly. They had added an Alouette II, XN132, and Auster 5 TJ569 was stored, having been refurbished ready for display. Another Auster AOP.9 had also been obtained.

The Humberside Aircraft Preservation Society was also expanding, and in doing so moved its museum from Elsham Hall to an area in Cleethorpes Leisure Park, which was duly named the Bomber County Aviation Museum. Despite the name, its next acquisition was a fighter! A four-man team – Christian Brydges, Ken Foster, Peter Aird and Mike Peart – oversaw the move of 'their' Mystere IVA from Sculthorpe to the large new site, which was at the southern end of Cleethorpes Promenade.

Not far away, the South Yorkshire Aviation Society had been forced to leave its site at Nostell Priory and set up a new base at Home Farm, Firbeck, near Worksop. Carl Speddings, then the Chairman, had plans to create a museum, but in the meantime the society operated workshops at the farm. Among their newer acquisitions were a Canberra nose, XM279, and a rather more recent Socata Tobago, G-BGTB, Cessna Centurion, G-BAGE, and the fuselage of a Cessna 150, G-AWFH. In addition, the Aeroplane Collection had loaned its Flying Flea and Bensen gyroglider, which were handy as mobile exhibits.

The seventy-seventh BAPC meeting was to be held at Firbeck in 1986, and this date spurred the South Yorkshire Aviation Society into getting the museum ready to open the following week. Chairman Ray Liversedge welcomed the delegates, and was able to show them the remains of a crashed Wellington that had been recovered by the society from its crash site near Braemar in Scotland.

MUSEUM SUCCESSES AND FAILURES

Clearly, the aircraft-museum scene was expanding, so it was sad to hear news of the impending closure of the pioneering Historic Aircraft Museum at Southend. It had been fighting a battle for survival for some time, but the announcement of its final closure, set for 27 March 1983, nevertheless came as a shock. All the aircraft in this fine collection were to be auctioned by Phillips on 10 May.

For an aircraft museum to be successful, all the conditions had to be right. Southend had been opened in a blaze of publicity, with a fine purpose-built building full of interesting aircraft, and with a degree of financial backing, but that was not enough. The aircraft had been acquired as much for their availability as because of any relevance to Southend, to Essex or to one another. Many of them had come from the previous British Historic Aircraft Museum on the other side of the airfield, which had not even got as far as opening.

Although there was always a large voluntary element in the labour force at Southend, it was not a volunteer-led organization, and therefore lacked the enthusiasm and drive that that often implied, which were much in evidence at places such as Newark and Coventry. Neither did it have the backing of a large national organization, like the Imperial War Museum or the Science Museum, or the local council, like the new museums at Manchester and Southampton. The lesson was clear – a shed full of assorted old aircraft did not necessarily guarantee a viable aircraft museum.

Although not volunteer-led, Southend did have a voluntary element, the Historic Aviation Society, and this did not fold with the museum. Although its numbers were smaller, the group continued in the Essex area, using the fuselage frame of Short Scion G-AEZF as its ongoing project. Other items owned by the society were loaned out, including the Flea G-ADXS, to the Rebel Air Museum at Andrewsfield, and the V-1 launching track, which went to Duxford.

Much further north, the Strathallan Museum was also showing signs of difficulty. It had carried on after the sale of many of its aircraft, had acquired a few extra exhibits such as the Rolls-Royce 'Flying Bedstead' VTOL rig, on loan from the Science Museum, and was continuing with the restoration of its Fairey Swordfish. However, it announced late in 1983 that it was to sell its airworthy Hurricane G-AWLW. Strathallan was an atmospheric collection on a delightful airfield, but suffered perhaps from a location that was just too far away from the major centres of population.

EIGHT VULCANS

Periodically, the RAF would retire one of its aircraft types, and immediately afterwards a number of examples would be released for the aircraft-preservation movement. In 1983 the retiring aircraft was the mighty Avro Vulcan, which had received a stay of execution because of the Falklands War, adding to its aura. Eight examples were being offered for the nominal sum of £5,000 each, plus the expense of airborne delivery. Acquiring one of these charismatic aircraft suddenly became a must for every aircraft museum that had an adjacent runway. (Dismantling, transporting and then re-erecting a Vulcan was beyond the abilities and pocket of all but the professionals of the Royal Air Force, who were about to do just this for the new Bomber Command Museum at Hendon.)

The first of the Vulcans to be delivered from their base at Waddington was XL319, which flew to Sunderland Airport for the North East Aircraft Museum on 21 January. Four days later, XJ863 was flown to Carlisle Airport for display alongside the aircraft of the Solway Aviation Society, having been bought by society members Tom Stoddart and David Hutchinson. Another 'private purchase' was XL391, which was bought by a syndicate of Austin Williams of Manchester, Alan Fletcher of Stockport and Brian Bateson of Blackpool. The aircraft was kept at Squires Gate, and, although they hoped to keep it in flying condition, flying costs of £2,000 an hour meant an annual bill of at least £50,000, even if the CAA would give such a complex aircraft a Permit to Fly.

Shortly afterwards, XM575 was flown to Castle Donington for the Loughborough & Leicester Aircraft Preservation Society. Later in the year they were to consider moving their base to Bruntingthorpe, a little further south, but re-siting the Vulcan was to be a major stumbling block in this plan. The smaller aircraft, Hunter, Vampire, Mystere, Buccaneer, F-100 and Anson, were in fact moved, but the mighty delta needed a Permit to Fly, even for the short journey to Bruntingthorpe. The permit was not forthcoming, even if LLAPS could have raised the £6,000 fuel costs.

On 30 January, XN612 was flown to Norwich Airport for the City of Norwich Aviation Museum, where one of the members, John Hale, had guaranteed a loan to cover the purchase price. Although the Vulcans were being sold for a price far below their scrap value, £5,000 was still a large sum for a voluntary group to find, as few had any kind of contingency funds. Money was usually spent as soon as it was raised – and in some cases even before it was raised!

The Midland Air Museum received Vulcan XL360, and immediately launched an appeal to the people of the city of Coventry to raise the necessary money. Newark was in the happier position of being the first organization to pay for its example, courtesy of Stewart Stephenson of the Lincolnshire Lancaster Committee, but was the last to take delivery, with XM594 being flown to Winthorpe on 7 February.

Two of the Vulcans were kept by the RAF: XM607, the aircraft that made the first raid on the Falklands, was retained at Waddington as gate guardian, and XM598, the aircraft that aborted from the first Falklands raid, went to the Aerospace Museum at Cosford, where it was to replace the Vulcan B.1 on display.

The Vulcan B.1 at Cosford was scrapped. It had been on display outdoors for some time, and was deemed beyond all economic repair, even to the point of becoming dangerous. This highlighted the problem the various new Vulcan owners had taken on. A large aircraft such as the Vulcan, which in all cases would have to be displayed outdoors, presented a gigantic ongoing maintenance problem. Even painting an aircraft with the surface area of a Vulcan was a mammoth task for a volunteer group. Nevertheless, the groups that had missed out on the first tranche of retired Vulcans were keeping an eye on 50 Squadron, which was still operating six Vulcan tankers at Waddington, and had noted that five other aircraft – three bombers and two reconnaissance aircraft – were still to be disposed of. They were pleased to reflect that there would be another chance to buy their very own Vulcan.

BAPC QUARTERLY MEETING

The new Bomber Command Museum, due to be opened by the Queen Mother in April, was the venue for the sixty-third Quarterly Meeting of BAPC. Not surprisingly, there was a bumper turnout. Two significant new members were voted in. The only new full member was the British Aerial Museum of Flying Military Aircraft, based at Duxford, with Graham Warner as its curator. This was to become synonymous with flying Blenheims. Among the associate members voted in at Hendon was the Berkshire Aviation Group. Chairman Phillip Davey announced plans to rebuild a Miles Master trainer, but it was not this that brought the group to prominence but the eventual creation of its museum at Woodley. Its appeal for Master parts almost immediately yielded a set of wings found by the Chiltern Historic Aircraft Preservation Group in the rafters at Booker. Project co-ordinator Paul Kiddell was soon in possession of other small items, including control boxes, instruments, canopies and seats.

Also at the meeting, the Aeroplane Collection, represented by Secretary Grahame Sparkes, finally announced a museum venture. With several of its aircraft going into the new Manchester museum, the group had obtained premises at a garden centre at Warmingham, Cheshire, which would operate as a small museum and workshop. Having striven to create a museum in the Manchester area for the last twenty years, it was ironic that they were now becoming an integral part of two, in the space of a few months.

The Lord Mayor of Manchester, Councillor Clifford Tomlinson, formally opened the 'other' museum, in Deansgate, on 29 March 1983. The usual ceremonies were accompanied by a fly-past by an Avro Vulcan, XL426. Keeper of the new museum was Peter Batson, who was still hoping for a Lincoln rather than the Shackleton AEW.2 that was the centrepiece. There were fourteen aircraft on display, including the Roe triplane replica and Avro Avian from the Aeroplane Collection. The first aircraft viewed from the entrance was the slightly incongruous Scottish Aviation Pioneer, although this would later be replaced by the far more appropriate Roe triplane, which was then next to it.

A refreshingly different display item was the Hawker Hunter, exhibited with large areas of its skin removed to show what went on underneath. Too often, museums believed that an aircraft on display had to be complete, but few people would have stopped to look at just another Hunter. By removing the skin, the museum gave visitors something different to see, in a way that was instructive about the structure and equipment of a 1950s vintage jet fighter.

In a similar way, the forward fuselage of Firefly WB440 was displayed with the Griffon engine exposed for all to see. A cockpit section is usually placed on display with the rear end blanked off, but a cockpit section, especially with the engine cowlings removed, gives a tremendous opportunity to show people features that they cannot see on a complete aircraft. At the same time such a policy means that an aircraft has to be fully restored beneath the skin, and not just re-painted externally.

AUCTIONS

The growing strength of the aircraft-preservation movement was reflecting in the increasing number of historic-aircraft auctions. In the spring of 1983 there were two in quick succession. The first, held at Duxford on 14 April, had over fifty assorted aircraft on sale and attracted around 2,000 people. Top price was paid for Spitfire LF IXB MH434, which made £260,000, and the Shuttleworth Trust's PR XI went for £110,000, but the Griffon-engined FR XIV G-FXIV received a top bid of only £180,000 against a reserve of £300,000. The former Skyfame Tempest 2 went to the USA for £85,000, but many of the lots, particularly the lighter aircraft, failed to sell.

At the sale of the Historic Aircraft Museum aircraft at Southend, the top price was achieved for the Sea Fury, which went for a mere £35,000. The Beverley was to stay on site, having been bought by the associated Queen's Moat Hotel for only £3,200, and the Lincoln was sold to Warbirds (UK) Ltd to yield spares for the Lancaster they had recently bought in Canada, which was under restoration at Blackbushe. The Science Museum purchased the de Havilland

Dragon G-ACIT, for £28,000, for its transport collection at Wroughton. This collection received a second aircraft from Southend when Marconi donated its Piaggio P.166 G-APWY, which had been on loan to the Historic Aircraft Museum for two years. The CASA 2.111 (He 111) and the North American Texan were purchased by Paul Raymond for his new, purely commercial Theatre of War venture in Central London, for which he had also bought the components of a Spitfire XIV at Duxford, as well as a Mustang. As it turned out, the CASA 2.111 would not fit in the Whitehall Theatre, but a CASA.1112 (Bf 109) bought from Biggin Hill and Storch D-EKMV did. The Theatre of War was arranged as a series of diaromas, with various aircraft, military vehicles and weapons, including a Sopwith Pup replica, N6542, suspended above. It opened in September 1983, and then closed shortly afterwards, as Raymond had failed to obtain council permission for a change of use.

The ex-Belgian Air Force F.84 Thunderstreak went to the RAF Museum, which entrusted its restoration to the Medway Branch of the Royal Aeronautical Society. Its members had finished their Meteor F.8, which was now on gate guardian duties at Rochester Airport, and the SAAB J-29 joined the Draken at Duxford.

To put these prices in context, a detached house in the Southampton area at the time cost £40,000. This particular house was 'Mon Repos', the former home of Australian aviator Bert Hinkler, which was due to be demolished to make way for an old people's home. The town of his birth, Bundaberg in Queensland, heard of this and arranged for the house to be demolished brick by brick, and shipped out to Australia to be reconstructed as a museum in his memory. The operation cost £40,000.

On Sunday 8 October 1983, the largest aircraft yet preserved in Britain, Boeing B-52D 56-689, landed at Duxford, ironically on the shortest runway ever used by the type. Just like its older relative the B-29, it had to be displayed outside for the time being, until suitable accommodation could be provided. Further down the non-Flight Line, the Viscount G-ALWF was finally getting some major treatment, being re-painted in BEA colours.

A rival in the size stakes arrived from Ireland at the Science Museum's store at Wroughton. Lockheed Constellation G-CONI had languished in Ireland for many years and was moved for the Science Museum by Aces High Ltd of North Weald. For a short time it even wore their name. It had actually been earmarked for a second series of the television drama *Airline*, but this had been cancelled and Aces High found themselves working for the Science Museum instead. The museum also bought a Boeing 247D and a Lockheed 10 Electra in the USA, to represent some of the earliest examples of all-metal airliners.

TERMS AND EXPRESSIONS

Over the years there have been long arguments within the aircraft-preservation movement about the correct terminology to be used for the various replicas/reproductions and full-scale models that have been built. As Editor of *Wrecks and Relics*, and the keeper of the BAPC Register for otherwise anonymous aircraft (which included many such constructions), Ken Ellis was well placed to lay down the law on the matter.

He decided that the term 'replica', which is the one most widely used, should be reserved for new examples of aircraft built in the same way, with the same materials as the original, and fitted with an appropriate engine. Of necessity these would have to be fully flyable aircraft, whether they eventually flew or not. The best examples of these would be the aircraft produced by the Northern Aeroplane Workshops – when T.O.M. Sopwith first saw their Triplane, he deemed it not a replica at all, just a late one off the production line! Strictly speaking, the term replica should refer only to an example built by the original manufacturer – in the case of the Sopwith Triplane, this would mean the Dunsfold Factory of British Aerospace – but was deemed just too nit-picking to make sense. The recent 'new' production Yak-9s built by Yakovel have Allison engines, and other differences from the wartime examples, so cannot be described as 'replicas', although there seems to be nothing to stop a manufacturer fitting any new engine to one of its products.

Ken Ellis reserved the term 'reproduction' for new examples of aircraft which looked the same as the original, but were built in a different way or of different materials. Good examples are the many 'World War One' aircraft built with welded steel-tube fuselages, and often fitted with modern engines. Reproductions should also be flyable but, again, this does not mean that they have to have flown, just that they need to have the potential to do so.

The term 'full-scale model' (FSM) is used to refer to those examples that look like the originals, but have been built of totally different materials, very often scrap materials or fibreglass. Of course, such models would never be capable of flight. The terms 'facsimile' or 'mock-up' might also be used for them.

Although a full-scale model would not be flyable, its construction could none the less be a major undertaking in its own right. One good example of this is the de Havilland Moth FSM, which was commissioned for the Gatwick Hilton. It was originally intended to be an aircraft built in the same way as the original, perhaps with lower-grade materials, but fire and safety regulations put paid to that. It had to be totally redesigned with an all-steel structure, covered with Class One fireproof material, with no rubber and only a limited use of fire-resistant glass-fibre. The entire airframe had to be designed, stressed and certified to a design factor of five for static loading, and this was extended to all fittings and suspension cables. The task was taken on by Shawcross (Models) Ltd, which had previously built an FSM of a Vickers Vimy for a film of Alcock and Brown's transatlantic flight, which was never made. Their Moth was built complete with its own internal winch, so that it could be lowered to the floor on its solitary cable for cleaning purposes – the world's only VTOL Moth!

Of course, although the design and construction of the Moth was an impressive achievement, the result was not an aircraft. Even if it was fitted with a real engine it would not be capable of flight. Nevertheless, it illustrated the aircraft in an accurate manner, just as many fibreglass Spitfires and Hurricanes serve the same purpose in static museums. (Indeed, in many cases, the aircraft in a museum might as well be made of fibreglass, for all the difference it would make to visitors.) There is a strong argument for putting FSMs on display in static museums and letting the real examples take to the air once more, where they belong.

The use of the correct terms for a specific project has often caused a great deal of head scratching, not least for one particular aircraft that began to appear in Yorkshire. In one of the 1984 editions of *Control Column* it was reported that the Yorkshire Air Museum, which had established itself on Elvington Airfield near York, was to rescue two poultry sheds from an island in the Outer Hebrides. The sheds were in fact fuselage sections of a Halifax bomber that had crashed on the Isle of Lewis.

The Yorkshire Air Museum was founded by Mrs Rachel Semlyen, who had the idea of preserving derelict airfield operations' buildings on a fenced-off 7-acre piece of land in the Elvington area, where she used to walk her dog. At the time, the airfield was in use as a satellite landing ground for the Jet Provosts from Church Fenton and Linton-on-Ouse. Mrs Semlyen got together with a group of aviation archaeologists from the area, to look at forming an aviation museum based on the derelict buildings.

One of the early members was Ian Robinson, a wartime Handley Page employee and pilot. When he heard of the Halifax hen coop, he raised the idea of recovering it and using it as the basis of reconstructing a complete Halifax. Rarely has the aircraft-preservation movement been faced with such a crazy idea. Recovering the 25-ft fuselage section from its remote location, and hoping to restore it after forty years' exposure to Hebridean weather, and pounds of chicken droppings, was an eccentric enough concept, but to think of building a Halifax from scratch seemed a daydream too far. Most people reading the item in *Control Column* quickly forgot about it, dismissing it as another non-starter scheme; just like an earlier idea – an appeal for volunteers to help build a replica of a Handley Page 0/400 – which really did come to nothing.

Volunteers at the Norfolk and Suffolk Aircraft Museum manoeuvre their Provost across the stream dividing the site, around 1980.

The Strathallan hangar at Auchterader crowded with aircraft and people in 1980.

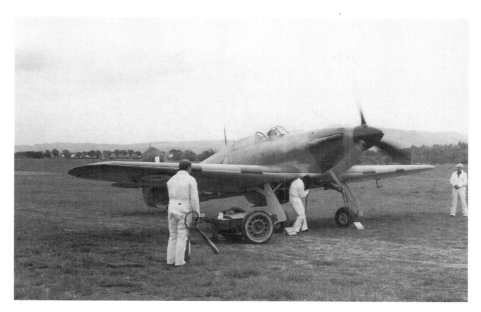

Strathallan's Hurricane being run up for flight in 1980.

Anson C.19 G-AWRS and Meteor F.8 WL181, early arrivals at the North East Aircraft Museum, Sunderland.

Two serving Norwegian Air Force officers, Lt Stig Halvorsen and Lt Peter Reymert, who had just flown the Saab Safir for presentation to the Newark Air Museum, in 1982. They are surrounded by museum members who had gathered to welcome the new arrival.

Supervisors from Dowty Boulton Paul Ltd present Derek Eastwood (fourth left), Curator at the Aerospace Museum, Cosford, with two power control units, from a Buccaneer (left) and a VC 10, with the Sea Balliol as a backdrop.

A volunteer applies rather more exciting markings to the Dumfries and Galloway Aviation Museum's Mystere IVA, 318, with its Meteor T.7, WL375, in the foreground.

One of the famous Vulcan sell-off, XM655, at Wellesbourne Mountford, where its taxi runs are rather more noisy than the usual Cessna movements.

The fuselages of Anson N4877 and Oxford V3388, training partners in war, ready to make the journey together from Skyfame to Duxford.

Some of Skyfame's aircraft lined up at Staverton for a last photocall before the journey to Duxford. Front to rear: Proctor LZ266, Sycamore G-48/1 and SRA.1 TG263.

The Hawker Hind at Shuttleworth, a refugee from Afghanstan.

The Percival Prentice at Newark, one of the longest residents.

Arthur Clover and Basil Carlin working on the Rapide within the Museum of Science and Industry in Manchester. Restoration work within the museum is a welcome feature of the displays, although it is slower than work in a separate workshop would be, as the workers often stop to answer questions from the public.

A fine example of what can be achieved: the Sopwith Triplane 'late production model', built by the Northern Aeroplane Workshops for the Shuttleworth Trust.

The Comet 1 fuselage in store at the de Havilland Aircraft Museum at London Colney, with its contemporary, the Vampire FB.6, alongside.

The magic of Old Warden. Volunteers from the Shuttleworth Veteran Aeroplane Society watch in front of the Hawker Tomtit as a rather more potent Hawker product, a Harrier, prepares for take-off.

Essential maintenance on Vickers Varsity WL626, at the East Midlands Aeropark.

The curse of preserving aircraft in bare metal – elbow grease. David Rogers of Autoglym helps polish the Vickers Viking at the Brooklands Museum.

Some of the Boulton Paul Association's workshop team in front of their Defiant full-scale model. Front: Jack Holmes (Chief Engineer) and Cyril Plimmer (Chairman). Back row, left to right: Dave Podmore, John Vaughan, Ray Simpson, Bill Pauling, Alec Brew, Brian Holmes, Colin Penny, Harry Law.

The Westland Dragonfly being rolled out after its restoration at Elvington.

CHAPTER 13

Maturity

TRANSPORTING MUSEUM PIECES

IN 1983 Newark Air Museum celebrated its twentieth anniversary. Pipped to the post as the first all-voluntary society in the country by the Northern Aircraft Preservation Society, Newark had got into its stride a little more quickly. By establishing a museum on a suitable site, and creating a large collection, it had swept to pre-eminence among the voluntary groups.

The value of its site at Newark Showgrounds, formerly Winthorpe Airfield, was incalcuable, and the presence of the runway (albeit little used), meant that several of the museum's aircraft had been flown to the site. While this was not vital with the first delivery – of Prentice G-APIY in 1967 – in the case of Hastings TG517 and the Vulcan, both bought by member Stuart Stephenson, it was immensely valuable. Despite having a runway at its disposal, the museum was also adept at dismantling and moving large aircraft, a process which often involved the organization of cranes and suitable transport, as well as liaison with police forces along the entire route. Their first experience of such an operation had involved the unique Meteor FR.9, but the museum had also moved much larger aircraft, including the Shackleton that they dismantled, transported and re-erected in only six weeks in 1977, and the Javelin (*see* page 103).

Sometimes, however, even their new-found expertise was not sufficient. In 1982, Newark's tender for Gannet AEW.3 XP266 was accepted, but the aircraft could not be easily split into a load of less than 19ft 6in wide, which would make a 'wide load'. It also stood at 16ft 10in high on its undercarriage, so a low-loader was essential.

Salvation came in the form of the Royal Navy's Mobile Aircraft Repair Transport and Salvage Unit (MARTSU). As soon as time could be found for a civilian job, MARTSU undertook the move in their usual professional manner.

The museum had averaged the acquisition of over one aircraft per year since its first tentative opening, in 1967. During the period 1980–82, it had obtained no less than nine new aircraft. These developments kept alive the interest of the public, and visitor numbers rose to an annual figure of 13,000 by 1982, a record that was to be easily surpassed in the museum's twentieth anniversary year.

Although the acquisition of new exhibits maintained interest, and therefore visitor income, and increased the museum's prestige, it brought with it huge new problems. In many ways the actual movement of an aircraft to the site was the least of these. Very often the museum was immediately faced with a huge amount of work just to bring the aircraft up to a suitable display standard. For example, the newly arrived de Havilland Heron G-ANXB, the first such aircraft preserved in Britain, was in a shocking state on its arrival, without engines or undercarriage. The first task was to fabricate new wing bolts so that the wings could be hung on. A team lead by John Manston and Paul Newton was put in charge of the Heron restoration; one of their assistants was an enthusiastic 12-year-old called Andrew Bakin.

Once an aircraft was in a presentable state for exhibiting, the museum was faced with the task of maintaining it. It was a never-ending job that strained the enthusiasm of voluntary members to the limit. Fetching a new aircraft and getting it in shape is always an exciting and rewarding experience, but the grim task of endless cleaning, re-painting and corrective maintenance soon becomes tiresome. With most of its growing number of exhibits displayed outside, Newark was faced with the twin assaults of the British weather and the British vandal. Its first Anson had been lost to an arsonist. The entire instrument panel of its Prentice had been removed by a thief and, after sixteen years' display, the aircraft was looking in very bad shape. It was urgently in need of a major restoration, once space was available in the small workshop building.

The construction of this workshop had been a major development, providing the museum with more covered accommodation to add to a few wooden huts and a Portacabin. Now, the financing of a large exhibition hall was becoming a priority, as a place to stow aircraft such as the Prentice, once restored, away from the reach of the weather and vandals.

The museum had established a 'team' system for the restoration and maintenance of each aircraft, but, as with any voluntary group, it had a finite number of working members. Much of the time needed to be spent on the basic operation of the museum and the maintenance of the site (simply cutting the grass was an immense chore). It was inevitable that a few members found themselves in several teams, and some aircraft found themselves orphans, without anyone looking after them until that fateful day when someone realized how tatty they had become.

Another tactic that could be used on such an orphan was 'The Blitz'. The Javelin, acquired in 1981, was a candidate for this two years later, with a large group of members descending on it over a few weekends, to strip it down, repair where necessary and then re-paint it. After the work was finished, the members would return to their usual tasks, or begin another 'Blitz', and the Javelin could be returned to display for a few more years until another refurbishment was needed.

Help was at hand via government employment schemes. From 1982, a YTS scheme in Newark had young people working on various maintenance and construction projects around the museum site. This was of immense value, especially when the Vulcan was due to arrive. The Winthorpe runway had to be completely swept, and all the holes filled in, and then fences had to be removed to get the aircraft on to the site. The team also built new toilet facilities and the new entrance/shop building.

The Manpower Services Commission also sponsored a Community Programme workforce at the museum, the largest such team in Newark, with twelve workers and a full-time supervisor, David Leggatt. As an ex-RAF apprentice, Leggatt had the right kind of experience to guide the team through a number of restoration projects on the museum's aircraft. Although the museum had to provide all the materials required, and workshop facilities, as a registered charity it was able to gain the full benefit of the Community Programme.

MIDLAND AIR MUSEUM

Although it had begun four years after Newark, the Midland Air Museum had followed a similar sort of path. It was now well established on an airfield site, albeit a rather busier one, at Baginton, and had a substantial and rapidly growing collection of exhibits, in many cases quite similar to those at Newark, and often obtained at the same time, through the same channels. These included the recently acquired Canberra PR.3 WF922, and Saro Skeeter XL765. The buildings on the museum site, which covered 6,000sq yds, were restricted to a small entrance building and a workshop, plus an old cattle lairage just off the site that was used to store many of the old wooden airframes that had been among the early acquisitions.

Chairman John Berkeley and the rest of the committee also recognized the need for a large exhibition building and had launched the Sir Frank Whittle Hangar Appeal. Although the fund grew steadily, sufficient finance seemed a long way off. Salvation was eventually to come from an unusual source. When the West Midlands County Council was wound up, with all the boroughs in the artificially created county being handed all authority over their own affairs, it found it had money left in its coffers. It was decided to dole out this money to suitably worthy causes, and the Whittle Hangar Appeal duly received £100,000, allowing construction to begin.

The use of Sir Frank Whittle's name also reflected a definite theme which had been applied to the museum's collecting policy. They were using the fact that Whittle was born locally, and did his early work on jet engines just down the road at Lutterworth, to define the development of the jet engine as the main focus of the museum's acquisitions, together with the general history of aviation in Coventry and the locality.

This conveniently fitted in with the acquisition of early jet aircraft, which was a trend that MAM and all such groups were following anyway, but it was also an excellent way to encourage support from the local council. When the museum outgrew the first site, and wished to move to a new 4.5-acre site alongside, not only was the council in full agreement, but it also donated £10,000 towards the costs. The reception area/shop, workshop, toilet block and store were duly painted in the museum's colours of grey/white/blue stripes, ready for the Lord Mayor of Coventry, Councillor Walter Brandish, to lead a ceremony naming the Vulcan *City of Coventry*. In this way, the museum's links with the city were further cemented.

The Armstrong-Whitworth/Whittle jet heritage themes were further explored with the acquisition of Sea Hawk WV797, in January 1986, followed by the loan of Meteor NF.14 WS838 from Cosford. Finally, in February 1987, five years of work by Chairman John Berkeley resulted in the arrival of the last but one flying Armstrong-Whitworth Argosy G-APRL, donated by the ABC Group. Wearing its Elan Parcels colours, it made its last-ever flight to Baginton, before its engines were removed for further use.

Newark was slightly more fortunate in its collecting policy, as almost any aircraft acquired had some connection with aviation in either of the two adjoining counties of Lincolnshire and Nottinghamshire. Newark could snap up any airframe and be fairly sure that it would fit in with its historical theme.

MAM had the same sort of manpower problems as Newark, and in 1983 took advantage of government policy to set up an £80,000 Community Programme Scheme. Sponsored by the museum, in collaboration with the Manpower Services Commission and the Warwickshire County Council, it envisaged the provision of two full-time employees and twenty trainees at the museum. They were divided into two teams, one involved in building work related to the development of the site and the move to the adjacent location, and the other refurbishing aircraft in a small new workshop hangar. The Folland Gnat fuselage was to be the first to receive their attentions.

In 1988 MAM decided to release the fuselage of Fox Moth G-ACCB for restoration to flying condition. It had been in store since they acquired it, and would not be part of any restoration programme in the foreseeable future. The decision was made to release it to someone who could put it back into the air, especially as it no longer fitted in with the museum's collecting policy. The fact that they had saved the Fox Moth, which had been derelict since a crash in 1956, was a strong argument against all those who had claimed that many of the voluntary groups were preserving scrap. If the museum had not saved G-ACCB in the days when it was the Midland Aircraft Preservation Society, and desperate to acquire any aircraft, the world would have one less Fox Moth gracing the skies today.

APPEALS FOR UNDERCOVER SPACE

Located on the Norfolk/Suffolk border, the museum at Bungay was another featuring similar aircraft on a large outdoor site. It did not have a runway adjacent, so all aircraft had to be dismantled to be transported in. This did not entirely prevent delivery by air, however. In 1983, the museum acquired Vickers Valetta VX580 from the Norfolk Scout Association, and it was flown in from Norwich Airport – suspended beneath a RAF Chinook helicopter! This museum also quickly recognized the need for a new hangar and soon launched an appeal fund.

Other voluntary-run museums were realizing the importance of getting at least some of their collection indoors. In Kent, the Battle of Britain Museum launched an appeal to raise £15,000 to erect a hangar they had already acquired, at Hawkinge Airfield. When complete it would be known as the Lord Dowding Memorial Hangar. The museum was at its third home by now, having first opened in 1971 at Littlecourt Langley, and then having moved later to Chilham Castle.

The group had been formed in 1966 by Mike Llewellyn, and specialized in the investigation of Battle of Britain crash sites. At Hawkinge, it incorporated the collection of Brenznett Aviation Museum, and displayed a massive collection of crash-site artefacts. When it was opened, in 1986, the Lord Dowding Memorial Hangar featured former Battle of Britain film FSMs of Spitfire, Hurricane and Bf 109, the latter in a suitable 'shot-down' pose, as well as a Beaverette armoured car. The museum also incorporated the Hawkinge control building and the former armoury.

The opposite approach was being taken at a new museum venture at East Kirkby airfield in Lincolnshire, which was to prove another chapter in the long saga of the ex-HAPS Lancaster NX611, G-ASXX. The Lancaster had been on RAF Scampton since just after its purchase by Lord Lilford at the Blackpool auction, but he had now sold it to Lincolnshire farmer Fred Panton. Panton had purchased 23 acres of East Kirkby and intended to create an aircraft museum as a memorial to his brother, Chris, who had been a flight engineer on Halifaxes, and was killed on the infamous Nuremburg Raid of 30/31 March 1944. The Panton family had already become involved in the aircraft-preservation movement when they presented a building to the Lincolnshire Aircraft Museum at Tattershall, as a memorial to Chris. The building was known as the Panton Wing, and contained several assorted displays.

The East Kirkby site included the control tower, which was under restoration to wartime condition, and the base for a hangar. Fred Panton had no intention of moving the Lancaster until he had erected a T.2 hangar on the site, and the aircraft could be housed indoors for the first time since its arrival from New Caledonia over twenty years before. He then intended to refurbish the aircraft until the engines could be run, and hoped perhaps even to put it back in the air.

On 9 July 1984 Lord King, Chairman of British Airways, opened the new British Airways Hall, attached to the side of one of the top two hangars at the Aerospace Museum, Cosford. The hall contained only models and memorabilia, but the entrance was flanked by the Museum's Viscount in BEA colours and Comet 1 in BOAC colours. Further down the hill, the Trident, VC-10 and Boeing 707 received new coats of paint in honour of the occasion. Len Woodgate, Curator of the Aerospace Museum, was at pains to point out that the paint used was chosen more for its weather-keeping properties and cost-effectiveness than for its authenticity. The collection of airliners was shortly to be joined by Bristol Britannia 312 G-AOVF; its engines would follow later. Eventually, the Britannia too would receive a BOAC colour scheme.

SAD LOSSES

In 1984 two significant figures in the world of aircraft preservation died. The early months of the year saw the death of BAPC Chairman Doug Harmer. He was replaced by Mike Hodgson, who was Chairman of the Lincolnshire Aircraft Museum and co-author of *Airfields of Lincolnshire since 1912,* as well as being a local farmer. One of his first duties was to welcome the sixty-ninth meeting of the BAPC to Tattershall.

On Sunday 19 August Mike Twite, Editor of *FlyPast,* was killed in the crash of Vickers Varsity G-BDTF/WJ897. The aircraft was owned and operated by the Leicester Aircraft Preservation Group, and had been flying from its base at Syerston to the Liverpool Air Show. It landed at the East Midlands Airport to refuel, and to pick up Mike Twite, who was writing a feature about the group. The aircraft suffered engine problems 38 minutes after taking off again, and crashed at Marchington in Staffordshire, killing eleven of the fourteen people on board.

Mike Twite had edited *FlyPast* from the first edition. Before that he had edited and written for motoring magazines, but he always had an affinity with aviation, having worked as an air traffic controller and being the holder of a pilot's licence. Working virtually as a one-man band, he had turned *FlyPast* into essential reading for anyone interested in historic aviation and aircraft preservation, displacing *Control Column,* which was shortly to close.

Mike Twite was replaced as Editor of *FlyPast* by teacher Ken Ellis, who had compiled the 'Preservation News' section in the magazine, and had previously edited *Flypast* – that is, the magazine produced by the Merseyside Society of Aviation Enthusiasts – from 1974 to 1981. He was also editor and compiler of *Wrecks and Relics* and the author of several other books, as well as being the compiler of the BAPC register of unregistered aircraft.

FlyPast instituted a Mike Twite Memorial Trophy, to be awarded every year to the most meritorious achievement in aircraft preservation, as voted by the magazine's readers. The trophy was made from the centre part of the propeller from a Gipsy III engine, and was accompanied by a cheque for £1,000. The first winner was to be B-17 Preservation, the operators of the B-17 'Sally B'. Elly Salingboe accepted the award at the Sally B Supporters Club AGM, held at the Crest Hotel Gatwick, and the trophy was presented by Mike Twite's widow, Pat. The second winner was Graham Warner's Blenheim IV restoration.

FACING CLOSURES

Amidst all the progress with new hangars and new museums in 1984, the news that the North East Aircraft Museum at Sunderland faced imminent closure came as a shock. Sunderland Airport was earmarked as the site of the new Nissan car factory, and the museum was in the way. Extensive negotiations were to follow involving museum chairman John Stelling and Sunderland Council, with BAPC making intensive representations. In July 1984 came the good news that the museum was saved and would be re-housed on a new 3-acre site with a long lease. They would also have a Romney Hangar, a new hangar and the former parachute club building, as well as a section of hard-standing which used to be a tennis court. The threat of closure actually boosted attendance over the following few weeks, so much so that the museum contemplated a regular announcement of closure!

The Vulcan had to be towed past the former airfield main entrance, through a hedge and over a service road, but that was the most difficult of the aircraft to move. The members were faced with a lot of work just getting the new site ready, but by the time of the BAPC meeting was held there the following year, the whole museum was in a very impressive state. By late 1985 they were sufficiently well organized for aircraft collecting to begin again in earnest with the acquisition of a Republic F-84 and a F-86D Sabre from the Greek Air Force.

In 1985 another museum was faced with closure, when the Lincolnshire Aircraft Museum's lease at Tattershall finally ran out. The site was required for redevelopment, unless the museum could buy the freehold for £50,000. They immediately began an appeal to raise the money, but looked around for other alternatives in the mean time. Roger Byron-Collins offered them a site at the former RAF Hemswell, if they could raise £67,000, but Lincs preferred to stay on its existing site. The Panton brothers then offered the group a home at their new museum at East Kirkby. The offer was accepted and the exhibits were moved from Tattershall to their new home on 10 and 11 December 1985, with a plan to open the new museum in May 1987.

Finding a site for a museum was a problem for many groups and, without security of tenure, the threat of eviction was ever-present for those who had thrown open their doors to paying visitors. As long as they did not own the freehold of the land they occupied, any plans for major exhibition hangars, for example, were irrelevant.

Another group in this situation was the Nene Valley Aviation Society, which discovered in 1984 that its site at Sywell Airfield had to be vacated because of redevelopment work. A new site was located at Sibson Airfield near Peterborough and its collection of two Whirlwinds, Vampire T.11, Javelin cockpit, Auster fuselage frame, and Luton Minor (on loan from NEAM) was duly moved. Its Buccaneer remained at RAE Bedford, awaiting developments.

They were just settling when they were forced to move out again, as they were refused planning permission. This time, they gave up the ghost, and the aircraft were dispersed. The Whirlwind HAS.7 went to the City of Norwich Museum, the Whirlwind HAR.10 to Snowdon Mountain Aviation at Caernarfon, and the Vampire T.11 to the South Yorkshire Aircraft Preservation Society at Firbeck.

FURTHER DEVELOPMENTS

The Booker Air Museum had been opened shortly before by the Chiltern Historic Aircraft Preservation Group, under the care of Curator Gordon King and his brother Derek, who acted as Secretary. They obtained a secure area of Wycombe Air Park and, with the co-operation and encouragement of Wycombe District Council, and Wycombe Air Park companies such as Personal Plane Services, created a small but professional-looking museum. Two large buildings were soon erected, housing a treasure trove of smaller items. They opened at weekends and on Monday and Wednesday evenings. A Vampire T.11, Provost and Harvard fuselage were loaned by Barry Parkhouse, and the 'Friends of Biggin Hill' Group loaned a Nord Norecrin, G-BAYV, a Vampire NF.10 and a Whirlwind.

Another collection on the move was that of the Loughborough and Leicester Group, which fell out with the management of East Midlands Airport over its plans to create an air park. Its entire collection was moved to Bruntingthorpe Airfield, which was owned by the Walton family. The one problem was its Vulcan, XM575. Plans were made to fly it on the short hop, and it was duly registered G-BLMC, but the CAA was not ready to issue a Permit to Fly to anything so complex, so the Vulcan remained at East Midlands Airport. It was eventually incorporated in the new East Midlands Aeropark and Visitor Centre. The Loughborough and Leicester group renamed itself the Phoenix Aviation Museum, but was forced to sell its Hunter to cover debts incurred; in addition, its Super Sabre was reclaimed by the USAF and shipped to Germany.

The closure of Paul Raymond's Theatre of War venture (*see* page 111) brought about another major vintage-aircraft auction in 1985. The CASA2-111, which had never fitted into the Whitehall Theatre, was sold for £24,000 to Kermit Weeks of the USA, but all the other major lots remained in Britain. Robs Lamplough bought back the Buchon, G-BJZZ, for the sale's top price of £34,000, as well as the Spitfire XIV 'kit of parts' that had been sold at the Duxford auction, for £30,000. The Mustang, MM4292, a derelict example that had been tarted up for the venture, was sold to Aces High for £9,000, and the Storch went to Des McCarthy for £19,000. The Sopwith Pup replica went, for £19,000, to the Fleet Air Arm Museum, which was steadily increasing the number of its First World War replicas. Finally, the Proctor went for only £500 to a private buyer.

During 1985 the first example of the latest must-have item for the aircraft museum inventory appeared on the gate at Duxford. There had been Spitfire replicas before, mostly notably those built for the *Battle of Britain* film, which had been eagerly sought by museums that had no chance of affording the real thing. Now Specialised Mouldings Ltd of Huntingdon built a private-venture glass-fibre Spitfire full-scale model (although they called it a 'replica'), and placed it on loan at the gate at Duxford, believing that this would be a good shop window for their new product. However, at £20,000 each, the price was generally well beyond the voluntary groups, no matter how much they coveted a Spitfire. Three or four retired jet fighters could normally be bought for that sort of money. However, the visually completely accurate FSM would prove attractive to any organization that had real Spitfires on display out in the weather, something which made no sense at all in an era when Spitfire prices were escalating.

The year 1985 was to finish with a significant event when, on 9 December, the Imperial War Museum's 'Superhanger' at Duxford featured a 'roll-in' of new exhibits. Never before had there been a museum building so large that a Boeing B-29, Avro Vulcan and Short Sunderland could be simply rolled in through the doors. And when Lancaster KB889, bought from Doug Arnold's Warbirds of Great Britain, arrived the following year, it could just be tucked away in a corner.

At the other end of the scale, the first steps were being taken the following year towards the creation a new aircraft museum at Wellesbourne Mountford in Warwickshire, as the water was pumped out of the prospective building! The Wellesbourne Aviation Group was restoring its Vampire T.11, XK590, on the concrete top of the wartime underground HQ building. As they could not afford a pump, they had to remove the water by means of a chain of buckets.

Chairman Peter Sommerton arranged further help for the restoration of the building, a valuable aeronautical relic in its own right, from the Manpower Services Commission, which would pay for a force of ten people, with Wellesbourne Aviation Group member Dell Paddock in charge. The Vampire was still exposed to the elements above, but it was eventually protected to some extent by a temporary shelter, with only the outer wings and tail protruding. It was an imaginative way to display an aircraft outside, providing reasonable protection from the weather, at minimum expense.

At the same time another aircraft museum was being established in North Wales, on Caernarfon Airfield, by Snowdon Mountain Aviation. Two Vampire T.11s, XD599 and XK623, were early arrivals, followed by a Sycamore helicopter from RAF Finningley, and the Whirlwind from the folding Nene Valley Group. As is often the case in the world of aircraft preservation, one group's misfortune was another's opportunity.

ATTRACTING MORE VISITORS

All aircraft museums suffered from the same problem of trying to keep going on the income provided by a steady influx of aircraft enthusiasts alone. This was reflected in a clumsy re-name for the Torbay Aircraft Museum, which, on 1 April 1984, re-opened for the summer season as the Torbay Trains, Robes and Roses Aircraft Museum. A new 70-ft gallery housed the Devonshire collection of period costume, and there was also a large OO scale model-railway layout, together with the three-quarter-acre rose garden that had always been a feature of the Museum. The new name was an attempt to convince the holidaymaker in the Torbay area that there was something for all the family at Higher Blagdon.

In a similar move in 1987 the Cornwall Air Park, next to RNAS Culdrose, was re-named the Flambards Triple Theme Park for the 1987 season, with displays based on the successful *Flambards* television series. This process of conversion from a pure aircraft museum to an attraction that was more theme park, with aircraft as one of the features, was to continue at Helston.

Events at Southend had already shown that it was not enough simply to put on display a number of old aircraft, of limited historical importance, without being an entirely voluntary-run operation. A collection with a meaningful connection to the local region, or with truly rare and historic aircraft, might survive on its own merits, but even then it had to make provision for 'the bucket and spade brigade' – those visitors who might have heard of a Spitfire or a Vulcan but would not know a Vampire from a Provost. A superb city-centre museum with historic aircraft and important local connections, such as Manchester, was able to attract 135,000 visitors in its first year, but even they recognized that special attractions had to be laid on to keep the visitors coming.

Oddly enough, one aircraft museum had problems because it attracted too many visitors. The East Midlands Airport Aeropark, a £100,000 centre created with the help of a new volunteer group and the support and financial help of the Leicestershire Museums Service, attracted no less that 177,000 visitors during 1986. They had succeeded in diverting people away from the airport's terminal buildings, and received a prestigious Certificate of Outstanding Achievement in Air Education. Despite this, and to the great displeasure of the Leicestershire Museums Service, the airport authorities decided to cut back the Aeropark venture, moving full-time staff to other parts of the complex, obstensibly to reduce the number of visitors to the facility!

On 19 December 1986 the last-but-one airworthy Vulcan, XL426, touched down at Southend Airport, for its new owner Roy Jacobsen, who had already bought the Vulcan at Wellesbourne Mountford. The Vulcan had just been replaced in the RAF's Vulcan Display Flight by XH558, but Mr Jacobsen fully intended his new acquisition to be put back on the air-show circuit during 1987. Heavylift Engineering at Southend was mooted as a suitable organization to maintain the aircraft, but XL426 had made its last flight.

EXPORTS AND FIRST FLIGHTS

During 1987 there was a fierce debate in the aeronautical press and at BAPC meetings about the RAF Museum's disposal of the last Airspeed Consul, G-AJLR, from its store at Cardington, to Singapore Airways in return for a 'donation' of £2,000. BAPC and others were concerned that a rare British aircraft had been 'given away' to an airline on the other side of the globe, without the various British aircraft-preservation groups being offered the chance to restore it.

Dr Tanner of the RAF Museum argued that the Consul was only a basket case, not really an aircraft at all, without engines, undercarriage or any metal fittings, and that SIA and its vast resources represented the only real chance of its complete restoration. SIA was anxious to obtain the Consul because that was the type with which the airline had started its operations forty years before. The idea was for it to go on display in Singapore International Airport for the anniversary celebrations. In the event, it was restored to pristine display condition in only 137 days.

The debate about the export of historic aircraft has been raised again and again over the years, whenever a significant aircraft has been exported. On the other hand, objections are rarely raised when aircraft are imported into Britain, depriving another country of one of its historical artefacts. The traffic in vintage aircraft had always been a two-way trade, enriching all concerned in the process.

In 1987 this argument was illustrated in spectacular fashion. On 22 May a Blenheim flew for the first time for forty years. A Canadian-built example, the aircraft was really a Bolingbroke IV, which had been imported into Britain without a whimper of complaint by the Canadians. After a nine-year restoration Graham Warner's British Aerial Museum team had put Blenheim V6028 G-MKIV into the air, at the hands of John Larcombe, accompanied by John Romain, who had 'grown up' with the restoration.

Originally, the aircraft had been imported by the late Ormond Haydon-Baillie, but it had been bought from his estate by Graham Warner in 1979. The volunteers who had laboured away on the restoration in Building 66 at Duxford – Nick Goodwin, John Gullick, Chris Hollyer, Bill Kelly, Roy Pullan, Hugh Smith, John Smith, Bob Sparkes, Colin Swann, David Swann – were able to enjoy the admiration of the entire aircraft-preservation movement, expressed by the well-deserved award of the Mike Twite Trophy.

It was a great month for British aircraft preservation. Just five days before, another aircraft had taken to the skies for the first time in nearly fifty years, when the Shuttleworth Trust's long restoration of the DH.88 Comet G-ACSS finally reached its conclusion. It was BAe test pilot George Ellis who took the aircraft aloft from Hatfield for its first flight since 1938. Remarkably, the two aircraft were contemporaries – one all-wood, one all-metal; one civil, one military – and both benefited from the skills of a dedicated team of engineers. For a short time at least, the beautiful restorations that were the result were to thrill air-show audiences.

A few weeks before, on 31 March, the prototype Civilian Coupe had also achieved flight once more after being in store since 1938. An example of the only aircraft type ever made in Burton-on-Trent, the Coupe was part of Mike Dunkerley's private collection housed at Biggin Hill.

GOOD NEWS AND BAD NEWS

The issue of *FlyPast* that reported all these first flights also showed pictures of the Yorkshire Air Museum's Halifax, which brought the project firmly back into the public consciousness. The occasion was the unveiling of the restored Hebridean chicken coop, on its return from the tender loving care of the apprentices at British Aerospace, Brough. The original fuselage section, beautifully restored and painted, was put on display wearing the serial HR792. Remarkably, it was fitted with a Boulton Paul Type A Turret cupola, which had been presented by the Cotswold Aviation Recovery group, and, over the wing, a fuselage 'covered wagon' section, which had been obtained from Linton-on-Ouse. The restored fuselage was shown attached to the centre section of the Hastings wing that would be used in the restoration, re-converted to Halifax standard. The outer part of these wings were found to be too badly corroded to use, but amazingly the team was able to track down brand-new outer wings, still in their packing cases, from a southern scrapyard.

The unveiling was carried out by Lord Halifax, before a gathering of former Halifax aircrew, including ATA pilot Lettice Curtis, who discovered that she had actually ferried this very aircraft. Gatherings of Halifax men were to be an increasing feature of the restoration; as the Halifax grew, so did the crowds which came to see it.

In the same issue of *FlyPast*, the recovery of the front turret for the Loch Ness Wellington, and the acquisition of an Elan Argosy by the East Midlands Airport Aeropark and a Danish Starfighter by the Midland Air Museum were also reported.

So, there was good news for the aircraft-preservation enthusiast, but it was countered by bad news the following month. The de Havilland Comet ground-looped and was heavily damaged while landing after its display at the Hatfield Open Day on 4 July. It had been based at Hatfield, rather than Old Warden, because of the longer runways there, and had been fitted with a tailwheel for use on the paved runway. Without the help of a tailskid, an already tricky aircraft to land had become even more difficult.

Worse news was the crash of the Blenheim while performing an ill-advised touch-and-go at Denham Air Show. Luckily, the three men on board, pilot Roy Pullan, John Romain and John Smith, were not badly hurt, but the aircraft was written off after a brief but glorious month in the air. Graham Warner and his team were understandably shattered at seeing the destruction of nine years of work, but resolved immediately to do the job again.

The Canadian Warplane Heritage offered one of its spare Bolingbroke IV airframes, and the Imperial War Museum also offered the use of its Bolingbroke airframe, which had been in store for some years. In the end, the Bolingbroke airframe owned by the former Strathallan Collection was purchased to form the basis for the new restoration. With certain accessories recoverable from G-MKIV, the British Aerial Museum team hoped to complete its second restoration in rather less than the nine years that it had taken to restore the original. To aid them, the Blenheim Society kicked off at Duxford on 28 November 1987 with the largest gathering of former Blenheim aircrew since the Second World War. BAM also proved that it was not a one-aircraft band when it put into the air John Romain's Chipmunk, G-BNZC, in striking Canadian colours.

Better news in the same month was the Berkshire Aviation group's progress towards creating a museum. The AdWest group, the successors to Miles Aircraft, donated a Robin hangar, and the local council offered a piece of land on a thirty-year lease. It was located on the edge of what had been Woodley Airfield, now a housing estate. The group's Miles Master project had already been significantly advanced with the acquisition of a Mercury engine and propeller from Miles Martinet G-AKOS, from a wood near Staverton Airport, enabling the Master to be planned as a Mark II. They had also found a complete Martinet canopy in Somerset to add to their growing Miles collection, which was further enhanced by Graham Johnson's Miles Magister rebuild, L6906, which had been started all those years ago in Bristol, and had been in store for many years at Wroughton.

Another new museum actually opened in June 1987. The Fenland Aircraft Preservation Society, famed for its crash-site investigations in the Fens and its subsequent engine restorations, opened the Fenland Aviation Museum, attached to Bamber's Nurseries, close to the Wisbech bypass. A little further north the Lincolnshire Aviation Centre, run by the Panton brothers, with help from the Lincolnshire Aircraft Recovery group and the Lincolnshire Aviation Society, opened on 19 July 1987. The East Kirkby site did not yet feature the T.2 hangar which was deemed necessary before the Panton brothers' Lancaster could be moved from Scampton, but the control tower was fully restored, and three large wooden barrack blocks and a Nissen hut had also increased the accommodation on offer.

The Bomber County Aviation Museum at Cleethorpes was closing. A new site had been offered at RAF Hemswell, and the difficult job of moving the exhibits was put in hand. Whirlwind HAR.10 XP339 went in a different direction – to Germany. It was privately owned and on loan to the museum, and its owners had exchanged it for a Luftwaffe Starfighter. The Starfighter was transported to RAF Binbrook in time for its air show, and covered accommodation was then sought.

The aircraft-preservation movement was to show time and again its fluidity, as groups closed or moved, split, re-formed, and sometimes re-emerged far stronger, having learned the hard way how not to do it.

CHAPTER 14

Out of the Depths

ON 21 September 1985, one of the most remarkable stories in the history of aircraft preservation in Britain unfolded in the glare of the world's press. Wellington bomber N2980, 'R for Robert', emerged from the depths of Loch Ness, where it had lain since being ditched on 31 December 1940. *FlyPast* had been born with the story of the intended salvage of the Wellington, but, until the moment when the battered airframe broke the surface for the first time, many did not believe it would ever happen.

'R for Robert' was not the first aircraft that had been salvaged from a watery grave. The RAF Museum's Halifax, 'S for Sugar', was one, and in 1983 the Ulster Aviation Society, with the co-operation of No.655 Squadron Army Air Corps and its Lynx helicopters, and the Ulster Sub-Aqua Club, raised Grumman Wildcat JV482 from Portmore Lough in Northern Ireland. It had lain in the lake partly submerged for forty years. The operation was sponsored by the Heyn Group, a Belfast company, whose Chief Engineer Jim Walsh planned the venture, and was a stalwart of its execution, along with his son Ronan. The UAS Chairman Ernie Cromie, Ray Burrows, Cecil Hamilton, Kevin Johnston, John Hewitt and Michael Cromie were also closely involved. On 30 April the airframe, minus the tail and the engine, were lifted from the Lough by a Lynx, having first been de-silted, and was dropped into a nearby field, where it attracted a great number of visitors.

By early May Ray Burrows had managed to get the wing-folding mechanism to work, and with the wings folded the aircraft could be raised up by crane, and the undercarriage lowered. The Wildcat could them be transported to the UAS workshop where the long process of restoration could begin.

The recovery of the Loch Ness Wellington was an epic on a much larger scale. The Loch Ness Wellington Association, which raised the funds for the operation, was headed by Robin Holmes, of Heriot-Watt University, Edinburgh, who had headed the group that first found the Wellington. The technical side of the lift was organized by Oceaneering Ltd, and the Weybridge Museum in Surrey provided a destination for the aircraft in its forthcoming Brooklands Museum, where the Curator was Morag Barton. The Weybridge-based Vintage Aircraft and Flying Group, which had already built replicas of a Vickers Gun-Bus and a Vickers Vimy, was to have charge of the restoration.

The raising of 'R for Robert' was the subject of a television documentary, filmed as it happened, and the television producers had all the dramatic twists and turns that they might have wished for. The specially designed lifting frame buckled and bent during the first lift and the aircraft had to be jettisoned, to fall 35ft back to the bottom of the loch. All seemed lost. Plans were made to return the following year and much of the press departed. Then a new plan to lift the airframe with air bags was instituted, operating on the limits of sub aqua capability. The attempt worked and suddenly a wing tip of 'R for Robert' broke the surface for the first time in forty years.

The aircraft was lifted from the loch by crane, although the rear fuselage and nose turret had broken free and remained on the bottom. The airframe was loaded on to a barge and moved to a point where it could be put on a truck, courtesy of British Aerospace, and transported to Brooklands. Plans were then put in hand to recover the missing tail and nose sections, so that 90 per cent of the aircraft could be put on display – the only operational Wellington bomber left in the world (the Wellington in the RAF Museum was a post-War T.10 trainer, converted back to bomber status).

The Loch Ness Wellington Association devised an imaginative funding initiative to finance the recovery of the nose turret of 'R for Robert' during 1987. They offered to sell rounds of ammunition, complete with their link, from the turret for the sum of £4 plus £1 for postage. In this way, people could own their own memento of the aircraft. Thanks to this initiative, the turret was eventually recovered. Afterwards, members of the RAF Kinloss Sub-Aqua Club scoured the bottom of the loch, working in the almost freezing water by touch alone, to bring to the surface a large number of small components that had fallen off when the Wellington hit the bottom for the second time, after the abortive first lift.

The wings for the Wellington were taken to Luton Airport where the Luton Branch of the Royal Aeronautical Society had agreed to undertake their restoration in a corner of a hangar provided by Monarch Airlines.

Co-ordinator of the Brooklands Museum and organizer of the Wellington project was Morag Barton. The two main sponsors were the museum's neighbours, British Aerospace, feeling very paternal about the aircraft as it had originally been built at Weybridge, and Gallaghers, which was developing one end of the Brooklands site, and had already donated a section of the curved racetrack as well as some land to the museum. There were many other sponsors. Frazer-Nash took on the restoration of the tail turret, and it was delivered to their premises by Budget Rent-a-Car. Dasics, manufacturers of auto-corrosion treatments, took on the task of stopping any further decay of the airframe, with every part being assessed and treated.

Having achieved its initial aim of raising the aircraft from the depths, the Loch Ness Wellington Association now threw its efforts into supporting the restoration. It was a long process, watched with admiration by the aircraft-preservation movement, and by Wellington veterans everywhere.

CHAPTER 15

Private Projects

THERE have always been private collections in the world of aircraft preservation; after all, the movement practically began with the personal collections of Shuttleworth and Nash. Over the last couple of decades, however, they
have become much more common – a situation reflected in the growth of the
'aerojumble'. Of these collectors, a small number set themselves a personal
project for the restoration of an aircraft, which becomes all-consuming. Such
projects draw admiration from all other enthusiasts active in the movement,
who know that restoring an aircraft to display condition is hard enough with
the support of a group, let alone on your own in the own back yard.

Tony Agar's quest to build himself a Mosquito night-fighter was one such
personal project, although the scale of the venture meant that his efforts were
forced to expand, to include a small team.

Many of the people who initiate such projects begin working within the
confines of a group, with all the attendant frustrations and conflicts. Too often,
much of a group's working meetings are taken up with chat – many aircraft
get 'restored' during a tea break – to the endless frustration of the few who
only wish to get on with the job. One or two enthusiasts then decide that they
would prefer to work on their own personal venture, dictating the course of
events and the working hours.

One such private venture is Bernie Salter's Lancaster in Lee-on-Solent.
Having worked on the Lancaster at Hendon as a member of the Friends of
the RAF Museum, and also having been a radio ham, a world in which ex-
RAF equipment features heavily, Salter evolved a scheme to create his own
Lancaster W.T. station. As with many such schemes, the simple initial goal
soon expanded into the creation of an entire Lancaster cockpit. The two parts
of an all-consuming passion fell into place. With the typical collector's obses-
sion, Salter made contacts and deals all over Britain, filling in the gaps in his
collection of the equipment and instruments needed to complete all the crew
positions in his cockpit. At home, planning the construction of the cockpit,
and designing a construction system that would be within his capabilities,
would be followed by long hours in the garage.

In 1984 Bernie Salter's project was featured for the first time in *FlyPast*, and
was admired by everyone who read it. The next time it appeared in the magazine, a number of years later, readers were astonished by the progress made,
as they were with a number of other well-known long-term projects.

Jeremy Hall, a customs officer in Surrey, followed the same route taken by

Bernie Salter. He began by building a Lancaster instrument panel to hold his collection of instruments, then acquired a Lancaster throttle quadrant, and conceived the idea of creating a complete Lancaster cockpit. His plans also soon expanded to encompass the creation of the complete forward fuselage of a Lancaster, kitted out with all the correct equipment, constructed not simply of wood but of aluminium, to original plans. He will soon be well on the way to achieving this.

Equating more closely with Tony Agar's Mosquito, Brian Nicholls became the instigator of the Hampden Project in 1987, when he acquired the remains of Hampden AE436, which had crashed in the Tstata Mountains of Northern Sweden on 4 September 1942. Discovered in 1976, after a hotter than usual summer had melted its snow covering, it was brought down from the mountains and the wreckage was divided between the Swedish and Royal Air Force Museums.

When the RAF Museum handed over its share to Brian Nicholls and his small team, they began work at the Hobbies Club at RAF Coningsby where Nicholls was an armourer. From the following year the project was based at the Lincolnshire Aviation Heritage Centre at East Kirkby, with the immense restoration task beginning in a small building, with few facilities and less money. Two years later the Swedish Air Force Museum handed over its share of the wreckage to the project. Soon afterwards the RAF Museum acquired its own Hampden wreck, from Russia, and Brian Nicholls' team no longer had an exclusive project.

Making new aluminium components of the Hampden by hand, without even so much as their own metal-folding machine, to replace those too far gone in the original, is a long, slow process. Buying in commercially made parts was out of the question, with a project funded only by a collection box in their small building. Such a project can only proceed with resolute persistence, and an ability to ignore the feeling that no progress is being made. Sometimes, it is hard for those closest to the project to see any results.

The Hampden Project suffered a massive blow in 1996 when, after a long illness, Brian Nicholls died, at the age of just 34. His widow Janet was determined that the Hampden should be finished, as a tribute to her husband. The project continued, with a new name, 'The Brian Nicholls Hampden Project', and with Janet herself taking a more active role. Perhaps one day this example of the Handley Page Hampden will be wheeled across an English airfield, for the first time in half a century.

In Leicestershire, a small team was working on the rebuild of another Second World War twin-engined bomber, the Douglas Boston. Richard Nutt became fascinated with the Boston/Havoc when he worked for a while on Gosfield Airfield, where the USAF 410th Bomb Group operated Havocs. Nutt and Roy Bonser began research into British use of the aircraft, collecting parts, drawings and data.

The centrepiece of the collection became components from the crash site of Z2186 in Carnedd Dafydd. Once Richard Nutt retired, the search was on for a house with space for a Boston workshop. When the workshop was ready, Nutt then began constructing a revolving jig in which to build the forward fuselage of a Boston IIIA, alongside a main undercarriage leg and wheel from a Boston stand in a working rig.

Steve Milnthorpe set out to build or re-create Hurricane P3717 at his home in Leicestershire. The family car was thrown out of his garage, and the painstaking reconstruction of the fuselage began in the resulting space, which had to be lengthened. The Hurricane is of labour-instensive construction, and Milnthorpe had to learn a number of skills as he went along. By 1998 he had reached the point where he needed to mate the fuselage with the centre section of the wing, and the garage area was no longer large enough. The answer was to build a workshop just large enough to hold a completed Hurricane; thanks to friendly neighbours, Milnthorpe was able to cross all the planning permission hurdles. He had by now gathered a small team of helpers around him, not least his long-suffering wife Sandra. With their help, the possibility of an increase in the world's population of Hurricanes is now assured.

Although the private collector usually has to content himself with a single project, occasionally an enthusiast finds himself in a position to create his own personal museum. In 1990, Graham Revill, who farms near Pershore and flies his own Cessna from a private strip, acquired Meteor T.7 WH166 at a Ministry of Defence sale. He followed this up with a Vampire T.11, XE979, and a Sea Hawk, WN105. His private museum was located on land adjacent to his farm buildings, and visible from the nearby Evesham road; it was guaranteed to intrigue all passing aircraft enthusiasts, but was not open to the public. The collection now numbers six, with the addition of Vampire T.11 WZ425, Hunter F.6 XF526 and Jet Provost XN632.

Farmers are fortunate in that they usually have plenty of land, and sometimes even spare buildings in which to store vintage aircraft. Another farmer who was able to create his own personal aircraft museum during the 1990s was Roy Jerman, who lived with his wife Sue on a farm near Welshpool.

Jerman had collected flying kit for some time and in 1993 he acquired two cockpits, a Canberra T.17, WK192, and Buccaneer XT277, to add to his collection. He had joined the ranks of the cockpit collector, and a Lightning F.6 duly arrived the following year. In 1995 he went really overboard and acquired three more cockpits, Harrier GR.3, Canberra PR.7 and Hunter FGA.9, and then had to bite the bullet and consider a building in which to house them. With the building completed, the Jermans had their own personal aircraft museum. For a time, they took a step in another direction when, in 1996, they acquired a complete aircraft for the first time, de Havilland Dove G-ANUW. As others had found before them, a complete aircraft has a completely different set of implications, both in terms of space and cost. When a Vulcan nose became available from another cockpit collector in Burntwood, who had decided his hobby was just too much, the Dove had to go, and was replaced by the nose of the V-bomber.

The Jermans' collection later also included the cockpits of a Sea Hawk, Canberra B.2, Whirlwind HAR.10 and Sea Vixen, as well as a Jet Provost procedures trainer. With good connections with the local ATC unit already established, the Jermans are now considering opening their delightful little collection on a limited basis with the occasional open day.

CHAPTER 16

More Warbirds

THE warbird movement had begun to expand considerably in the 1980s, and one of the major fleets on the air-show scene was the distinctive all-red aircraft owned by Spencer Flack. On 2 August 1981 this fleet was reduced by one when his Sea Fury G-FURY crashed near Waddington. Flack was flying the aircraft himself in company with his Spitfire XIV, piloted by Stefan Kowowiski. He was returning to his base at Elstree from a display at South Humberside when the Centaurus engine began to run hot. He diverted to the nearest airfield, which was Waddington, but the engine cut completely on the approach at an altitude of about 200ft. The Sea Fury ploughed into a potato field short of the runway, and disintegrated. Luckily, the pilot was able to escape from the wreckage suffering slight burns and a broken leg – Kowowiski had landed at Waddington expecting to find his friend dead. The experience lead Spencer Flack to declare that he would never fly a similar aircraft again.

On 28 April 1984, one of the most significant fleets of warbirds to grace British skies moved from its base in Switzerland to take up residence at Duxford. Stephen Grey's private 'Air Force', which would become known as the Fighter Collection, was relocated to the most important base for historic aircraft in Europe. The collection at the time included Mustang, Bearcat, Wildcat, Spitfire and Hurricane, but would grow as time progressed.

There was a significant addition to the warbird movement in February 1985 when Arthur Gibson, John Watts and Paul Warren-Wilson bought Catalina C-FMIR, and put it on the British register as G-BLSC. After a long restoration programme and operated as Plane Sailing Air Displays, the aircraft was destined to become a familiar part of the air-display scene for the next thirteen years. This was longer than originally anticipated – a crack had been found in a wing spar during the work, and this had had to be repaired. Like *Sally B*, the Catalina, soon known as *Killer Cat*, had the sort of charisma that would attract its very own fan club, the Catalina Society.

Another potential warbird operator, which was organized on the lines of the Confederate Air Force in Texas, was the British Air Reserve. Started by Patrick Luscombe after his purchase of Sea Fury WJ288, at the Southend auction, it was based at Lympne. There, the restoration of the Sea Fury began, aided by the purchase of a new engine from Spencer Flack. This was followed by the purchase of Fiat G-46 MM53211; the Piper Super Cub G-PULL was also taken on. There were also stated plans to buy DC-6B G-SIXA, which had resided at Manston for some time, to refurbish it for charter flights, although this proved a scheme too far.

One of the private collections often to be seen flying at air shows could not have been further away from the warbird theme, although a couple of the aircraft within it did wear roundels. Mike Russell had founded his Russavia collection with the acquisition of a number of vintage gliders in the 1950s. Gliders and ultra-light aeroplanes such as the BAC Drone, formerly restored by Bob Ogden, and the DH.53 Humming Bird reconstruction, were to be a feature of the collection, but the most unique thing about Russavia was not an aircraft but a piece of paper. It was the only all volunteer-run organization to hold an Air Operator's Certificate, allowing its Dragon Rapide, Tiger Moth and Chipmunk to take paying passengers aloft on joy flights from Duxford. Mike Russell's day job as a Britannia Airways Boeing 767 pilot undoubtedly helped Russavia achieve this unique accolade.

One of the early lodgers at Duxford, using Building 63 as a workshop, Russavia offered a refreshing change to the military aircraft and large airliners that were the main features of the airfield, although the Rapide was painted in the colours of the Royal Navy Ferry Flight, and the Tiger Moth also wore RAF roundels. Also within the collection was a DH.2 replica, which helped cement a certain de Havilland theme.

A new collection of warbirds was created during the 1980s in Hampshire by Charles Church, a housing developer in the area. With an intense interest in classic warplanes, and in particular those powered by the Merlin engine, Mr Church had set up Charles Church (Spitfires) Ltd. It was managed by Dick Melton, who had been with the Battle of Britain Memorial Flight, and then with Doug Arnold's Warbirds of Great Britain, where he had worked on the famous Spitfire 'assembly line', restoring a large number of examples. Another Spitfire 'assembly line' was established at Charles Church, with three Spitfire IXs, including a two-seat conversion, and a Spitfire XIV. Also acquired from Robs Lamplough was the ex-Theatre of War Hispano Buchon Ha.1112, and from the USA a P-51D Mustang.

It was not Charles Church's intention to let others fly his classic aircraft once they were back in the air; he intended to do that himself. To build up his hours on a relatively high-performance tailwheel aircraft, he bought Pilatus P.2 G-CJCI from Doug Arnold in mid-1984. Its Argus engine was a little out of place among all the Merlins, but, in the absence of a two-seat trainer such as a Merlin-powered Boulton Paul Balliol, the P.2 was probably the best trainer for the job.

Charles Church was to add to his Merlin-engined collection during 1987 with the purchase of Strathallan's Lancaster, G-BCOH, and Fairey Battle, R3950. With them came Dick Richardson, who left Strathallan for Charles Church's employ. The Battle went for restoration to Dave French's workshop by the Solent, alongside Charles Church's Buchon, but the Lancaster was too big for either French's or Church's facilities. After a canvas of the various units in the country's aerospace industry, the BAe factory at Woodford agreed to take on the Lancaster's restoration. This seemed like good news at the time, but when the aircraft was at Woodford, dismantled and being worked on, the hangar roof collapsed, severely damaging it.

At about the same time, another part of British Aerospace, the former Folland factory at Hamble, took on the restoration of Folland Gnat F.1 XK740. The Gnat had been on display at the Aerospace Museum, Cosford, in totally false Red Arrows colours. It was to be refurbished at Hamble and placed on display in the Southampton Hall of Aviation.

Jet aircraft did not yet feature much in private hands – air-show performers were still largely in the hands of the military – but at Bournemouth Mike Carlton had built up a pioneering collection with his two all-red Hunters, single-seat G-HUNT and two-seat G-BOOM being the stars. When the collection was sold at an auction at Bournemouth Airport on 1 October 1987, it set a benchmark for the price of classic jets; until that time there had not been much of a market on the British side of the Atlantic.

The top bid for G-HUNT was £150,000 and G-BOOM attracted a top bid of £100,000, but the other aircraft in the collection went for far lower sums. Jet Provost G-JETP sold for £55,000, and its companion, G-PROV, went for £5,000 more. Other aircraft in the auction came from the Thorpe Park Collection, which was being replaced by more conventional theme-park attractions. Also sold were Charles Church's Fairey Battle and Roland Fraissinet's Spitfire PR XI, which he was entering for his second sale, the aircraft having failed previously to reach its reserve. The top bid for each aircraft was as follows:

Sopwith Camel replica G-BFCZ	£32,000
Fokker Dr.I static replica	£2,800
SE.5A static replica	£5,000
Fokker Dr.VII static replica	£2,700
Bristol M.1C static replica	£4,800
Supermarine S.6B static replica	£3,200
Macchi M.39 taxiing replica	£2,800
Curtis R.3C2 static replica	£6,000
Sopwith Baby static replica	£1,100
Deperdussin monoplane static replica	£600
Spitfire PR XI G-PRXI	£300,000
Fairey Battle R3950	£38,000
Jet Provost G-PROV	£60,000
Jet Provost G-JETP	£55,000

Meteor T.7 G-AJETM	£1,300
Meteor TT.20 G-LOSM	£22,000
Sea Hawk G-JETH	£1,500
Sea Hawk G-SEAH	£5,500
Hunter G-HUNT	£150,000
Hunter T.8	£100,000

Duxford remained the centre of warbird operation, at least in most people's minds and by 1995 the Fighter Collection's fleet had grown to include Mustang, Kingcobra, Skyraider, Wildcat, Hellcat, Bearcat, Hurricane, P-38 Lightning, Mitchell, Thunderbolt, and Spitfires IXE and FR XIV. This was the largest warbird fleet in Britain, indeed, outside the USA.

The other major warbird fleet at Duxford was Ray and Mark Hanna's Old Flying Machine Company, which was able to boast Spitfire, Mustang, Corsair, Fury ISS, Hispano Buchon, T-33 Silver Star, Sabre, MiG-15 and Hans Dittes' Bf 109G. Also at Duxford was the British Aerial Museum with its second Blenheim restoration, Auster AOP.9, Morane-Saulnier MS505 and the Beech 18.

Away from Duxford, apart from the Fleet Air Arm's Historic Flight, and the Battle of Britain Memorial Flight, there were the Shuttleworth Collection's aircraft at Old Warden and Intrepid Aviation at North Weald, which operated a Mustang, Folland Gnat, Beech 17, Boeing-Stearman PT.17, Harvard and Yak-11.

Many of the other aircraft on the warbird circuit were singletons owned by enthusiasts, who often banded together. This was the case with the Harvard display team and the Tiger Moth display team – The Diamond Nine. Increasingly, these privately owned aircraft were to feature jets, particularly newly retired Venoms and Vampires from the Swiss Air Force, and jet trainers such as the Jet Provost T.4s retired by the Royal Air Force.

These warbird operators existed for the personal enjoyment of the aircraft owners/operators, but also to provide aircraft for the air-show circuit. They constantly reinforced their side of the perennial argument between those who would preserve aircraft in 'safety' on the ground, and those who believed that the right place for an aircraft was in the air. During the summer of 1996 extra ammunition was provided for the safe-not-sorry side of the argument when three rare aircraft crashed within a short period of time. 'Hoof' Proudfoot lost his life when the Fighter Collection's Lockheed Lightning crashed during a display at Duxford. The Mosquito T.3 operated for many years by British Aerospace, and fresh from a recent major overhaul, crashed at Barton, killing pilot Kevin Moorhouse and engineer/navigator Steve Watson and the Bristol Freighter C-FDFC, recently introduced to the European air-show circuit, crashed on take-off at Enstone, fortunately without major injuries to the crew. These were the sole flying examples of all three aircraft in Europe.

Of course the accidents did not render the types extinct. Even if they had been the only examples of their breed, the recent restoration to pristine static-display standards of the last Bristol Bulldog, itself a victim of a major crash, shows that even the crash of the last example of a type does not necessarily relegate that type to history. And, as major fires in Canadian and San Diego museums and a hurricane in Florida have shown over the years, even confinement inside an aircraft museum does not necessarily guarantee absolute security.

CHAPTER 17

1987 – Lightnings

COLLECTING POLICIES

IN 1987 the British Aircraft Preservation Council celebrated the twentieth anniversary of its formation with a conference at the East Midlands Airport. The underlying theme of the meeting was an introspective look at the movement. Chairman Mike Hodgson opened proceedings and then handed over to Keith Fordyce for the key-note speech. Fordyce set the trend of the conference, questioning whether every group was living up to the full meaning of the word 'preservation', which his dictionary took to mean, 'conservation', 'restoration', 'to keep safe', 'to guard', 'to rescue', and 'to keep in good condition'. He also urged museums to cater for the 99 per cent of the population who were not aircraft enthusiasts, something he had clearly been trying to do at Torbay.

David Lee, Vice-Chairman of BAPC and Deputy Curator of the Imperial War Museum at Duxford, backed up Fordyce's statements, being severely critical of many groups that were collecting 'wrecks and eyesores'. He highlighted in particular the rush to buy a Vulcan by groups that had failed to consider whether they were in a position to maintain it. He considered this 'the ultimate folly', after the widespread duplication of exhibits in the shape of the Vampire T.11, and the ex-American/French aircraft, the Mysteres, T-33s and Super Sabres. He felt that groups should be collecting aircraft not just because they were available, but that they should have a definite collecting policy to reflect their own local interests, and their own ability to restore and maintain the resulting exhibits.

Many a local amateur group would argue that they just wanted to be associated with the restoration and preservation of old aircraft but could not always afford to be too selective in their collecting. They may have hoped to have exhibits of local significance and national importance, but on the whole they had to settle for what they could get – and what they could afford.

They would also argue that local aircraft museums have an importance all their own. The major national museums were few in number, and, though the aircraft enthusiast would trek any distance to visit them, for the average person with only a passing interest in aviation, a visit to Duxford, Hendon or Yeovilton was something only to be considered if they happened to be in the area. A local museum was something for families to visit on a Sunday afternoon; something to interest those who might just be able to tell a Spitfire from a Hunter, and a place to inspire the young. They would be unlikely to know (or care) that there were twenty-five other Vampires or Flying Fleas preserved in Britain; their local one would be the only one they were ever likely to see. It might seem the 'ultimate folly' to have eleven Vulcans preserved, but if this charismatic aircraft drew non-enthusiasts to a museum, surely every one of those aircraft should be protected from the scrapman – even if only temporarily.

In addition to his, how many and which of those eleven Vulcans would survive into the distant future? Some would have argued that the preservation of three Blackburn Beverlies was one or two too many, considering the relative importance of the type. In fact, with the apparently secure examples at the RAF Museum, Hendon, and at the Southend Historic Aircraft Museum, eventually succumbing to the scrapman, the movement owed the Humberside Aero Club a debt of gratitude for its 'folly' – preserving a third example at Paull. After its move to the Museum of Army Transport at Beverly, this is now the only one left. Too often, the efforts of amateur preservationists have been disparaged, yet it is they who have acquired and treasured aircraft wrecks and eyesores, saving them from destruction, so that later they could be restored and even flown.

Eleven Vulcans had been acquired because it was a charismatic aircraft being retired from RAF service. Indeed, the last aircraft still flying in the RAF's Vulcan Display Flight actually won *FlyPast*'s Mike Twite Trophy for 1987; clearly, keeping a Vulcan in the air was very important to the magazine's readers, who voted for it.

ACQUIRING LIGHTNINGS

In 1988 the English Electric Lightning was serving out its last days at RAF Binbrook, and many groups were desperate to get their hands on an example. With even former surface decoy Lightnings being put back into the air, to eke out the last airframe hours on the fleet, the wait was a long one. One of the major problems facing groups was the reluctance of the Lightning to come easily apart for road transportation. Unless a deal could be struck that involved delivery by air, ingenuity was required to avoid cutting off the wings.

The Battle of Britain Museum at Hawkinge was one of the first to get its hands on a Lightning, a Mark 3, XP701, located at Binbrook. They decided on an airborne delivery, suspended beneath a USAF Sikorsky Ch-53C Jolly Green Giant. However, the Ch-53C could only lift 13,000lb on such a long lift; even with the engines removed, the Lightning weighed 16,000lb. A careful examination with the experts at British Aerospace identified items that could be removed to bring the airframe down to the required weight, and on

17 December XP701 was ready for its last flight – or flights, since it required several hops, via Sculthorpe, Woodbridge and Manston, before arrival at Hawkinge.

Stuart Scott and John Jackson also bought a Binbrook Lightning F.3 and identified a more novel way of moving it the 4 miles to Logh, where it was to be restored. Having removed the fin to avoid cutting a swathe across the Lincolnshire telephone system, they simply towed it behind a tractor on 20 December, with the help of a police escort. They were then in a position to call themselves the Lincolnshire Lightning Preservation Society, a rather presumptuous title given the continuing efforts of No.11 Squadron back at RAF Binbrook.

The Cranfield-based Vintage Aircraft team also acquired two Lightnings, a T.5, XS451, which they hoped to put back into the air, and F.2A G-27-239, as a source of spare parts.

The ambitions of some organizations to put Lightnings on to the air-show circuit were to come up against the same impossible hurdle that prevented any of the Vulcans taking to the air again – the CAA. It refused to issue a Permit to Fly to such complex aircraft, and T.5 XS451 was eventually sold in the USA.

In April 1988 the Air Ministry released tender documents for the sale of 22 Lightning F.6s, all without engines. It was the scrapmen who led the queue to obtain them. With No.11 Squadron receiving its first Tornados the following month, the writing was well and truly on the wall for the rest of the Lightning fleet.

Over the next few months a number found their way both to museums and to organizations hoping to put them on to the air-show circuit. Road transport in a dismantled state was the usual means of removal, with a police escort for the resulting wide load. The moves of XR755 from Binbrook to Castle Air in Cornwall in June 1988, and XR771 from Binbrook to the Midland Air Museum in mid-July, were typical. Most of the aircraft that left Binbrook had their outer wings cut off to facilitate transportation. One that did not was XR770, which was presented to the town of Grimsby and was dismantled with the help of the base personnel.

A rather lighter exhibit was moved to a new museum site at Long Marston airfield near Stratford-on-Avon at around the same time. The Stratford Aircraft Collection was inaugurated with the arrival of a Slingsby TX-3 Cadet and a Grasshopper TX-1, which joined the Sea Venom of the Midland Warplane Museum, which was already on the site. The museum had taken the step, which was commendable for a new group, of stating its collecting theme from the outset – 'All in training' – but it remained to be seen how closely they would keep to this.

The Yorkshire Air Museum at Elvington had the advantage of a very long runway adjacent to its site. When it acquired Lightning F.6, XS903, delivery was no problem, and on 18 May the aircraft was flown in by Wing Commander Jarron. It was soon joined by its stablemate, Canberra T.4 WH846, which was brought by road, having been dismantled at British Aerospace's airfield at Salmsbury. The Canberra was one of a number that BAe released from its stock for preservation groups, at a nominal fee, following the similar 'giveaways' of Hunters and Vampires. The Canberras were shortly to be followed by a number of Lightnings, particularly ex-Saudi Air Force examples, returned to Britain as part of the sale of Tornados.

The trail of Lightnings then began to lead from Warton as well as Binbrook, as the two Lightning concentrations were dispersed. The Midland Air Museum secured a two-seat T.55, ZF598, to go with its single-seat F.6 from Binbrook, and a single-seat F.53 went to the Solway Aviation Society at Carlisle. East Midlands Aero Park took ZF588 and the Wales Aircraft Museum at Rhoose took ZF578.

DOOMED TO FAILURE?

The Wales Aircraft Museum had been the subject of critical debate a few months earlier. The words of Keith Fordyce and David Lee at the BAPC twentieth Anniversary Meeting were echoed in a letter to *FlyPast* in August 1988, by F.W. Reynolds of Swindon, who had visited the Wales Aircraft Museum at Cardiff Airport, and was shocked by what he found. He likened the site to 'something between a scrapyard and a graveyard', with aircraft standing in long grass on deflated tyres. He found the paintwork on the aircraft cracked and peeling, with the laminations of the plywood nacelles of the Vampire and Venom already splitting. He found aircraft lying around in a dismantled state, and a Meteor T.7 without part of its canopy, and nothing to cover the gap, to protect the cockpit from the elements.

Mr Reynolds' remarks were prescient, in view of what eventually became of the Wales Aircraft Museum. When it folded it was really turned into a scrapyard, with only a handful of the aircraft saved by other collections. The whole sorry episode showed once again that merely obtaining an aircraft as an exhibit was only the beginning of the task of preserving it. Collections that did not have a restoration and maintenance policy were doomed to failure.

Often, the problem lay with the make-up of the volunteers who created the collection. Any voluntary group can rely on only a low percentage of members who are willing to turn up and help on a regular basis, probably a dozen for every 80–100 who pay their subscription. Among that small group of 'workers' it is always necessary to have a hard core of 'movers and shakers', to get things going and, more importantly, to keep them going. They need someone with the personality to organize for the future, and the perseverance to carry through long-term restoration projects. Too many committee members see the glory in leading in a low-loader with a newly acquired aircraft. They are happy to contribute the burst of energy needed to dismantle it and then re-erect it on site, but few will take on the weekly drudgery of rubbing down an aircraft to bare metal by hand, and spraying on the etch primer.

Two months after Mr Reynolds' letter in *FlyPast* there were replies both for and against his sentiments. One supporter, Chris Simmonds of Malden, had visited the RAF St Athan collection on the same day, and had drawn the same unfavourable comparison (somewhat unfairly, since St Athan had the benefit of all the skills and facilities that could possibly be required for the preservation and restoration of aircraft). Alex Murison of County Durham, on the other hand, urged support for collections like that at Rhoose, and even suggested the donation of a tarpaulin to cover the gap in the Meteor's canopy as a simple way of helping the situation.

Perhaps Reynolds was right, although, in defence of the volunteers at Rhoose, those aircraft that were eventually saved from the museum might have already been scrapped if not consigned to their interim care. On the other hand, since they lacked the means to acquire suitable grass-cutting equipment, or tarpaulins to cover holes in aircraft, it was surely a dubious decision to acquire another large aircraft such as a Lightning.

In October 1988 the aircraft at the Torbay Aircraft Museum were entered into an auction at Sotheby's. Keith Fordyce claimed that his museum was seeking a new location, and that he was whittling down the numbers in preparation. With hindsight, it was the beginning of the demise of a museum that had struggled to survive for years as a tourist attraction for the Torbay area. As Southend had already discovered, not enough tourists were prepared to leave the beaches and pay the entrance fee to a local aircraft museum.

Neverthless, a new 'seaside' aircraft museum, Snowdon Mountain Aviation Museum at Llandwrog, snapped up several of the exhibits, including the Anson, Dove, Sea Hawk and Dragonfly. The highest bids of £4,000–5,000 came for the three *Battle of Britain* film full-scale models – the Spitfire, Hurricane and Bf 109 – although these still failed to reach the auctioneer's estimates.

Snowdon Mountain Aviation eventually opened its new museum as the Caernarfon Air Museum, and was able to offer flights in its own Rapide G-AIDL, the last Rapide with a Public Transport Certificate. Filling a geographical gap in the coverage of British aircraft museums, Caernarfon also had a definite theme – mountain rescue in the adjacent mountains of North Wales.

SEMINAR ON COLLECTING POLICY

On 20 April 1989 the three major national aircraft collections – the Science Museum, the Imperial War Museum and the RAF Museum – came together for the first time at a one-day seminar at Duxford on their aircraft-collecting and preservation policies. Some would say that a national policy was long overdue, with the remit of these three national institutions in particular overlapping by some way. There were, for instance, airliner collections at Duxford, Cosford and Wroughton, although not all were owned by their parent bodies. With, for example, a Trident standing in the elements at all three sites, it would seem to the outside observer that rivalry played a bigger part in decision-making than co-operation.

Also represented at the seminar were the 'other' national aircraft museums – the Fleet Air Arm Museum, the Museum of Army Flying and the Royal Scottish Museum – as well as other regional museums, such as Brooklands and Shuttleworth's. Even more welcome was the invitation to the more mature of the amateur collections, which were represented by Rodger Smith of the Midland Air Museum and Dave Westacott of Newark. Also attending were delegates of the warbird operators, with Stephen Grey of the Fighter Collection, Ray Hanna of the Old Flying Machine Company and Graham Warner of the British Aerial Museum.

Although most of the speeches involved the various delegates outlining the existing policies of their own museums, there were some examples of a new co-operation. The RAF Museum had allowed its Polish MiG-15 to go to the Imperial War Museum at Duxford, making room for its own Swift to come to Hendon from St Athan; and there had been a short-term agreement to allow the Benson Bf 109G to be operated by the Imperial War Museum at Duxford, on the air-show circuit.

New Names and Acquisitions

At about the same time, another 'national' museum was opening. The International Helicopter Museum, easily the largest collection of rotorcraft in the world, opened its doors to the public at Easter 1989. It dated back to 1959, and the personal collection of Elfan ap Rees, initially of documentation relevant to the helicopter, and then increasingly actual helicopters. The British Rotorcraft Museum, as it was first styled, based itself at Weston-super-Mare, the former home of Bristol helicopters, later part of Westland. Although it opened to the public in 1974 for a brief period, problems with its tenure of the site meant it had to close and go into hibernation for a long while.

When it was reborn, in the late 1980s, its new title – the International Helicopter Museum – was intended to reflect the international nature of its exhibits. It opened for a brief preview period at Easter 1988, and then permanently the following year. Initially, most of its huge number of helicopters were displayed outside, with only two small buildings housing smaller exhibits, but plans were in hand for a larger building. Westland Helicopters proved very supportive, even supplying a 'stock' of Westland 60s for trade. Elfan ap Rees, now Chairman of the Trust Committee, was able to look forward with confidence, having a secure niche within the preservation movement, and a collecting policy that almost decided itself.

At the ninety-first quarterly BAPC meeting, held at the Manchester Air & Space Museum, the council decided to change its own name to the British *Aviation* Preservation Council, in order to reflect the varying nature of the activities of many of the members. This was aptly illustrated when Sqn Ldr Mike Dean's historical radar archive was welcomed to membership. Another new member was a more traditional volunteer-based aircraft collection, the Macclesfield Historical Aviation Society, which was able to announce the recent acquisition of a two-seat Hunter T.53.

Later in the year, at Easter, the traditional opening period for most new museums, the Stratford Aircraft Collection began opening on all weekends and bank holidays. Instigated by collector David Cotton, and co-operating with the Midland Warplane Museum, it was based on Long Marston Airfield, west of Stratford. The collection featured a number of training aircraft to highlight its main theme, and the most impressive exhibit was the Shackleton MR.3 WR985. Most of the aircraft were displayed outside, but there was also a small display hangar.

At the ninety-fifth meeting of the BAPC, held at Old Warden, the new position of Honorary President was created, and Chairman Mike Hodgson was able to welcome Sir Charles Masefield, a stalwart of the preservation movement for many years, to the position. At the same meeting David Reader stepped down from the role of Secretary and Don Storer took over, with his wife Shirley becoming Council Administrator.

During 1991 another Viscount was saved from the axe when G-APIM, which had suffered a ground collision with a Shorts 330 at Southend, was externally repaired and dismantled before transportation to Brooklands. On loan from British Air Ferries, it was returning to its place of birth. An airliner about to make a similar return was the first production Handley Page Herald, G-APWA, acquired by the Herald Group of the Museum of Berkshire Aviation, also from British Air Ferries, which was proving to be a great friend of the preservation movement. Both airliners were little more than shells, however, having been stripped by BAF to provide spares for the rest of its fleet; their restoration would take many years.

The Museum of Berkshire Aviation opened for the first time on 4 May 1991, earlier than planned because of a visit of people from the French town with which the local community of Wokingham was being twinned. The official opening date was 27 March 1993. The museum was based in a Robin hangar formerly used by the Miles Technical School, and donated to the Museum by AdWest Ltd, which operated from the former Miles Factory. The hangar had been moved to a stretch of parkland on the edge of what had by now become the vast Woodley housing estate – mirroring the fate of so many airfields.

The Brooklands' Viscount was joined on 28 June 1991 by its predecessor, the Vickers Viking G-AGRU, the twelfth production Viking, which had been in the British Airways collection at Cosford since 1979. The move was undertaken by British Airways, which also undertook to refurbish the aircraft. Other Vickers stablemates at Brooklands were the Loch Ness Wellington, the Sultan of Oman's VC-10 and a Vickers Varsity.

The ranks of preserved airliners were to be joined by an example of the Bristol Britannia, G-ANCF, an ex-British Eagle example that had ended its days with Invicta at Manston. It became an almost personal crusade of Roger Hargreaves of Proteus Aero Services to save this airliner from the fire crews at Manston. He had had an on/off/on relationship with the Britannia since a brief period employed by British Eagle just before its collapse, and he had been instrumental in seeing a Monarch example preserved at Duxford.

He was able to provide the fire crews at Manston with a Viscount that his company had the job of stripping, and was then faced with the unprecedented problem of moving the Britannia by road and finding it a new home. Initially, once the job of dismantling had been achieved, various parts were stored all over the place. The fuselage, in two parts, went to Brooklands in May 1988, where it was safe at least for a while. The wing went to RAF Quedgley in Gloucestershire, but its width meant that the entire trailing edge had to be removed before it could take to the road. Mick Bates of Proteus had the small task of removing the thousands of rivets.

A new organization, born in Bristol to preserve the products of the Bristol Aircraft Company, and called the Bristol Aero Collection, heard of the problems of finding the Britannia a home, and offered space on land it was negotiating for at Banwell. The offer was gratefully accepted. A team of a dozen volunteers from Bristol Aero Collection then descended on the wing and began the process of preserving it.

Another collection in the same neck of the woods, the Gloucestershire Aviation Collection, acquired the Gloster Javelin FAW.9, XH903, from the gate at Innsworth. Not dedicated entirely to the products of Gloster the aircraft company, but to those of Gloucestershire the county, the new group was nevertheless ensconced in the former Gloster buildings at Hucclecote, with the assistance of H.H. Martyn & Co., one of the founders of the Gloucestershire Aircraft Company. There, the Javelin joined Meteor T.7 WL760. Ironically, it was replaced on Innsworth's gate by the Meteor T.7 just restored by the neighbouring Cotswold Aircraft Restoration Group. The Gloucestershire Aviation Collection was shortly to announce the commencement of construction of a non-flying replica of a Gloster Gamecock, using plans acquired from Finland.

A PERSONAL STORY

This trend of volunteer groups dedicated to the memory of particular aircraft manufacturers had begun with the Mosquito Aircraft Museum's association with de Havilland. While writing a history of Boulton Paul Aircraft, I had been

struck by the apparent lack of interest in the company's eighty years in aviation within the confines of what had become a branch of Dowty Aerospace. I
was particularly concerned about Dowty Boulton Paul's photographic archive
– 20,000 negatives, including 7,000 glass plates – which had been left to gath-
er dust after the closure of the photographic department many years before.

In 1991, the company began trading as Dowty Aerospace Wolverhampton,
and the words 'Boulton Paul' were taken down from in front of the factory. I
feared that the name of another great British aircraft manufacturer would be
consigned to the scrap heap, and decided to form the Boulton Paul Society,
dedicated to preserving the history of the company. I contacted Jack
Chambers, who had worked for the company for forty-seven years, and had
spent the eight years of his retirement researching its history. I knew that the
new group would be likely to fail unless there were definite projects on which
to work, and we instigated two immediate goals from the outset. The first was
the creation of an exhibition of Boulton Paul's history, to be displayed at the
nearby Cosford Aerospace Museum. The second was to borrow the Boulton &
Paul P.10 wing, the oldest British metal aircraft wing in existence, from
Norwich, and to create drawings of it with a view to building a replica.

A hastily arranged makeshift show at Wolverhampton's local history fair
drew a response from a number of ex-employees, and the new society was on
the move. With financial and practical support from Dowty Aerospace, and the
company's former parent Boulton & Paul Ltd, still in Norwich, the 220ft long
exhibition was built. Erected at Cosford in the spring of 1993, it centred on the
Sea Balliol, and featured a number of other borrowed exhibits that were relevant to the company's history, including the P.10 wing.

Former BPA draughtsman Cyril Plimmer began preparing drawings of the
wing, but the P.10 project was superseded when entreaties made to the
Pennine Aviation Museum led to their donation of two Boulton Paul Balliol
cockpits, WN149 and WN534. They had remained in storage in Lancashire
since their rescue from the Failsworth scrapyard ten years before. Dowty provided a workshop for their restoration. In April 1993, they duly arrived back
at the factory where one of them, WN149, had been made (WN534 had been
built by Blackburn Aircraft). With definite projects on hand, a clear objective,
and a secure home, the society made steady progress, with an increasing membership, made up of former employees and ex-Defiant aircrew. The name was
also changed; if it became the Boulton Paul Association, thus preserving the
initials BPA, it could purloin the Boulton Paul Aircraft Company logo.

MUSEUMS AND LOCAL COUNCILS

Elsewhere, the two pre-eminent amateur museums both achieved significant
landmarks during 1991, centred on new exhibition hangars. Newark took

delivery of the RAF Museum's newly restored Oxford and Harvard on a two-year loan. The new building was essential for the museum to be trusted with these aircraft; it was a mark of the respect that the museum had built up among 'the professionals' over the years that the loan was even considered. Newark was also in receipt of the Mike Twite Trophy from *FlyPast* magazine for 1990, because of its new hangar.

The Midland Air Museum took delivery of the largest surviving pieces of an Armstrong-Whitworth Whitley, on loan from the RAF Museum, and the Meteor NF.14, on loan from RAF Cosford. To celebrate the fiftieth anniversary of the first flight of the Gloster E.28/39, the Whittle Jet Heritage Centre was formally opened on 21 May by Lord King's Norton, with the Martin-Baker Meteor T.7 flying overhead.

These two museums were seen by their local councils as a positive asset for the community, featuring in any list of places of interest. When Newark was in the final throes of fundraising for its new 200 × 100ft building, Newark and Sherwood District Council came up with a grant to add to the total. Turf was first cut on 2 November 1989, and wherever possible the museum's volunteers undertook parts of the job themselves. To save £10,000 the hardcore was sourced from local building rubble, and moved and laid by the middle of January 1990.

The roll-in of the first aircraft was on 11 April and, with the new roof over their heads, the completion of a number of restorations could take place, notably the Anson. Roger Bryan accepted the Mike Twite Trophy and the accompanying cheque from Pat Twite on 11 September 1991; at the same time, the museum was hosting a meeting of a number of local mayors and councillors, who could witness for themselves the civic benefits that a bunch of local aircraft-preservation enthusiasts could bring to a town.

Many councils have a negative view of aircraft collections and possible museums, and planning consent is often hard to achieve. One such council was Mole Valley, covering Gatwick, where local private collector Peter Vallance had built up a large collection of aircraft in a very short time. Vallance ran an industrial estate called Vallance Byways at Charlwood, adjoining Gatwick, and had been offered a Jet Provost to be pole-mounted as a gate guardian in 1987. The council turned down his planning application. He then bought a Sea Hawk at the auction of the Hunter One Collection, and this was positioned by the gate in October 1987. Over the next four years this aircraft was followed in short order by a fleet of others, including two Shackletons, Buccaneer, Sea Vixen, Venom, Canberra, Gannet, Meteor, Hunter, Pembroke, Sea Prince and Whirlwind.

Vallance applied for planning permission to build a large hangar and to open as an aircraft museum, with a strong educational element. He was turned down again, and a long, bitter struggle with the council began.

Peter Vallance's problems with Mole Valley Council remain unresolved but the Gatwick Aviation Museum, as it is now called, is open on several selected Sundays each year throughout the summer.

BAPC ANNIVERSARY

On 16 May 1992, BAPC celebrated its twenty-fifth anniversary with its 100th meeting, one of the largest ever. As they had been five years before, the speeches were largely introspective. The meeting was hosted by the Midland Air Museum, which was celebrating its own twenty-fifth anniversary the same weekend. None of the delegates could be too churlish about the progress made within the movement in the face of MAM's marvellous progress. They had begun as a group of volunteers holding meetings in pubs and collecting any old wooden aircraft wreck that became available, and had become the proud organizers of a large regional museum.

MAM Chairman John Berkeley was able to greet delegates with a run-down of that progress. The Whittle Jet Heritage Hangar was open, with a new 'Wings over Coventry' gallery being constructed on the first floor, above the office/entrance complex. Further down the site, a wartime Robin hangar was being erected as a workshop, entirely funded by the museum, and an education centre was due to open shortly. At the same time the museum had been collecting exhibits to fit in with its twin themes of local aviation history and the development of the jet aircraft. It had made the most of its excellent relationship with the USAF and had acquired a Danish Starfighter, a Phantom and no less than two Voodoos.

Perhaps MAM's fine example had a tempering effect on David Lee, whose speech demonstrated that he was far more optimistic about the future. He seemed to be satisfied with the progress that had been made in the five years since his hard-hitting criticisms at BAPC's twentieth-anniversary meeting of groups collecting 'wrecks and eyesores'.

It was Ken Ellis, Editor of *FlyPast*, which was sponsoring the meeting, who ended the day with a cautionary note. He referred his comments to the sixty-six council members (from a total of ninety-seven) that were exhibiting aircraft, either in their own museums, or on loan to other museums. He suggested six reasons why members of the public might arrive at any particular museum: 1. Word of mouth, 2. Advertising, 3. Love of aircraft, 4. Saw the sign, 5. Sheer desperation, or 6. Got lost! He then listed six reasons given at an aircraft museum survey in New York State for people to return: 1. Cafe/Restaurant, 2. Covered area for displays, 3. Easy parking, 4. Relaxed atmosphere, 5. Bookshop/gift-shop, 6. Good toilets.

Ken Ellis pointed out that there was no mention of exhibits in either list. Apparently, the aircraft on show in an aircraft museum are not the main attraction for the non-enthusiast member of the public, who simply wants to be entertained and looked after. Too many groups, like the Wales Aircraft Museum, saw the acquisition of new exhibits such as the Lightning as the way to pull in new visitors, and to bring old visitors back. In fact, a nice children's play area and a cup of tea in a friendly café are far more likely to attract the public than a shiny new jet fighter in the aircraft park.

CHAPTER 18

Volunteers

A small number of groups followed a different course from most in the preservation movement. They never attempted to build their own aircraft collection, or aspired to the eventual goal of creating their own museum, but were content to work on restoration projects for others, concentrating on the things they enjoyed doing, without indulging in the complications of running a museum. Not for them the weekly grass-cutting chore, or the long hours waiting on the door to deprive visitors of their entrance money. They wanted to work on aircraft, to preserve their skills, and in many cases to learn new ones.

The Northern Aeroplane Workshops was one such organization, constructing exact replicas of First World War aircraft for the Shuttleworth Trust. The Medway Branch of the Royal Aeronautical Society was another, with a steady stream of aircraft passing through its hands, mostly for preservation by various branches of the Royal Air Force Museum. After a two-year restoration, the derelict Meteor F.8 WK914 was put on gate guardian duties at Medway's 'own' airfield, Rochester. This was followed by the F-84 Thunderstreak, which had been acquired by the RAF Museum after the demise of the Southend Museum.

Medway also undertook the restoration of aero-engines. In 1984 they took on the restoration of the port outer Merlin XX from the Halifax 'S for Sugar', that had been raised from the bottom of a Norwegian lake, and had been on display in an unrestored condition at Hendon. For the Battle of Britain Museum at Hawkinge they were also restoring a Daimler-Benz DB.603 engine, taken from an Me 410 crash site. This engine had looked like a lump of chalk when it first arrived.

After three years and 12,000 man hours of work, the Medway team handed over Hurricane LF751 to the RAF on 22 April 1988, for display in the Manston Memorial building alongside its Spitfire restoration, TB752. In 1997, the group took the Fairchild Argus from storage at Cosford, for a complete restoration, in a break from the usual run of fighters.

The third main group of dedicated restorers without ambitions for a museum of their own were the Cotswold Aircraft Restoration Group (CARG). Its members like to think of themselves as a 'maintenance unit' for the rest of the movement, not just restoring aircraft for other groups but also tracking down parts both from their own spares holding, and elsewhere. CARG was born out of the closure of the Skyfame Museum, when many of the Skyfame Supporters

Club were left at a loose end, pining for old aircraft to work on. Skyfame's Auster AOP.9 and Flying Flea formed the basis for a new group. Tony Southern was instrumental in its formation, and became its Chairman.

With the experience of Skyfame as a warning, CARG intended from the start to avoid the pitfalls of trying to create its own museum. Its 'home' became two large barrack-type buildings within the bounds of RAF Innsworth, where successive COs gave help and encouragement. In return, CARG restored Meteor T.7, VW453, to be displayed at the station's gate.

Members ranged from Chief Engineer Fred Eagles, who ran Classic Aeroplanes at Staverton, to Martin Clarke, who had started at Skyfame as a fourteen-year-old ATC Cadet in 1964, and had gone on to become an engineer at Dowty Rotol. Secretary for the group was Steve Thompson, who shared the workload even though he lived quite far away, in Leominster, by doing the vital administration work.

Apart from these dedicated groups there were also supporters' associations attached to most of the major aircraft museums, made up of volunteers who were happy to give up their time to work on the aircraft as directed by the museum staff. Some museums, such as Duxford, had several full-time conservation officers, each working on a different group of aircraft. Ted Haggar, for example, was in charge of the restoration of the B-17, B-29 and B-52, but was totally reliant on the volunteers assigned to each of these aircraft. The B-17 'Mary Alice' had a volunteer crew consisting of Ron and Steve Bones, who joined in April 1979, Graham Douglas, Andy Height, Martin Perman and Dave Sewell. This team was responsible for bringing the aircraft up to full 8th Air Force standard. Right across the huge Duxford site there were similar groups of volunteers working away on 'their' aircraft, with no reward other than the satisfaction of a job well done.

Virtually every museum in Britain benefits from such volunteers, and most could not operate without them. In 1999, the Aerospace Museum at Cosford became the RAF Museum Cosford, a title that recognized it as one of the finest aircraft museums in the world, in its own right, rather than an adjunct of the Hendon Museum. It has a large supporters' club, and although, as always, only a relatively small percentage of the membership are seen on a regular basis, those who do turn up are invaluable to the running of the museum. They serve as guides, make up an instant labour force whenever aircraft need to be shifted or dismantled, and undertake their own restoration projects, always within the museum itself.

Although the Skyfame Supporters' Club was the first, the Shuttleworth Veteran Aeroplane Society is now the oldest of these museum-helpers groups, with members graduating from helping the trust only by paying their subscriptions, to hands-on restoration and display organization work.

CHAPTER NINETEEN

The Nineties

TOP-RANKING MUSEUMS

A RGUABLY the greatest restoration project of the amateur preservation movement, the re-creation of a Halifax by the Yorkshire Air Museum (YAM) at Elvington, came one step closer near the end of 1992. Its new display hangar/workshop was opened, allowing the museum considerably more elbow room, although the newly restored fuselage could still not be mated with the ex-Hastings wings, even in the space available, which also had to house its Buccaneer and its Lightning.

Moving the Halifax into the new building freed up the old Romney hanger for Tony Agar's Mosquito night-fighter. Twenty years after first acquiring the cockpit of HJ711 for £7 from the Reflectaire sale, Agar's small night-fighter preservation team was working against time to have the aircraft up on its wheels by the fiftieth anniversary of the Mosquito's first flight. This was duly achieved on Elvington's Mosquito Day, which featured the arrival of British Aerospace's Mosquito T.3.

The night-fighter was a long way from being complete, even after twenty-four years of work. The engines were not yet installed, the leading edges of the wings were not attached, and there were dozens of other little jobs to do. Still, when the aircraft was pushed across the grass to join its flying sibling, the event was a marvellous testament to what had been done. The tiny team had taken on on a huge task – for instance, they had replaced 10,000 little brass screws in the refurbished wings. The parts had come from all over the world; the nose cone was from New Zealand, while the elevators were from Israel.

Once the anniversary celebrations were over, the Mosquito had to be dismantled again to get it back into the new workshop, but plans were soon announced for a new building to house it. In the event this ambition was merged with that of the Halifax team, when the museum acquired a T2 hangar. As soon as the Yorkshire Air Museum had its T2 hangar the Mosquito could be fully assembled, and work continued until the aircraft's official roll-out on 6 September 1996, with the correct Merlin 25s fitted. There was still much work to be done, even after twenty-seven years of endeavour, but no one could deny that Tony Agar had created the only Mosquito NF II in the world, and it was one of only two night-fighter Mossies.

Soon afterwards, the Halifax was also rolled out, having been given a new identity. Previously known as HR792, from the original rear fuselage shell that formed the basis for the project, it was now decided to paint it in the markings of LV907, 'Friday the 13th', a Halifax that had completed 128 operations during the war. A week after the Mosquito was rolled out, the only complete Halifax in the world was the star of a similar ceremony. On Friday 13 September 1996, it was revealed in daylight for the first time. Again, despite eleven years of hard work from a large band of dedicated volunteers there was still much to be done to the interior of the Hali-bag.

The new building and the prestige of 'Friday the 13th', as well as other jewels in its crown, such as the Mosquito, had propelled YAM into the first rank of volunteer-run museums, alongside Newark and Midland.

Midland had recently acquired three more exhibits: a Spey engine, Sea Vixen FAW.2 XN685, and the cockpit of Sea Vixen FAW.2 XJ579. The number of naval aircraft on display at Coventry had led the museum to contemplate the creation of a 'carrier flight deck', with a section of the external display area decked out with steel plates. This imaginative idea was to take some years to come to fruition; when it did, it was inside a hangar, and at the Fleet Air Arm Museum at Yeovilton, in its ground-breaking 'Carrier' display.

CREATING MORE EXHIBITION SPACE

Following YAM on a rapid path to major acceptance as a frontline volunteer-run museum was the Tangmere Military Aviation Museum. Beginning life as a wreckology-based collection, centred on two ex-RAF huts rented from the local Tangmere Parish Council, the museum was initially led by Chairman Jimmy Beedle, ex-43 Squadron. After his death, in 1989, the guiding lights were co-directors Andy Saunders and Peter Dimond. The museum had gone the usual route of acquiring an ex-Danish Hunter F.4, E-412, from Dunsfold, and an ex-French Air Force T-33, 19252, from the USAF, together with the Wessex Aviation Society Meteor F.8 WA984. Visitor numbers to the museum rapidly reached 30,000 per annum, aided by the famous aerojumble event, but the directors recognized that the future lay with a large exhibition hall. The result was an appeal fund for an £85,000 building.

As Newark, Midland and Yorkshire had already discovered, a new exhibition hall immediately brought credibility, and respect from 'the professionals'. The result was the loan from the RAF Museum of two world air-speed record-breaking aircraft, Meteor IV (Special) EE549, and Neville Duke's Hunter F.3, WB188. With them, Tangmere gained a second major theme; after the history of RAF Tangmere itself, it would focus on high-speed flight. The hall was also soon to house high-quality commercially built FSMs of the Hurricane and Spitfire, the latter paid for by the family of Pilot Officer Axel Anders Svendsen, who went missing while flying from Tangmere on 24 April 1942.

The North East Aircraft Museum at Sunderland became the next volunteer-run museum to build a large display hanger, in summer 1993. Established on its new site, over the road from the Nissan car plant, the museum had decided to call a halt to its rush to collect new aircraft, apart from those paid for by its members, and decided to put aside funds with a view to building a 100 × 80ft display hall. A proper business plan and registration with the Museums and Galleries Commission gave the museum further credibility with the local council, and a new building was the result.

With many of the exhibits lodged in this new facility, the old display building was converted to a display of naval aircraft. As Chairman Andrew Parkin savoured the new building he was already planning the further security of the site, with a new boundary fence. The need for this was to be tragically demonstrated in the not too distant future.

Newark Air Museum was soon in the enviable position of being able to send back its two RAF Museum loan aircraft, the beautifully restored Harvard and Oxford. With the donation of a Saab Draken by the Danish Air Force, which arrived on 29 June 1994, and the imminent arrival of a Tiger Moth, restored for Newark by members of the Costwold Aircraft Restoration Group, the space occupied by the loan aircraft was needed.

Tying in With Veterans

In Essex, the Rebel Air Museum had managed to find its own secure niche in the aircraft-preservation movement. Created largely by Stan Brett and his son David, the museum first appeared at Andrewsfield in 1978; it was open at weekends, in a hanger that it was obliged to vacate during the week! After Stan's death this arrangement came to an end, and the museum went into storage for four years, before a generous interest-free loan from a supporter enabled the group to build a 7,000sq ft building at nearby Earls Colne airfield.

That corner of Essex was the home of the USAF's 9th Air Force, and this force, and in particular its Martin Marauders, became the museum's speciality. A small handful of working members created an artefact-based museum that was well laid out; an ex-scrapyard Marauder rear fuselage was their pride and joy. The only complete aircraft were the Fairchild Cornell, which came originally from the old Historic Aircraft Museum at Southend, and a Flying Flea.

The museum came to be something of a Mecca for 9th Air Force veterans, and gained many exhibits that way, with the collection being kept open by a hard core of about half a dozen members. Sadly, by 1997, the museum was forced to close, and the collection was dispersed, except for the Marauder exhibits, which were kept as a purely private collection.

A tie-in with a particular group of veterans was also to serve the Yorkshire Aircraft Museum well. The area had been the home of large numbers of Canadian aircrew, and links forged with the Canadian Armed Forces led to the acquisition of a Canadian-built CT-133 Silver Star. At the same time, Elvington, formerly the home of two French Halifax squadrons, had used its links with

France to bring from French Air Force Noratlas Transports the Hercules engines for the Halifax re-build, as well as other parts. The link was also later to yield the only Mirage III to be displayed in Britain.

Also at Elvington the night-fighter preservation team had recently acquired a de Havilland Venom NF.3, WX788, previously held by the Midland Warplane Museum, and before that by the Wales Aircraft Museum. They were also shortly to acquire a relic of another night-fighter, the engine and propeller of Defiant, N1766, which had been on display at the Manchester Air & Space Museum after excavation from its Peak District crash site.

Manchester Air & Space Museum was unaware that in Wolverhampton the Boulton Paul Association was busily collecting Defiant parts from any source, in order to come as close as it could to creating the world's second Defiant in the town of its origin. Not yet a member of BAPC, the association was yet to discover the benefits that membership could yield – in this case, a Merlin engine.

COCKPIT COLLECTORS

One phenomenon that began to gain ground during the 1990s was that of the cockpit collector. With a cockpit, the average person or small group could preserve an important chunk of aviation hardware on a limited budget and, more importantly, with limited space. Many of these enthusiasts began with a collection of aircraft parts and instruments, and graduated to creating fully equipped instrument panels. It was a natural step to want to see these panels installed in a cockpit. Once one cockpit was fully kitted out, leaving the collector at a loose end, the next step was to acquire a second.

A sub-group calling itself the Air Defence Collection was formed in 1993 within the Wiltshire Historic Aviation Group, based on a collection of five cockpits – Chipmunk, Gnat, Hunter, Swift and Hurricane. A Wiltshire member, Steve Arnold, also owned the cockpit of a Hunter as well as a Spitfire V under restoration. The Phantom Restoration Group, based at Bruntingthorpe, owned not one but two Phantom FGR.2 cockpits, and then expanded somewhat with the purchase of the cockpit of Viscount XT661. At New Milton in Hampshire Peter Burton bought a Sea Vixen cockpit to go with his Buccanner S.2 cockpit.

In Market Drayton in Shropshire, Roger Marley, a member of the Warplane Aircraft Recovery Group, an aviation-archaeology group of long standing, acquired the cockpit of a Hunter from the Staffordshire Aviation Heritage Society. (The society had tried to start a museum at Seighford airfield near Stafford. The rest of the Hunter was scrapped, and the Staffs group's Canberra T.4, which lay in a dismantled state at Seighford for several years, was finally bought by Ian Hancock, who already owned Lightning F.1 XG329. Both aircraft had been at Seighford during their career to be modified by Boulton Paul

Aircraft, and both were to join one another at the Norfolk and Suffolk Museum at Flixton.)

Having caught the Hawker aircraft bug, once his Hunter was fully kitted out, Roger Marley acquired a Harrier cockpit. He later sold this to another cockpit collector to help fund his rebuild of a Typhoon cockpit. In 1993, Colin Mears in Sidcup obtained the cockpit of Vulcan B.1 XA903, which created problems all of its own. Fortunately, according to the local council it was 'incidental to the property', despite being nearly 11ft high, so planning permission was not needed – just understanding neighbours.

The mother of all cockpit collections was the Robertsbridge Aviation Society based at Bush Barn, in the Sussex countryside. RAS had been formed as long ago as 1964, as a wide-ranging society for the local aviation enthusiast. In 1973 a site with some deserted chicken sheds became available, and the society set about creating a museum to display its large collection of artefacts, including many from its aviation-archaeology activities. The sheds became a treasure trove of aviation-related items, but could hardly include many complete air-craft. A Mystere IVA was the only whole airframe displayed, but this was on loan from Lashenden. Bush Barn also presented the cockpits of a Lightning, Cadet TX.3, Jet Provost and Meteor T.7, and the fuselage of a Tiger Moth. By the end of the 1990s these had been augmented with the cockpits from a Sea Vixen, Canberra PR.3, Tornado and Sukhoi Su 7.

Further evidence of the strong links that the Midland Air Museum had devel-oped with the USAF came with the arrival of a McDonnell F4C Phantom, a Vietnam veteran with one MiG victory to its credit. The museum had also been allocated a Polish-built MiG-15 by the USAF, but now faced the problem of moving it from Arizona. The Royal Air Force Museum continued to place its trust in the Midland Air Museum, having already loaned Armstrong-Whitworth Siskin and Whitley parts, as well as a Meteor NF.14. The Aerospace Museum at Cosford passed on its Lockheed T-33, to join MAM's own. The intention was to convert one of them into a replica of a Lockheed P.80 Shooting Star, to fur-ther complete the collection of early jet fighters.

DISPOSING OF VICTORS

One of the last great retirements of RAF bombers came with the cessation of No.55 Squadron's Victor tanker operations. The disposal of the fleet did not create the same sort of scramble to acquire examples as the Vulcan retirement, despite the fact that the Victor was a more beautiful and effective aircraft, and a veteran of two wars, not just one. Most of the retiring Victors were destined for fire practice training or for the scrapyard.

The proximity of a runway was a pre-requisite for obtaining a Victor. The Yorkshire Air Museum was grateful to Gerry Tempest for purchasing a Victor, XL321 'Lusty Lindy', for delivery to Elvington. Photographed alongside its

Halifax, it would make an interesting Handley Page comparison. Astonishingly, the first flights of the two types were only thirteen years apart.

The Walton family, who owned Bruntingthorpe, purchased XM715 'Teasin' Tina', and this was delivered for display next to their Vulcan. Bruntingthorpe was rapidly becoming a major aviation heritage centre, with the Cold War as its main theme. Its Big Thunder air display was its very noisy shop window, with high-speed taxiing displays, not only by the Vulcan, but also by the Lightning Preservation Team's two Lightning F.6s. Apart from the Walton family's own collection, Bruntingthorpe was soon to house others, such as the Vintage Aircraft Team and Canberra operator Classic Aviation Projects.

The only other place where the two greatest V-bombers were to be preserved alongside one another was the Aerospace Museum, Cosford, where XH672 'Maid Marion' was delivered. Because Cosford's single runway was too short, the Victor was flown to Shawbury, to be dismantled and transported by road. The Bomber Command Museum at Hendon did not have room to show the three V-bombers together, but contented itself with having the nose of XM717 'Lucky Lou' to stand alongside its Vulcan and Valiant.

VOLUNTEERS GO FROM STRENGTH TO STRENGTH

David Lee, now Chairman of BAPC after the retirement of Mike Hodgson, was shortly to host the fourth BAPC conference, 'Stopping the Rot', which was held at the RAF Museum restoration and storage centre at Cardington. Unsurprisingly, since it offered the chance to look round this important venue, the conference was well attended.

There was evidence of increasing maturity at some of the volunteer collections, with large exhibition halls springing up at many, freeing up smaller buildings for use as workshops, and planned restoration programmes being put into effect. The bleak picture of 'wrecks and eyesores' was becoming a thing of the past.

The growing respect for the volunteer movement was reflected in the fact that the aerospace industry was prepared to support its efforts. British Aerospace had always been a benefactor, with a number of welcome disposals of its aircraft – Vampires, Hunters, Canberras and the like – at minimal prices. Different parts of the BAe empire had also provided help and encouragement in their own neck of the woods. Brough had obtained its own Buccaneer to recall its days as Blackburn Aircraft, and continued to provide help to the volunteers just up the road at Elvington. Much of the rear fuselage and tail of the Halifax there was refurbished or built new, as part of the factory's apprentice training. The factory also restored two Swordfish to flying condition for the Fleet Air Arm's Historic Flight, and built an FSM of a Blackburn Lincock in just forty days, for exhibition at one of its open days.

At Woodford, they were determined to preserve their Avro identity; having acquired a Vulcan, and the cockpit of a second aircraft, they also acquired an Anson 19, G-AHKX. The volunteers of the Avro Heritage Society began its restoration to flying condition.

At Hatfield there had always been support for the Mosquito Aircraft Museum, and its de Havilland aspirations, and the Brooklands Museum was enjoying help from both the former Hawker and Vickers divisions of BAe. Its hangar, containing the Loch Ness Wellington restoration, was designated the Vickers Hangar, and there were plans to build a Hawker hangar alongside. Even when the Vickers factory at Brooklands closed, the museum was allowed to rescue a number of relevant artefacts, including glass panels etched with Vickers types, furniture, period photographs and even world time clocks.

Westland Aircraft continued to support the International Helicopter Museum at Weston-super-Mare, a museum that was steadily gathering together an international collection of rotorcraft. Even Mil-1 and Mil-4 helicopters were arriving from behind the quickly rusting Iron Curtain.

Dowty Boulton Paul Ltd in Wolverhampton, and its new Managing Director Paul Strothers, continued to support the Boulton Paul Association. It even turned over the whole of a 10,000sq ft building, which was officially opened in 1997 by former Chief Test Pilot A.E. 'Ben' Gunn, as the Boulton Paul Aircraft Heritage Project. Inside, the restoration of Balliol cockpit WN149 continued, but it was now to be incorporated at the heart of an FSM of a Balliol. The technique used for the new parts – applying an Alclad skin to a wooden frame – inspired the commencement of the construction of a Defiant FSM. The parts of Defiant N3378 had been collected from all over the country, as well as from the crash site itself, high in the Peak District. They were displayed as found, in a re-creation of the crash site, as a memorial to the two men who died in the incident. The Defiant FSM alongside, incorporating many original parts, would bring to life the Black Country's highest-profile contribution to the Second World War.

As the idea of building full-scale models of Boulton Paul Aircraft took hold, a third FSM was started. This one came from a different era. The Boulton & Paul P.6 biplane of 1918 had been built as an experimental machine, but it was used after the war as the company's own transport, and made the first official business flight in Britain, on 1 May 1919. The P.6 was to be formally unveiled on 5 August 2001, by Paul Strothers, MD of the whole Dowty Aerospace Group, now Smiths Aerospace after a recent takeover.

The surviving Boulton Paul archives, including 20,000 negatives, were moved to the Heritage Centre. Next door an education centre was created, containing the company's technical library, with books going back to 1913, when J.D. North worked for Grahame White Aviation. The donation of further collections of memorabilia and historic items is encouraged, whether connected to Boulton Paul or not, and for this reason the collection was renamed the West Midland Aviation Archive.

The inspiration for the official opening of the Boulton Paul Aircraft Heritage Centre was the First National Aviation Heritage Week, sponsored by BAPC and *FlyPast* magazine. All over the country, groups and museums dreamed up special events for the week, in some cases opening their doors to the public for the first time, as at Wolverhampton. Such was the success of the week that the two sponsors decided to repeat it, on a biennial basis.

Elsewhere, the flow of Lightnings to collections continued. The Fenland Aviation Museum at Wisbech, a collection created by an aviation-archaeology group, made a significant step into the world of owning whole airframes with the purchase of not one but two Lightning T.5s, XS420 and XS459. Many miles further north, Lightning F.3 XR749, owned by Ken Ward and sited at his cottage on the North York Moors, was threatened with the axe. Teeside Airport offered it a home in one of its hangars while Ward and his friends restored it to pristine condition. Once finished, it went on display in a small compound in front of the terminal building.

Ken Ward had long collected items from crash sites, especially on the North York Moors, which were practically his back garden. His cottage at Chop Gate, at the end of an unmade track up on to the moors, soon became the home of his personal museum. A small building housed a massive collection of small items, until it was almost impossible to move around inside, and a nearby compound slowly began to be filled with complete airframes and cockpits. These soon included a Vampire T.11, and the cockpits of a Meteor NF.11, Lightning F.1A, Jet Provost, and Buccaneer S.2B. Ken Ward also owned a Vickers Valiant nose, but he placed this on loan at Bruntingthorpe, where it made a fitting companion to the Vulcan and Victor.

Ken Rimmell's Museum of D-Day Aviation at Apuldram in West Sussex specialized in aviation relating to the D-Day landings. It placed a heavy emphasis on the Hawker Typhoon, with a cockpit on display, and was much frequented by members of the Typhoon/Tempest Association. A fibreglass Spitfire FSM guarded the door, but there were no other full-size aircraft. The site was rather lost in the Sussex countryside, attached to a garden nursery, so, when the chance of a site at Shoreham Airport came along in 1994, the museum moved there.

The acquisition of Buccaneer cockpits and complete airframes was becoming more and more common, as the Brick was retired and replaced by the Tornado. One of the groups that considered the Brick to be an excellent addition to their collection was the Ulster Aviation Society. The society was now based at Langford Lodge, where its Grumman Wildcat restoration was still progressing. The rest of its collection had a definite emphasis on Ulster aviation, and a Shorts 330 was the largest lump on display. There were also a Sea Hawk and the inevitable Vampire T.11. Having its own runway, the society was able to arrange the aerial delivery of its 'Bucc', XV361. It was probably the shortest delivery flight ever – 92 seconds from RAF Aldergrove.

FLEAS

In the mid-1990s, with preservation groups around Britain busily obtaining Buccaneers and Lightnings, it was hard to recall the time twenty-five years earlier when these aircraft were in frontline service, and the most that the infant preservation groups could aspire to was the discovery of a Flying Flea in a local barn or outbuilding. In fact, it seemed impossible that there were any Fleas left to be discovered, but this was not the case.

In the 1930s, Bill Pennington, who lived in a tiny village by Coniston Water, Cumbria, bought a Flea just for its engine. He installed it in a car he was building and the aircraft was stored away in an outbuilding for the next fifty years. After his death, in 1990, his widow Doreen contacted the RAF Museum to see if they wanted the Flea. Henri Mignet's creation had never been in service with the RAF, and the museum was not interested (although a Flea has since gone on display at the RAF Museum, Cosford). They contacted Ken Ellis, Editor of *FlyPast*, keeper of the BAPC's register of anonymous aircraft, on which a large number of Fleas appear, and author of a Flea book. He arranged for this 'new' Flea to go to Haverigg Prison, which was sited on the former RAF airfield of Millom. An RAF Millom Project had been created within the prison, to display the history of the airfield and aviation in the immediate vicinity. It had strong links with the Dumfries & Galloway Aviation Museum, not far away, north of the border. Haverigg was looking for a complete aircraft to add to its small collection, so, when David Reid, Dumfries' Chairman, heard about the Flea, he put the two together. The Flea was soon obtained, to be restored in the prison's workshops.

Dumfries & Galloway Aviation Museum was itself based at the former control tower of the RAF airfield of Tinwald Downs. The group had formed in 1973, and the museum did not open until 1982, becoming Scotland's only independent aircraft museum in 1988 when Strathallan finally closed down for good. The aircraft park alongside the tower contained the usual Vampire T.11, Super Sabre, T-33 and Mystere IVA, as well as a Meteor T.7, Sycamore, and a Varsity cockpit. The latter was retained when the group decided to scrap the whole aircraft, which it had obtained from the Glasgow Airport Fire department, but was deemed too large for them to cope with.

Most of the 'quality' items at the museum were the smaller bits and pieces, many of which had come from crash sites; they were displayed within the tower. Two rescues had been the 'Blue Peter' Spitfire and the 'Loch Doon' Spitfire, both of which were under restoration on site, one with considerable help from inmates of Haverigg Prison.

FUNDING DIFFICULTIES

While the aircraft-preservation movement had been mushrooming right across the country the Shuttleworth Trust had continued to function at Old Warden, much as it always had, slowly restoring new aircraft from time to time, including the Hawker Hind, Desoutter Monoplane and DH.88 Comet. Occasionally, a shortage of cash led to the sale of the odd aircraft deemed outside the normal scope of the collection, like the Provost, Spitfire XI, Auster AOP.9 and Anson, but in mid-1994 it came as something of a shock to discover that the Trust was running at a loss. It would need a large cash injection from the sale of some of its prime aircraft just to survive. There was considerable furore when Jean Batten's Gull was sold to her native New Zealand, as part of this financial restructuring process.

In 1994, the National Lottery provided a new source of funding, and a number of museums, including Brooklands and Elvington, were soon looking into making claims for new building work. However, Lottery funding could not be used to pay running costs. Other collections could only dream of being in a position to make a Lottery application; simply obtaining planning permission from the local council was difficult enough. At Gatwick, Peter Vallance continued his long fight with the Mole Valley District Council (see page 158). Given a year to comply with the decision that his collection should be dispersed, he felt that the date for any sale had been put back to September 1995.

Meanwhile, the Macclesfield Historical Aviation Society fell foul of the greenness of the Cheshire countryside. It had established itself in the open on a farm near Chelford, with a Canberra, Hunter and Jet Provost as its main exhibits, but the Macclesfield District Council decided after eight years that the collection had become an eyesore. The society was ordered to remove it, although it was granted a period of grace.

The Fleet Air Arm Museum's marvellous 'Carrier' exhibition was opened in 1994. Built inside the museum's original hangar, the exhibit re-created a carrier flight deck, with one wall taken up with the carrier's superstructure, and the others featuring a painted diorama of a sunrise at sea. Visitors were 'flown' to the carrier inside a Wessex helicopter, entering through one door, and, after a suitably effective experience of flight, stepping on to the flight deck through the other. Here, they found ten historic naval aircraft, with a Phantom ranged on the carrier's catapult forward, and 'wind' blowing over the deck (from fans hidden in the Phantom's jet pipe). The experience did not end with the flight deck, as the visitor could pass through many of the normal departments of a carrier, with interactive displays giving a feel of what it was like to be at sea in the 1950s and 60s.

'Carrier' was recognition on a grand scale that an aircraft museum had to be more than a collection of old aircraft standing in a hangar, or, even worse, outside in a field. It was the conversion of an aircraft museum into an aviation theme park, something already undertaken at Thorpe Park and Helston. It represented an acceptance that, if the place was to survive and expand, the general public as a whole, not just the aircraft enthusiast, had to be attracted through the door.

Even at the RAF Museum, the ultimate hangar full of old aircraft, there were new projects to create a wider appeal. Dioramas of what it was like in the Blitz for the civilian population were housed in the Battle of Britain Museum, and then the Sunderland interior was opened up, with interactive commentary, for visitors passing through. Aircraft museums had to become a dynamic part of the 'leisure industry', competing with many other leisure-related activities.

An imaginative and commendable way to protect the wooden pod of a Vampire T.11 – the Wellesbourne Wartime Museum's 'car port' for XK590.

Canberra T.19 WJ975 at the Bomber County Aviation Museum at Hemswell in Lincolnshire.

Dick Melton's Walrus;
there is a marvellous
chance that this
restoration will see the
breed return to the air
once again.

The 'Loch Ness Wellington', as it will always be known, on display at Brooklands after its mammoth restoration.

The Lancaster at East Kirkby, NX611, fires up its Merlin engines once again, a routine that now includes regular taxi runs.

'Sally B', Britain's only flying Boeing B-17, and a star of the air-show circuit for over twenty years, at Duxford in 1990.

The Fighter Collection's Hurricane, KZ321, in the organization's own hangar at Duxford in 1990.

The Gannet guarding the entrance to the Flambards Theme Park at Helston.

Perhaps the finest ever Vampire T.11 restoration, XE998, winner of the 1993 Mike Twite Trophy for the Fenland and West Norfolk Aviation Museum. It was later moved to Brooklands and is now at Farnborough.

The Vampire T.11, XD534, at the Barton visitor centre, with the Canberra T.4 cockpit behind.

The RAF Museum's newly restored Airspeed Oxford, MP425, on loan at the Newark Air Museum, showing that the most professional of the amateurs can be trusted by the professionals.

Hurricane PZ865 and Lancaster PA474 of the Battle of Britain Memorial Flight enjoy the sunshine at Coningsby in 1994.

The ex-Saudi Lightning T.55, 55-713, at the Midland Air Museum, Coventry

The decaying Shackleton, WR985, at Long Marston. Star exhibit in the Stratford Aircraft Museum, it is owned by the landowner and is not connected to the Jet Heritage Preservation Group, despite being in the group's compound.

The composite Hunter at Long Marston, which the Jet Heritage Preservation group hope to turn into an FR.10.

Tony Agar's Mosquito being erected at Elvington for its first roll-out, in 1991.

The wings of Anson VS962 flanking the entrance to the RAF Llanbedr Museum at the Maes Artro leisure village. The fuselage was under restoration inside this facility which, once closed, has now re-opened.

Not Johnny Johnson standing by his Spitfire, but Keith Jones, by his fibreglass FSM, with its original cockpit and other parts, on display at the Warplane Aircraft Recovery Group's museum at High Ercall. It has since gone to Sleap.

The Black Country Aircraft Collection's Canberra cockpit WJ576 and Antonov An-2 fuselage, RA-01641, after their arrival in the same week at Smiths Aerospace, Wolverhampton.

The Defiant FSM, 'L7005', unveiled at the Boulton Paul Aircraft Heritage Project on Battle of Britain Day 2002, a fine example of how to fill a gap in a collection without access to vast funds.

CHAPTER 20

Into the Twenty-First Century

AMATEUR SUCCESS

ONE of the first great successes of the amateur aircraft-preservation move-ment in Britain was the return from Noumea of the ex-French Lancaster NX611, by the Historic Aircraft Preservation Society in 1965. The sad odyssey of this aircraft and its gradual decline to the ignominy of the Reflectaire sale in Blackpool seemed to prove that the 'amateurs' had bitten off more than they could chew; for a while the Lanc was returned to the care of the 'profession-als', taking up gate guardian duties at RAF Scampton in 1974.

In 1983, NX611 was purchased by Fred and Harold Panton, destined to become the star of their new East Kirkby Lincolnshire Aviation Heritage Centre. It was installed in the new hangar in 1989, and the brothers then set about getting the aircraft going. In 1994 the first of her Merlin engines burst into life once more, after lying idle for twenty-two years. It took Roy Jarman and Ian Hickling, the two full-time engineers involved in this marvellous achievement, about three months of work to get each engine running once more. During 1995, NX611 was able to taxi under her own power again.

The Panton brothers had proven quite spectacularly that the amateur air-craft-preservation movement had really come of age, able to resurrect even its own major failures. In a different sense, another resurrection took place in Gloucestershire during the 1990s.

Home of the pioneering and long-lamented Skyfame Museum, Staverton Airport saw the return of an aircraft museum with the re-location of the exhibits of the Gloucestershire Aircraft Collections. Formed in 1985 and locat-ed at Hucclecote for many years, building up its collection of aircraft related to the county, GAC had also established a strong relationship with the local councils, even obtaining grant aid from them. When the collection needed to be moved from its industrial-estate site, Chairman Tim Kershaw was able to find a new home in an old Bellman hangar on Staverton airfield, and thoughts turned to the preparation of a National Lottery application.

During 1996 the Yorkshire Air Museum learned that its Lottery application had borne fruit. As a result, it was able to proceed with the construction of a T.2 hangar to house its Halifax, Tony Agar's Mosquito, and many of the other aircraft in its collection, including the newly arrived Mirage IIIE.

A slightly more significant application was to be made by the Imperial War Museum, which was seeking £6.5 million towards the total cost of £11 million for its American Air Museum, to house all the American aircraft in the collection. It would be a spectacular building, big enough to hold both the B-52 and the B-29, apart from all the other 'smaller' aircraft. The museum was faced with the twin mammoth tasks of raising the rest of the money itself, and restoring all the aircraft to a suitable condition for installation in the museum once it was built. Stripping down a B-52 was to prove a considerable problem in itself, requiring a novel approach; vacu-blasting inside a tent.

WALES AIRCRAFT MUSEUM

The long foretold demise of the Wales Aircraft Museum came about early in 1996, and the final fall was sudden and very swift. There had been a reduction in the number of aircraft in 1990, when the airport took back some of the land for a new maintenance base. At the same time, the organization of the museum was taken out of the hands of the volunteers and invested in Aircraft Museum (Wales) Ltd, a company charged with attracting more visitors.

Aircraft were repainted in more 'attractive' though inappropriate schemes. The one really rare aircraft, the nose of the Avro Ashton, was swapped with the Avro Heritage Group at Woodford for ATP and Jetstream 41 fuselages, to give the public more aircraft to climb aboard. The changes were too little too late, and in its last year of operation the museum saw just 5,000 people pass through its gate, or an average of twenty-four per day. In the end, further airport expansion brought down the final curtain, but the spiral of decay had been such that no one really wanted to fight at the end.

Aircraft on loan, such as the Fleet Air Arm Museum's Gannet, were removed, and most of the rest were scrapped, even the three on loan from the USAF (the T-33, Super Sabre and Mystere). The corrosion on them was just too bad to consider trying to save them. In some cases the cockpit sections were saved when the airframes were scrapped. Long years of standing out in the open and the effects of the salt air at Rhoose had ensured that many were riddled with corrosion; without any intrinsic value, they were condemned to the scrapman as the only option.

The Fleet Air Arm's Gannet T.5 was passed on to the Museum of Berkshire Aviation at Woodley, and several of the cockpits ended up at Phoenix Aviation at Bruntingthorpe, which was becoming well known as a purveyor of aircraft cockpits. One of them was the cockpit of Canberra T.17, WJ576, which was bought by Tom Atkinson in Lancashire. It soon adorned the front of his house, to the delight of his children and the horror of his wife.

FINDING THE RIGHT LOCATION

In 1996, the East Midlands Aeropark was also having to find itself a new home. The highly successful Aeropark had been run by a small team of enthusiastic

185

volunteers. As in Wales the exhibits were outside, but there were only nine airframes. It was a number that was easily managed by the volunteers, who kept the Aeropark in tip-top condition, helping to attract 100,000 visitors in a year, twenty times the number attracted by Wales Aircraft Museum, which had far more aircraft. Because of cargo apron extensions at the East Midlands Airport, the Aeropark had to be moved but, after a lot of hand-wringing and thoughts of the aircraft having to be scrapped, the airport authorities were able to find a new location away from the developments.

Finding a secure location to display a collection has always been the most difficult problem facing an amateur group. One route is to find a business with spare land or buildings available, and to convince them that a small on-site aircraft museum would be an extra attraction to pull in more punters. Ideally, the host business would do most of its trading at weekends, traditionally the only time that amateur groups could man their collections on a regular basis. For a couple of groups the local garden centre seemed to fit the bill, offering an out-of-town location, sometimes with a great deal of land, and a large car park.

The Aeroplane Collection finally managed to open its own museum at a garden centre at Warmingham, Cheshire. In Wisbech, the Fenland Aircraft Preservation Society had mostly cut its teeth digging wrecks from the soft, preserving soils of the Fenland, and, unlike many such groups, restoring its finds to pristine display condition. The society entered into an agreement with Bamber's Garden Centre at West Walton, near to the very busy A47 road. The owner of the garden centre, Lee Bamber, believed that an on-site aircraft museum would represent a positive way to attract more customers.

The Fenland group started with a building packed with its wreckology collection, in displays that were well thought out, and opened its doors for the first time on 20 June 1987. It was two years before its first aircraft arrived on the site, in the shape of the inevitable Vampire T.11, XD434. This aircraft went through a major restoration at RAF Marham in 1993–94. In 1994 the museum acquired two Lightning T.5s from Roger Sheldrake's private collection at Narborough. Twenty members clubbed together to buy XS459, while one of the museum's two Keepers of Aircraft, Murray Flint (the other was John Springett) bought XS420 himself. Roger Sheldrake was so impressed with the museum that he lent his Jet Provost, XM402. Also acquired were a Slingsby Grasshopper and a crashed Piper Colt, but these were placed in store to await a larger display building. The museum was such a success in attracting people to the garden centre that in 1995 Lee Bamber organized a doubling of its floor space.

With most of Roger Sheldrake's Wellesley Aircraft Collection now at Wisbech, some of his former helpers – Hadyn Block, Nigel Clayton and others – found themselves at a bit of a loss. They decided to band together, as the Terrington Aviation Collection, and began to collect and restore mainly cockpits, starting with Buccaneer, Lightning and Phantom. They also forged links with the Fenland Museum, placing much of their collection on display there.

Although the garden centre/aircraft museum symbiosis seemed to work well in East Anglia, in Cheshire the Warmingham garden centre folded, and the Aeroplane Collection was forced to vacate the premises. Salvation seemed to appear over the horizon in the shape of the Griffin Trust, a new organization formed to preserve the historic hangars at Hooton Park, and to house a transport collection within them. On the surface it seemed a marriage made in heaven. On the one hand the trust had historic buildings and needed to fill them and on the other the Aeroplane Collection needed a home for its large exhibits.

Graham Sparkes, Chairman of the Aeroplane Collection, was optimistic, but in the end the two sides could not come to a suitable arrangement. Sparkes was forced to oversee the dispersement of the Warmingham exhibits to museums all over the country, and TAC concentrated its efforts on supporting the Manchester Air & Space Museum.

Finding the right location for a museum was always difficult, and security was one of the main issues. The North East Aircraft Museum had apparently found the right place at Sunderland Airport, only to have its existence threatened by the construction of the Nissan car plant. When it acquired a new site at Usworth, with the help of Nissan, its troubles seemed to be over, but early in 1997 vandals attacked the Vickers Valetta and it was burnt out. The need to preserve more than one example of an aircraft was highlighted once again, as the RAF's medium transport of the 1950s was down to just two examples, at Flixton and at Cosford.

Three examples of the Valetta's heavy counterpart, the Blackburn Beverley, had been preserved, apparently securely, at the RAF Museum, Hendon, the Historic Aircraft Museum, Southend, and at the Museum of Army Transport at Beverley, near Hull. To the horror of the aircraft-preservation movement, the Hendon and Southend Beverleys had been broken up for scrap, but at least there was another example of the breed securely preserved in Yorkshire in a major museum, with the backing and financial support of the local council and the help of the Beverley Association. In January 1997, however, it became clear that the Museum of Army Transport was in desperate financial straits and, with no more financial help forthcoming from the council, it was forced to close. It became very likely that avaricious scrapmen would descend on the last Blackburn Beverley in the world, but the Beverley was saved when local businessman Alan Bushell took control of the museum, and was able to re-open it later in the year.

VARYING DEVELOPMENTS

On 1 August 1997 Duxford's American Air Museum was opened by the Queen. A building worthy of the twenty-first century had been created to commemorate American air power's military assistance to Europe through two world wars and the Cold War – in other words, for much of the twentieth century. The ceremony was backed up by flypasts and displays by some of the warbirds based at Duxford, the B-17 'Sally B', two Mustangs and a Thunderbolt. These were then followed by a thunderous pass by four F.15Es from USAF Lakenheath, illustrating America's continued commitment to NATO and the defence of Europe.

The building was heavily funded by the National Lottery Heritage Fund, a source of financing that has had a dramatic effect on the preservation, restoration and exhibition of aircraft throughout Britain. Other museums to benefit have included the Yorkshire Air Museum at Elvington, and the RAF Museums at Hendon and Cosford. The latter was able to build a visitor centre, providing a new entrance, shop, café and conference facilities.

The growth of the museum at Cosford was somewhat haphazard. One of the few RAF stations with a secure future, as the only home of technical training in the service, it was almost the only RAF facility that was actually expanding during the late 1990s. The demand for building space and land was of necessity in conflict with the needs of the museum. It would probably have been better if the RAF Museum's second site had been located on an abandoned RAF airfield, perhaps one of particular importance, such as the Imperial War Museum's home at Duxford. Cosford's museum simply carried on growing, and in the end became too big to move, especially in view of the many British Airways airliners preserved there (in itself an odd choice of location).

Aircraft museums come into being in many different ways. In 1996, the Island Aeroplane Company Museum appeared on the Isle of Wight in a way that had never been seen before – it was imported in its entirety from abroad when Josef Koch, vintage aircraft collector and operator, brought sixteen of his aircraft from Germany to a new purpose-built facility at Sandown airport. The whole history of aviation was represented, from a Blériot replica to aircraft from post-war days.

The museum operated for less than two years before Koch removed most of his aircraft, but the site was taken over by three enthusiasts, Mark Kirby, John Tinckner and Steve Vizard, who re-opened it as the Front Line Aviation Museum. It housed some of Koch's aircraft, some other aircraft that had been loaned to Koch's museum, and new exhibits, not just aircraft, but also a large display of aviation-archaeology items collected by Vizard over many years. Sadly, this valiant attempt to resurrect the museum was itself doomed to failure.

The private collector is an increasingly visible feature of the preservation movement, often with a collection of artefacts and just one aircraft, or more often a cockpit, the pride and joy of the individual enthusiast. Collectors often enjoy their hobby by themselves, deriving their satisfaction from initiating and completing a restoration or collection. Others start with membership of a preservation group, which gives them the confidence to take on their own project.

After six years of helping, as a member of the Boulton Paul Association, to restore the cockpit of Balliol WN149, and learning a certain amount about metal aircraft structures in the process, the opportunity arose for me to acquire a wooden aircraft, the fuselage of a Slingsby Cadet TX.1 glider. The fuselage was broken in two and had been stripped of parts and my offer of £100 was accepted. I then acquired an 80 per cent share in Canberra T.17 WJ576 from Tom Atkinson and moved it to Wolverhampton. In the week it arrived I bought the fuselage of an Antonov An-2 from a Coseley scrapman, and suddenly I had my very own aircraft collection. I decided to name it the Black Country Aircraft Collection.

Other groups in Britain holding single examples of aircraft or cockpits include the ATC squadrons (and Air Scout troops), which look after nearly fifty such aircraft or cockpits, representing a sizeable pool of vintage aircraft, although of a relatively limited number of types. In most cases these aircraft belong to the Royal Air Force and are 'fathered' by the nearest RAF station, but this arrangement is sometimes seen as too confining by some ATC squadrons, which have acquired their own aircraft.

Peter Alcock and Vaughan Meers of No.196 (Walsall) Squadron wanted a cockpit of their own so that they and their cadets could enjoy hands-on restoration. They tracked down a Jet Provost, XR662, in Bicester, whose owner said they could cut the cockpit off. They hated to do that, so they bit the bullet and took the whole aircraft. Aware of the huge difference between keeping a cockpit, which can usually be housed inside, and a complete aircraft, which usually has to be kept outdoors, exposed to the weather and the local vandals, they negotiated with the Boulton Paul Association to keep the JP at the BPA's Heritage Project in Wolverhampton. Although the JP's Dowty undercarriage was the only tenuous connection with Dowty Boulton Paul, it was seen as an instant added attraction for BPA's open days.

The cadets were able to help with the aircraft's restoration to display condition, learning a great deal about the innards of a modern aircraft in the process. The connection with the ATC was to be further cemented with the acquisition of a number of gliders from various sources, resulting in the finest collection of Slingsby's ATC gliders anywhere.

CHAPTER 21

Where Next?

IF the 1900s were the century of the aeroplane, aircraft preservation and restoration represented a phenomenon that existed only in the last forty years of that century. In the 1950s, there were only two museums in Britain that were open to the public displaying aircraft, the Science Museum and the Imperial War Museum (although the Air Historical Branch/RAF possessed a large but scattered collection often to be seen on RAF station open days). Today, there are more than fifty museums open on a regular basis with more than two aircraft on display, and four times that number of organizations concerned with aircraft preservation and restoration, from warbird operators to tiny amateur groups. Added to these is an unknown number of individual collectors.

There are several major national aircraft museums, of which Duxford is by far the biggest; indeed, it is probably the most impressive centre of aircraft preservation in the world. The Royal Air Force's two major museums, at Hendon and Cosford, are also among the best in the world, and the Science Museum's store at Wroughton has the potential to join them, especially if the National Aeronautical Collection in its attic in South Kensington were to be moved there. Other national museums of importance include the Fleet Air Arm Museum, the Museum of Army Flying, the Museum of Flight at East Fortune, and the Manchester Air & Space Museum.

Over the thirty-plus years it has been operating, the amateur preservation movement has created several sizeable regional aircraft museums, operating in a professional manner. The Newark Air Museum, the Midland Air Museum, the de Havilland Aircraft Museum, the International Helicopter Museum, the Yorkshire Air Museum, the Norfolk and Suffolk Aircraft Museum, Bruntingthorpe, and the North East Aircraft Museum all have twenty or more aircraft on display. All have large exhibition halls or hangars, to house many of them. In addition, there is the unique institution that is the Shuttleworth Trust.

The amateurs sustain many smaller museums, some of which might well one day join the ranks of their bigger brethren. The first of these in the new century appears to be the South Yorkshire Aviation Museum, based for many years at Home Farm, Firbeck (although it first opened its doors at Nostell Priory in 1976). In 1999 it signed the lease on a substantial tract of land on the former RAF Doncaster site, which included a Bellman hangar, workshop and two wooden buildings. Once this site was refurbished, and the museum's large collection of aircraft had been moved in, SYAM had the potential of rivalling the Elvington Museum north of the Humber. It soon acquired the new name of Aeroventure, to reflect its new circumstances.

The Ulster Aviation Heritage Centre at Langford Lodge also has all the ingredients to become a large permanent aircraft museum. Although its collection of aircraft is quite small, with just a Vampire T.11, Buccaneer, Sea Hawk, Short SD.330, Chargus hang-glider, Lavery Sea Hawker and, the jewel in its crown, the Wildcat restoration, it also has a hangar and two other buildings on an airfield site. Its only competition in the province is the Ulster Folk and Transport Museum, which keeps most of its aircraft in store.

The proliferation of small museums and organizations has been criticized, but it does tap into a demand from enthusiasts who wish to become involved in the preservation and restoration of aircraft close to home. There are a number of people who might otherwise be lost to the preservation movement because of the travelling involved. My own case is a prime example. I was a member of the Midland Air Museum for twenty-two years, but I lived too far away to become actively involved in hands-on aircraft preservation. Cosford was only 5 miles down the road, but I lacked the skills to be let loose on their precious aircraft. Helping to create the Boulton Paul Association just round the corner from my own house not only drew me and about twenty other people into regular participation in the movement, it also created a particular niche in the preservation of the history of one company.

Even today, following all the expansion, there are some areas of British aviation history that remain more or less ignored by existing groups, from particular manufacturers to post-war light aircraft. Where are the Cessna/Piper/Beech/Beagle light aircraft on display? These are the most common types in the skies of Britain over the last forty years, and therefore arguably the most important, so why are they not interesting amateur groups?

Strangely, the preservation of large civil aircraft, namely airliners, does not seem so much of a problem, with four substantial collections at Duxford, Cosford, Brooklands and Wroughton, and quite a number of other examples at places such as Woodley and Kemble. With the help of a friendly airline that is willing to donate a time-expired airliner to a museum with a suitable runway, in return for having its colours preserved on display for the museum's visitors, their acquisition is fairly straightforward. It also gives a museum a substantial instant exhibit, into which its visitors can climb.

Even so, the preservation of military aircraft over the years has been disproportionate compared with civil aircraft; where owners have had a choice of authentic military and civil schemes for their vintage aircraft, it is usually the roundels that have won the day. In 1999 BPAC hosted a conference, at Cosford's new conference centre, entitled 'G-DASH', to discuss the problems of preserving the civil side of aviation, and perhaps to redress the balance a little. The problems were brought to everyone's attention, but no solutions were forthcoming.

The development of small museums, often with only two or three aircraft, will inevitably continue. Small groups or individuals feel the need to place their restoration work on display for others to enjoy, thereby also bringing in a small source of income to help them widen their collection. Aircraft-archaeology groups are often involved in such activities, working for years to build up displays of the artefacts found in the ground, and keenly putting them on display, especially where there are strong local connections.

After the initial displays, it is a natural progression to want to include more complete chunks of aircraft on display, perhaps cockpits, or even complete aircraft. The Shropshire Warplane Aircraft Recovery Group first set up a museum in two small buildings on High Ercall airfield in 1996. It moved to larger accommodation at Sleap in 1999, operating from two wooden huts, one of which was also in use by the local flying club. Member Keith Jones placed his full-size fibreglass Spitfire (with original cockpit parts) on loan, and another member, Roger Marley, loaned his Hawker Hunter cockpit. These two also took on loan a full-size model of a Hawker Fury that had been on display at Cosford, keeping it in the blister hangar at Sleap and bringing it out when the museum was open at weekends.

Little museums such as this have come and gone in the past, as the initial enthusiasm of setting them up is replaced by the weekly grind of keeping them going, but sometimes they prosper. The excellent Tangmere Military Aircraft Museum, for example, began in two wooden huts displaying aircraft wreckology items. Indeed, the aircraft-preservation movement as a whole is an organic movement with a few permanent physical certainties, such as the RAF Museum and Duxford, and a greater number of organizations with a less certain future. Sometimes its hard to predict which aircraft museums and preservation groups will survive and which will wither on the vine.

For example, creating a volunteer museum on a busy airfield site might seem a recipe for success, with active runways on which to deliver aircraft and aircraft enthusiasts drawn there anyway to watch the flying. However, although the Midland Air Museum prospered at Coventry, as did the Aeropark at the East Midlands Airport, the Wales Aircraft Museum folded at Rhoose, Skyfame did not survive at Staverton, and neither did the Historic Aircraft Museum at Southend.

On the other hand, a group occupying a less-used or deserted airfield site, without the commercial pressures of a busier airfield, is no more likely to succeed. For example, Elvington and Newark have grown and achieved national recognition, while the Stratford Aircraft Museum faded away.

The Torbay Aircraft Museum in a rural non-airfield location did not last the course, but the Mosquito Aircraft Museum (now the de Havilland Aircraft

Museum) and Flixton developed into fine regional museums. The Aeroplane Collection failed in its location attached to a garden centre, but Fenland prospered in a similar situation.

So, why should one succeed, and another fail? Luck plays its part, of course. Sometimes, bad fortune overtakes a museum venture, like the sudden rent rise that killed Skyfame, while a sudden dose of good luck, such as the large donation by the West Midlands County Council to the Midland Air Museum, can save an ailing project.

However, there is more to it than that. The personalities of the volunteers involved is an important consideration, particularly those who find themselves running the show. Very often, committee members who are in at the very start remain there for a long time. It is vital that they have a clear idea of where the group should go, sensible ideas about how to get there, and the ability to persuade others to work towards that eventual aim.

It helps a lot if a group concentrates on the aviation history of its local area – perhaps a particular aircraft manufacturer, a local airfield, or a unit that flew from there. Groups that simply collect a few assorted aircraft of no real relevance to their area have almost always failed. Local tie-ins are more likely to elicit assistance from local councils, local companies and local people. If other interested groups, such as veterans' associations, can also be linked with a venture, there is further cause for optimism about its future. Yorkshire Air Museum, for example, has established strong links with the French, because of the two Free French squadrons that flew from Elvington during the war, and with the Canadians who flew from Yorkshire as a whole. They also attract veteran air gunners, to an air-gunners' museum within the site, as well as Halifax Association members. Collecting special-interest groups to a museum brings a plethora of special events, reunions and practical help.

If the creation of an aircraft museum is the ultimate aim of a group, rather than just the restoration of aircraft, perhaps for other museums (as at the Northern Aeroplane Workshops or the Cotswold Aircraft Restoration Group), it goes without saying that a secure, sensibly located site is vital. A group that relies for its premises on the goodwill of a commercial company, such as an airfield operator, is living on a knife edge. The rug can be pulled out from under any operation, at any time, unless some real benefit is perceived. Only the ownership of the freehold of a site, or a very long lease, is any security at all, at the same time allowing the development of that site with the construction of new buildings or the restoration of old ones.

The Lincolnshire Aircraft Museum, itself born from the demise of a previous volunteer group, had a lease on its site at Tattershall, and put a great deal of work into creating a very pleasant aircraft museum. When the lease ran out however, the writing was on the wall.

It is also clearly important for a group to become as professional as possible as quickly as possible. Becoming a limited company and either a registered charity or a non-profit-making trust not only gives the outside world a good impression, but makes sure the group has to operate on strictly professional lines. Formal committee meetings, with regular financial reports, may not be to the taste of many enthusiasts, but they are inevitable and necessary. Professionalism should also extend to the appearance of a museum. A display that looks tatty and disorganized will not create a favourable impression. A lick of paint (on buildings and exhibits) and cutting the grass can make a world of difference. As has been proven, the ambience of a museum is more likely to attract people back than new exhibits.

This is not to say that exhibits are not important. It helps immensely to have at least one jewel in the crown – for example, the Halifax at Elvington or the Lancaster at East Kirkby. The title of this book refers to the fact that there are ten museums in Britain that exhibit both a Vampire and a Flea, and three times as many that have one or the other. Having only a de Havilland Vampire T.11 and a Mignet HM.14 Flying Flea in a collection is not a bad way to illustrate part of the history of aviation, aircraft constructional techniques and the principles of flight, but aircraft museums usually do need something more than Vampires and Fleas.

British Aircraft Preservation Council Members and Museums

THE BAPC membership includes voluntary groups, commercial organizations, and national and municipal museums. Not all are directly involved with aircraft preservation. Over fifty feature museums at which one or more aircraft are on display. Some of these museums are open seven days a week, others at weekends, or even more infrequently, and some strictly by prior appointment only.

Aces High Flying Museum
Hangar 4, North Weald Airfield, Epping, Essex CM16 6AA,
01992 522949
Admission by prior permission only.
A commercial organization without voluntary element.

Aerial Application Collection
Bill Taylor, Fieldhouse, Eaudykes, Friskney, Boston, Lincs PE22 8RT,
01754 820202
Admission by prior permission only.
A private collection and archive relating to aerial spraying.

The Aeroplane Collection
12 Warren Hay, Wirral, Cheshire CH63 9TL
The oldest voluntary preservation organization, with airframes at Hooton Park, Manchester Museum of Science and Industry and elsewhere.

AeroVenture
Sandy Lane, Doncaster DN4 5EP,
01302 761616
Admission Thurs–Sun, 10am–5pm
Run by the voluntary South Yorkshire Aviation Museum.

Air-Britain (Historians) Ltd
James Halley, 5 Walnut Tree Road, Shepperton, Middlesex TW17 0RW
An organization for aircraft enthusiasts and serious historians alike, without active restoration involvement.

Aircraft Preservation Society of Scotland
Roy Corser, Museum of Flight, East Fortune Airfield, North Berwick,
East Lothian EH39 5LF
A voluntary group supporting the work of the museum.

Airfield Research Group
Peter Homer, 12 Trident Close, Walmley, Sutton Coldfield B76 1LF,
0121 3513035
Group of historians concerned with airfield history.

Airship Heritage Trust
Gp Capt P.A. Garth, 5 Orchard Lane, Brampton, Huntingdon PE1 8TF,
01480 457851
Voluntary group preserving artefacts and archives relevant to British airships.

Air Atlantique Historic Flight
Bob Pritchard, Hangar 5, Coventry Airport, CV8 3AZ,
01203 370566
Admission by prior permission only. Commercial organization.

Avro Heritage Society
Avro International, Chester Road, Woodford, Cheshire SK7 1QR,
0161 4305050
Not open to the public.
Voluntary element largely limited to employees and former employees.

Barton Aviation Heritage Society
Pennington Hangar, Barton Airport, Eccles, Manchester M30 7SA
Admission Sat–Sun 10am–5pm.
A visitor centre operated by a voluntary group.

Battle of Britain Memorial Flight
Visitors' Centre, RAF Coningsby, Horncastle, Lincs S81 9HJ,
01526 344041
Admission Mon–Fri except bank holidays, 10am–4.30pm.
Aircraft of the Flight may be away at displays even on weekdays.
No voluntary element in the restoration and operation of the Flight's aircraft.

Blyth Valley Aviation Collection
Cliff Aldred, Vulcans End, Mells Road, Walpole, Halesworth IP19 0PL,
01986 784436
Admission by prior permission only.
Restoring and collecting mainly aircraft cockpits; volunteers welcome.

Bomber County Aviation Museum
Martin Chiappini, 10a Partridge Drive, Rothwell, Lincs LN7 6BH
Admission Sun and bank holidays 11am–6pm.
At other times by prior appointment.
An aircraft museum devoted to the history of aviation in Lincolnshire; volunteers always welcome for all roles.

Boulton Paul Association
Chairman: Cyril Plimmer, 25d Bilbrook Road, Bilbrook,
Wolverhampton WV8 1EU, 01902 843118
Curator: Alec Brew, 35 Blakeley Avenue, Wolverhampton WV6 9HR,
01902 759696, email Alecbrew@aol.com
Admission Every Sunday 10am–4pm, and every Wed and Fri afternoon
2pm–5pm.
Operates the Boulton Paul Aircraft Heritage Project at Smiths Aerospace,
Wolverhampton. Volunteers of any skill level always welcome.

Bournemouth Aviation Museum
Hangar 600, Bournemouth Airport, Christchurch, Dorset BH23 6SE,
01202 580858, www.aviation-museum.co.uk
Admission daily Apr–Sept, 10am–5pm, winter 10am–4pm.

Brenzett Aeronautical Museum Trust
Ivychurch Road, Brenzett, Romney Marsh, Kent TN29 0EE, 01797 344747
Secretary: A.J. Moor, 190 Hythe Road, Willesborough, Ashford, Kent
01233 627911
Admission Sat and Sun from Easter to end of Oct, plus bank holidays
11am–5.30pm. Also July to end of Sept, Wed, Thurs, Fri, 11am–5.30pm.
Voluntary organization displaying aviation items of local interest. Volunteers
always welcome.

Bristol Aero Collection
A1 Hangar, Kemble Airfield, Cirencester, Glos GL7 6BA, 01285 771204,
www.bristolaero.com
Admission Easter and every Sun mid-April to October, 10am to 4pm.
Voluntary organization dedicated to the preservation of aircraft relevant to
Bristol, and linked with the Britannia Preservation Trust.

British Aerial Museum of Flying Aircraft
Graham Warner, Building 66, Duxford Airfield, Cambs CB2 4QS
Admission: *see* Imperial War Museum, Duxford.
Collection of flying aircraft operated in conjunction with the Aircraft
Restoration Co (ARCo).

British Aerospace North West Heritage Group
Geoff Ainsworth, 3 Kingsway Avenue, Broughton, Preston, Lancs
PR3 5JN, 01772 864469
Admission by prior permission only.
Voluntary preservation group operating within the former English Electric
factory.

British Aviation Heritage
Peter Harper, 39 Breycote, Shortstown, Beds MH24 0XD,
01234 742468
Admission every Sun 10am–4pm.
Operator of Bruntingthorpe airfield, which houses several vintage-aircraft
groups.

British Balloon Museum and Library
Norman Pritchard (Secretary), 75 Albany Road, Old Windsor,
Berks SL4 2QD,
01753 862977, email 101364.1534@compuserve.com
Not open to the public.
Collection and restoration of artefacts and documents relevant to the history
of ballooning.

Brooklands Museum Trust
Julian C. Temple (Curator of Aviation), Brooklands Museum,
Brooklands Road, Weybridge, Surrey KT13 0QN,
01932 857381, email brooklands@dial.pipex.com
Admission Easter–Oct, Tues–Sun, 10am–5pm; winter, 10am–4pm.
A large voluntary group supports the work of the Trust.

Buccaneer Preservation Society
Broderick Kelly, 47 Freshwell Gardens, West Horndon, Essex CM13 3NE,
01277 8325400
For enthusiasts of all things 'Buc'.

Canadian Aeronautical Preservation Association
R. J. McClure (President), 5112-52 Avenue, Stony Plain,
Alberta, Canada, T7Z 1C1

Catford Independent Air Force
Alan Partington, 100 Culveley Road, Catford, London SE6 2JY,
020 8697 6929
Private collection.

Chiltern Aviation Society
Keith Hayward (Chairman), 52 Pinn Way, Ruislip, Middlesex HA4 7QF,
01895 637872
Local aviation interest group.

City of Norwich Aviation Museum
Kelvin Sloper, Old Norwich Road, Horsham St Faith, Norwich,
Norfolk NR10 3JF, 01603 625309 (home)
Admission Jan–Mar, Nov–Dec, Sun noon–4pm, Wed 10am–4pm;
summer Sun noon–5pm, Tue–Sat 10am–5pm. Also bank holidays.
Voluntary group-operated museum.

Computair Consultants
Jeremy Parkin, 24 Staniland Drive, Weybridge, Surrey KT13 0XN,
01932 821106, email 100070.2607@compuserve.com
Private collection of helicopter artefacts and archives.

Cotswold Aircraft Restoration Group
Steve Thompson (Secretary), 'Kia-ora', Risbury, Nr Leominster,
Herefordshire HR6 0NQ, 01568 760371
Admission by prior appointment only.
Voluntary group famous for restoring other groups' aircraft.

Croydon Airport Society
Margaret White, 38 Long Walk, Tattenham Corner, Epsom, Surrey KT18 5TW,
020 8253 1009, www.croydon.gov.uk/airport-soc/
Admission first Sun of each month 11am to 4pm.
Support for the Croydon Airport visitors' centre, at Airport House, Purley
Way, Croydon.

De Havilland Heritage Museum
PO Box 107, Salisbury Hall, London Colney, St Albans, Herts AL2 1BU,
01727 822051, www.dehavillandmuseum.co.uk
Admission first Sun of Mar to last Sun of Oct Tue, Thurs and Sat, 2pm to
5.30pm, Sun and bank holidays 10.30am–5.30pm.
Volunteer-run museum.

Derby Industrial Museum
Roger Shelley (Senior Keeper of Industry and Technology),
The Old Silk Mill, off Full Street, Derby, DE1 4AR,
01332 255308, www.derby.gov.uk/museums
Admission Mon, 11am–5pm; Tues–Sat, 10am–5pm; Sun/bank holidays, 2–5pm.
Large collection of Rolls-Royce aero-engines; *see* Rolls-Royce Heritage Trust.

Derby Historical Aviation Society
W.A. Harrison, 71 Mill Hill Lane, Derby DE23 6SB,
email williamharrison@netscapeonline.co.uk
Voluntary society supporting the work of the Derby Industrial Museum.

Dick Melton Aviation
Repps Mill House, Martham, Great Yarmouth, NR29 4RB
Walrus restorer.

Douglas Boston-Havoc Preservation Trust
Richard Nutt, 17 Hinckley Road, Barwell, Leics LE9 8DL,
01455 845517
Boston restoration team.

Dumfries and Galloway Aviation Museum
Enterprise Park, Dumfries
David Reid (Chairman), 11 Ninian Court, Lockside, Dumfries DG2 9PS,
01387 259546, email david-reid-50@hotmail.com
Admission Easter–Oct Sat and Sun 10am–5pm,
Wed 6pm–9pm Jun–Aug.
Volunteer-operated museum. Volunteers and visitors always welcome.

Dundonald Aviation Visitors Centre
Frasers Garden Centre, The Crossroads, Dundonald, Ayrshire KA2 9BT,
01563 850215
John Hunter (Chairman), 62 McKinlay Crescent, Irvine KA12 8DW,
01294 312693
Admission weekends 9am–5pm.
Volunteer-run museum within garden centre.

Duxford Aviation Society
Trevor W. Scarr, Duxford Airfield, Cambs CB2 4QR,
01223 835593
Admission: *see* Imperial War Museum, Duxford.
Voluntary society working at Duxford, with its own collection of airliners.

East Anglian Aviation Society
Mike Killespy (Secretary), 3 Sainfoan Close, Sawston, Cambs CB2 4JY,
01223 562564
Admission by prior appointment only.
Society for aviation enthusiasts who run a museum in Bassingbourn
Barracks.

Fenland and West Norfolk Aviation Preservation Society
Bambers Garden Centre, Old Lynn Road, West Walton Highway,
Wisbech, Norfolk
Murray Flint (Chairman), Broadmeadows, Chalk Road, Walpole St Andrew,
Wisbech, Cambs PE14 7PN
Admission Mar to Oct weekends and bank holidays, 9.30pm–5pm.
Volunteer-run museum attached to a garden centre.

Fleet Air Arm Museum
RNAS Yeovilton, Ilchester, Somerset BA22 8HT,
01935 840565
Admission every day except Christmas, Apr–Oct, 10am–5.30pm,
winter 10am–4.30pm
Fine museum supported by a voluntary Friends of the Fleet Air Arm
Museum.

The Fresson Trust
Secretary, Head Office, Highlands and Islands Airport Ltd,
Inverness Airport, Inverness IV1 2JU,
01667 462445

Friends of the DC-3
John Woods, 3 Dalcross, Crown Wood, Bracknell, Berks RG12 3UJ,
01344 56774

Gatwick Aviation Museum
Lowfield Heath Road, Charlwood, Surrey RH6 0BT, 01293 862915,
email gpvgat@aol.com, www.gatwick-aviation-museum.co.uk
Open selected summer Sundays, 10am–4pm (*see* web site for dates).
Private aircraft museum.

Gosport Aviation Society
Ron Jones (Chairman), Priddy's Yard, Gosport, Hants PO12 4LE

The Griffin Trust
Hooton Park Exhibition Centre, North Road, Ellesmere Port,
South Wirral L65 1BQ, 0151 3502598
Admission by prior permission only, plus occasional open days.
Voluntary organization preserving the history of Hooton Park Airfield.

The Grimsby and Cleethorpes Aircraft Preservation Group
31 Montgomery Road, Cleethorpes, NE Lincs DN35 9JE,
01472 696344

Handley Page Association
Brian Bowen, 77 Bowershott, Letchworth, Herts SG6 2EU,
01462 679112

Harrington Aviation Museum
43 Greenhill Road, Kettering, Northants NN15 7LP,
01536 519272
Admission Easter–Oct weekends and bank holidays 10am–5pm.
Voluntary group operating the Carpetbaggers Aviation Museum at the former
Harrington airfield.

The Herald Society
269 Wykeham Road, Reading, Berks RG6 1PL,
0118 9699296, email snqfree@reading.ac.uk
Admission: *see* Berkshire Aviation Museum.
Voluntary group preserving Herald G-APWA at Woodley.

Historical Radar Archive
Sqn Ldr Mike Dean, Little Garth, High Street, Scampton, Lincs LN1 2SD,
01522 730338

Imperial War Museum
Duxford Airfield, Cambs CB2 4QR,
01223 835000
Admission daily except Dec 24–25 and New Years Day,
Apr–Oct 10am–6pm, winter 10am–4pm.

International Friends of the DH.89
Graham Simons, 67 Pyhill, Bretton, Peterborough, PE3 8QQ,
01733 256123

International Helicopter Museum
Weston Heliport, Locking Moor Road, Weston-super-Mare, Somerset,
01934 635227
Admission Nov–Mar, Wed–Sun, 10am–4pm,
Apr–Oct, Wed–Sun, 10am–6pm.
Major helicopter museum with a substantial volunteer element in the Friends
of the Helicopter Museum.

The Jet Age Museum
John Lewer, 40 Sutton Park Rise, Kidderminster, Worcs DY11 7NQ,
01562 515994
Voluntary-run collection currently in store awaiting new premises.

The Jet Aviation Preservation Group
Stuart Holder, 62 Avon Street, Evesham, Worcs WR11 4LG,
01386 765994
Admission by prior appoinment only.
Small voluntary group with a collection of aircraft at Long Marston,
Warwickshire.

LAASI International
D.R. Johnston, 52 Oak Road, Caterham, Surrey CR3 5TS,
01883 347801
Huge aviation enthusiasts society.

Lashenden Air Warfare Museum
Headcorn Airfield, Headcorn, Ashford, Kent TN27 9HX
Trevor Matthews (Secretary) 01622 890236
Admission Sun and bank holidays, 10.30am–6pm,
Easter–end Oct, 10.30am–3.30pm winter.
Voluntary group running a museum on Kentish aviation.

Leicester Museum of Technology
Peter Stoddart BA, 30 Rushton Drive, Leicester LE2 9HX,
0116 2775932

Lightning Association
Charles M. Ross, Secretary, Binbrook Airfield, Lincs LN3 6HF,
01472 398594
Admission by prior permission only.
Lightning enthusiasts who preserve XR724.

Lightning Preservation Group
R. Tuck (Secretary), 95 Thornhill, North Weald, Essex CM16 6DP,
01992 522047
Admission: *see* British Aviation Heritage.
Lightning enthusiats who preserve two aircraft at Bruntingthorpe, Leics.

Lincolnshire Aircraft Preservation Society
Graham Chaters (Secretary), 154 Park Street, Grimsby, S. Humbs
DN32 7NS, 01472 311210
Admission Easter–Oct, Mon–Sat 9.30am–5pm,
winter 10am–4.30pm. NB not open Sun.
Voluntary restoration of the Hampden and Proctor at East Kirkby.

Lincolnshire Aircraft Recovery Group
Dave Stubley, 13 Granville Avenue, Wyberton, Boston, Lincs PE21 7BY,
01205 369594
Admission: *see* Lincolnshire Aircraft Preservation Society.
Aircraft-archaeology group with recovered items on display at East Kirkby.

Lincolnshire's Lancaster Association
John Ball, 31 Knaton Road, Carlton in Lindrick, Worksop, Notts,
01909 732255
Support group for the Battle of Britain Memorial Flight.

Manchester Airport Archive
Patsy McClements, Archivist, Manchester Airport, Manchester M22 5PA,
0161 4893668

Medway Aircraft Preservation Society
AFIS Unit, Rochester Airport, Maidstone Rd, Chatham, Kent ME5 9TX,
01634 816492
Lewis Deal, 15 Amethyst Ave, Chatham, Kent,
01634 65028
Voluntary society restoring aircraft for other museums.

Midland Air Museum
Dianne James (Manager), Coventry Airport, Baginton,
Coventry CV8 3AZ, 01203 301033,
email midlandairmuseum@aol.com, www.midlandairmuseum.org.uk
Admission Apr–Oct, Mon–Sat 10am–5pm, Sun and bank holidays 10am–6pm,
winter 10am–4.30pm, closed Christmas and Boxing Days.
Voluntary-run museum.

Midland Warplane Museum
M.J. Evans (Secretary), 46 Arthur Street, Kenilworth, Warks CV8 2HE,
01926 522264, email mwm@couplandbell.com
Admission by prior appointment only.
Voluntary group.

The Miles Aircraft Collection
Peter Amos (Secretary), 4 Castle Bungalows, Storrington, Nr Pulborough,
West Sussex RH20 4LB,
01903 893444, email tkhome@ndirect.co.uk
Private collection not available for inspection.

MM Aviation
Michael Coghlan, 9 Park Hill, Charlton Marshall, Blandford,
Dorset DT11 9NE, 01258 455664

Montrose Aerodrome Museum Society
Waldron Road, North Montrose
P. Davies, 7 Lunan Ave, Montrose, Angus DD10 29DG,
01674 674210, email 106212.152@compuserve.com
Admission Sun noon5pm.
Voluntary-run museum.

Museum of Army Flying
Middle Wallop, Stockbridge, Hants SO20 8DY,
email daa@flying-museum.org.uk, www.flying-museum.org.uk
Admission daily 10am–4.30pm.
Official museum of Army aviation.

The Museum of Berkshire Aviation
Mohawk Way, off Bader Way, Woodley, Reading, Berks RG5 4UF,
01734 340712
Ken Foteskew (Curator), 45 Malvern Way, Twyford, Berks RG10 9PY,
0118 9340712
Admission weekends and bank holidays, Mar–Oct 10.30am–5pm.
During May–July also open Wed 11.30am–4pm, winter noon–4pm.
Voluntary-run museum, incorporating the Herald Society. Volunteers always
welcome.

Museum of Flight
East Fortune Airfield, East Lothian EH39 5LF,
01620 880308,
email Museum_of_flight@sol.co.uk, www.nms.ac.uk/flight
Admission daily except Christmas and New Year, 10.30am– 5.00pm.
Weekdays only Oct–Mar.
National aviation museum of Scotland supported by the voluntary Aviation
Preservation Society of Scotland.

Museum of Science and Industry in Manchester
Liverpool Road, Castlefield, Manchester M3 4JP,
0161 8322244,
email n.forder@msim.org.uk, www.msim.org.uk
Admission daily, 10am–5pm, except Dec 23–25.
Municipal museum heavily supported by the voluntary Aeroplane Collection,
and the Friends of the Museum.

Napier Power Heritage Trust
Mike Chowdry, 20 Heather Grove, Hartley Wintney,
Basingstoke, Hants RG27 8SE,
01252 843859
Volunteer group preserving the history of D. Napier & Co.

Newark Air Museum
The Airfield, Winthorpe, Newark, Notts NG24 2NY,
01636 707170,
email newarkair@lineone.net, www.newarkairmuseum.co.uk
Howard Heeley (Secretary), 4 Winterton Close, Woodthorpe View, Arnold,
Nottingham NG5 6PZ,
0115 9201536

Night-Fighter Preservation Team
Steve Hague, 197 Leeds Road, Kippax, Leeds, West Yorks LS25 7DZ,
0113 2865066
Admission: *see* Yorkshire Air Museum.
Voluntary group restoring and preserving Mosquito and Venom night-fighters
at Elvington.

Norfolk and Suffolk Aviation Museum
The Street, Flixton, Bungay, Suffolk NR35 1NZ,
01986 896644,
email nsam.flixton@virgin.net, www.aviation.museum.net
Admission Apr–Oct Sun–Thurs 10am–5pm,
winter Tue, Wed and Sun 10am–4pm.
Large volunteer-run aircraft museum.

Northampton Aviation Society
Mrs B. Reeves, 53 Palmerston Road, Northampton, Northants NN1 5EU,
01604 37043

North East Aircraft Museum
Old Washington Road, Sunderland SR5 3HZ,
0191 5190662,
email neam_uk@yahoo.com
Alex Murison (Secretary), 44 Tudor Road, Chester-le-Street, Co.
Durham DH3 3RY,
0191 3891702
Admission daily 10am–5pm, to sundown in winter.
Large voluntary-run aircraft museum.

North Weald Airfield Museum
Ad Astra House, Hurricane Way, North Weald Aerodrome,
Essex CM16 6AA,
email Arthur1@btinternet.com, www.fly.to/northweald
Admission Sat and Sun, noon–5pm.
Small, voluntary-run museum gem.

P.H.T. Green Collection
The Spinney, Irby-on-Humber, Grimsby, South Humberside DN37 7JR,
01472 371359
Private collection of aircraft photographs.

RAF Millom Museum
John Nixon (Secretary), HM Prison, Haverigg, Millom, Cumbria LA18 4NA,
01229 774284
Admission summer Sat–Mon, Wed, Fri, 10am–5pm; winter, Sun only.
Run by the South Copeland Aviation Group, in conjunction with the prison.

Real Aeroplane Company
The Aerodrome, Breighton, Selby, E. Yorks YO8 7DH,
01757 228838, www.realaero.aol.com
Nigel Ponsford (Manager), 94 Parkland Drive, Leeds LS6 4PT,
0113 2691564
Admission weekends and bank holidays 10am–4pm.
Working aerodrome with attached museum.

Restorations Unlimited
James Howley (Secretary), 1 Sheephouse Green, Wotton, Dorking,
Surrey RH5 6QW,
01306 886220.

Robertsbridge Aviation Society
Phillip Baldock, 53 Wannock Avenue, Willingdon, BN20 9RH,
01323 483845
Admission by prior appointment only.
Cockpit collection and museum run by volunteers.

Rolls-Royce Heritage Trust (Bristol Branch)
Peter Pavey, Whittle House Annexe, GP2-1, Rolls-Royce plc, PO Box 3,
Filton, Bristol,
0117 9564205
Admission by prior appoinment only.
Volunteers preserving history of Bristol and de Havilland aero-engines.

Rolls-Royce Heritage Trust, Derby and Hucknall and Coventry Branches
PO Box 31, Derby DE24 8BJ,
01332 249118,
email richard.haigh@rolls-royce.com
Admission by prior appointment only.
Voluntary groups preserving the history of Rolls-Royce and Armstrong-Siddeley aero-engines from a shared workshop.

RAF Museum, Cosford
Cosford, Shropshire TF11 8UP,
email cosford@rafmuseum.com, web www.rafmuseum.com
Admission daily 10am–4pm, except Christmas and New Year.
RAF's second museum, and conservation centre supported by volunteers, the Aerospace Museum Society.

RAF Museum, Hendon
Grahame Park Way, Hendon, London NW9 5LL,
020 8205 2266, www.rafmuseum.com
Admission daily 10am–6pm except Christmas and New Year.
Main RAF museum supported by the volunteers of the Friends of the RAF Museum.

The Science Museum
The National Aeronautial Collection, Exhibition Road, London SW7 2DD,
020 7942 4455, www.sciencemuseum.org.uk
Admission daily 10am–6pm.
Some of the most historic airframes preserved in the UK.

Second World War Aircraft Preservation Society
Lasham Aerodrome, Hants
Bob Coles, 8 Barracane Drive, Crowthorne, Berks RG45 7NU,
01344 774157
Admission Sun and bank holidays 10am–6pm, or sundown in winter.
Volunteer-run aircraft museum with post-war airframes.

The Shuttleworth Collection
Old Warden Aerodrome, Biggleswade, Bedfordshire SG18 9EP,
01767 627288, www.shuttleworth.org
Admission daily, April–Oct 10am–5 pm, winter 10am–4pm;
closed for 14 days around Christmas and New Year.
Delightful museum heavily supported by the voluntary Shuttleworth Veteran Aeroplane Society.

Skysport Engineering
Tim Moore, Rotary Farm, Thorncote Green, Hatch, Sandy, Beds SG19 1PU,
01767 627375
Admision strictly by prior appointment only.
Aircraft restoration company.

Solway Aviation Museum
Aviation House, Carlisle Airport, Crosby-on-Eden, Carlisle CA6 4NW,
01228 573823, email info@solway-aviation-museum.org.uk,
www.solway-aviation-museum.org.uk
Admission Mar–Oct Sun and bank holidays, Jun–Sept, Sat–Sun,
Jul–Aug Fri–Sun, 10am–5pm.
Expanding museum run by the former Solway Aviation Society.

Southampton Hall of Aviation
Albert Road South, Southampton, Hants SO1 1FR,
02380 635830,
email aviation@spitfireclub.com, www.spitfireonline.co.uk
Admission daily, except Mon and during Christmas, 10am–5pm;
Sun 2pm–5pm.
Excellent regional museum, which might soon move.

Southern Aviation Research Associates
Doug Revell, 26 The Brooklands, Wrea Green, Preston, Lancs, PR4 2NQ

Tangmere Military Aviation Museum
Tangmere Airfield, Chichester, PO20 6ES,
01243 775223,
email admin@tangmere-museum.org.uk, www.tangmere.org.uk
Admission daily 10am–5.30pm, Mar–Oct, winter 10am–4.30pm.
Closed Dec and Jan.
Fine volunteer-run museum.

Thorpe Camp Preservation Group
Mike Hodgson, Lancaster Farm, Tumby Woodside, Mareham-le-fen, Boston,
Lincs PE22 7SP,
01526 775223,
email mjhodgson@lancfile.demon.co.uk, www.thorpecamp.org.uk
Admission Sun and bank holidays, 2–5pm.
Voluntary group running the excellent Thorpe Camp Visitors' Centre at
Woodhall Spa, Lincs.

Ulster Aviation Society
Ray Burrows, 33 Old Mill Meadows, Dundonald, BT16 1WQ,
028 9445 4444, www.ulsteraviationsociety.co.uk
Admission Sat 1–6pm, Feb–Nov.
Voluntary group running the Ulster Aviation Heritage Centre at Langford
Lodge Airfield.

Ulster Folk and Transport Museum
John Moore, Cultra Manor, Hollywood, Co. Down BT18 0EW,
01232 428428, www.nidex.com/uftm
Admission daily except three days at Christmas; phone for current times.

Vulcan Restoration Trust
Richard Clarkson, 39 Breakspears Drive, St Paul's Cray, Orpington,
Essex BR5 2RX,
020 8309 1161, email Richard.Clarkson@avrovulcan.com,
www.avrovulcan.com
Occasional open and 'up-and-running days'.
Voluntary group preserving the Vulcan at Southend Airport.

Wellesbourne Aviation Group
Derek Powell, 167 Colebourne Road, Kings Heath, Birmingham B13 0HB,
email d-powell@iclway.co.uk
Admission Sun and bank holidays 10am–4pm.
Voluntary group running the delightful Wellesbourne Wartime Museum at
Wellesbourne Mountford airfield.

Wiltshire Historic Aviation Group
Tony Dyer, 8 Thurlow Close, Amesbury, Salisbury, Wilts SP4 7QG,
01980 625380
Admission strictly by prior arrangement only.
Voluntary group helping to create the Boscombe Down Museum project,
incorporating its Air Defence Collection.

Yorkshire Air Museum
Elvington, York YO41 4AU,
01904 608595, www.yorkshireairmuseum.co.uk
Admission weekdays 10.30am–4pm, weekends 10.30am–5pm,
late June–Sept, 10am–5pm.
Fine museum housing a number of voluntary groups.

APPENDIX II

A Flying Vickers Vimy

ONE of the most outstanding achievements of the amateur aircraft-preservation movement in Great Britain was the construction of a flying replica of Alcock and Brown's Vickers Vimy, to commemorate the fiftieth anniversary of the first non-stop transatlantic flight.

The team concerned had already built a flying replica of a Vickers Gun-Bus, to commemorate the 100th anniversary of the foundation of the Royal Aeronautical Society, in 1966. It had been built by the Weybridge branch of the society, and the type was chosen because of the local Vickers' connections, and its claim to be the first ever practical fighting aeroplane.

Assorted volunteers collected on 19 July 1965 at the Vintage Aircraft and Flying Association (Brooklands), and began to assess their resources. The group began with thirteen Air Board drawings of the Gun-Bus in the Science Museum, so a team of volunteers often had to work late into the evening to produce over 600 working drawings. The design team, led by Geoffrey Gregg, had to supervise the re-stressing of the entire airframe using traditional methods and formulae. The aircraft flew successfully, and eventually found its way to the RAF Museum, one of the founder exhibits at Hendon, where it has remained to this day.

When the decision was taken to build the Vimy it was quickly realized that the scale of the job, in comparison with the Gun-Bus, brought a whole new set of problems. The project would have to be run on almost professional lines. The British Aircraft Corporation loaned suitable premises within the former Vickers factory for after-hours work, as well as tools and other facilities. Late in the Vimy's construction, skilled men were also diverted from their normal work, so that the aircraft might be completed in time to be displayed at the Paris Air Show next to Concorde. One invaluable ally in the project was Sir Dermot Boyle, Vice-Chairman of BAC, and a trustee of the RAF Museum, where it was planned to display the replica after its flying life was over.

The Vimy had a head start on the Gun-Bus – around 150 drawings had been saved from the dustbin by some forward-thinking Vickers' employees. It was thought that only about 500 more would be needed, although in the event over 2,000 had to be produced. One another advantage brought to the project was the existence in the Weybridge area of a handful of survivors who had actually built Vimys, and were able to bring their expertise and inside knowledge to the construction of the replica.

A works sub-committee was formed out of the general committee of the association, the membership of which reached 800 by the time the project neared completion. Many of the other factories in the British Aircraft Corporation group formed branches of the association, including Hurn, Filton, Stevenage and Warton, but membership was not limited to BAC. There were also members who were employees of BEA and BOAC, the local Air Training Corps, Heathrow air-traffic controllers, technical college instructors, dental mechanics and even postmen.

One key to the whole project was the search for original Rolls-Royce Eagle engines. Eventually, a number were found in water-pumping stations in Holland. Some Eagle Mark IXs had been bought as war surplus engines to power standby pumps when the windmills were out of commission. It was found that the only difference from the Mark VIIIs fitted to the Vimy was the position of the induction manifold. Rolls-Royce apprentices at Derby took on the job of overhauling the two engines to flight standard.

The selection of timber for use in the airframe was entrusted to Vickers' establishment foreman carpenter, Stan Chidsey, who had been the chief timber expert at Weybridge when wooden airframes were still being built, and so was the ideal man for the job. To track down the many fittings that were required – electrical components, instruments, wiring, and so on – the Weybridge representative of Marshals of Cambridge took charge, and began badgering many companies in the aircraft industry. By the end of the project, over fifty firms had contributed items or services.

One of the biggest problems was the building of radiators for the engines. Over 6,000 thin-walled copper tubes were made by Imperial Metal Industries, each end-belled to a hexagon. These were then tightly packed into a matrix for each radiator, held in solely by friction as it was dipped in solder, which filled the gaps between the tubes by capillary action. The vintage-aircraft engineers who supervised this operation at Weybridge then held their collective breath as the radiators were air-pressure tested at five pounds per square inch in a water bath.

Despite an extensive search, suitable original propellers could not be found, so two of the four-blade units had to be made from scratch. One of the original Alcock and Brown propellers was on display in Terminal 3 at Heathrow, having been presented to the British Airports Authority by the Maxwell-Muller family. Percy Maxwell-Muller had been in charge of the working party in Newfoundland that had erected the Vimy for the transatlantic flight. He had been presented with it when new propellers were fitted to Alcock and Brown's Vimy for its display in the Science Museum; the originals had been damaged when the aircraft landed on its nose in an Irish bog.

Using the original propeller to provide data, blade profiles were drawn and then transferred to mahogany planks about an inch thick, eight for each propeller. These were then set up on stagger blocks to give the correct relationship to one another. Glue was applied to the mating surfaces, which were joined up to form the four-blade configuration. The whole assembly was clamped up and the glued-up propeller was then bored to take the hub. Rough shaping was done with an axe, then with a rabbet plane and spokeshave. It was finished off with a scraper and the propeller was then balanced on knife-edge pivots until the smallest touch could turn the unit on its shaft.

The huge voluntary input helped to keep the overall cost of the project within reasonable bounds, and further funding came from membership subscriptions, donations and small sponsorship deals. There was some urgency for the completion of the Vimy. It was due at the Paris Air Show on 6 June 1969 and immediately afterwards at the Alcock and Brown Commemorative Exhibition at Ringway, Manchester.

When the finished Vimy was wheeled out at Brooklands it brought the entire factory to a standstill, as everyone deserted their posts to watch. Sir Geoffrey Tuttle, director in charge of all air movements, ordered everyone back to their benches and desks, and the first flight took place quietly one evening. Only four days later, the Vimy successfully arrived in Paris, making the flight directly from RAF Odiham, but was only displayed at the back of a hangar. There had been the intention of flying it in the company of Concorde but the spectators were denied this magnificent sight; perhaps the French were reluctant to allow the British to steal any more that half the limelight.

The Vimy then made its way to Manchester, where, after only a total of eleven and a half hours of flight, disaster struck. After a month's display inside a nylon exhibition tent, it was removed on a very hot June day and, after standing in the sun for some time, suddenly caught fire. The combustion was thought to be related to a build-up of electrostatic energy while inside the tent, and the sun reflecting from the highly polished nacelles.

The limited company formed by the Veteran Aircraft & Flying Association to exploit the Vimy as an air-show attraction, possibly making it the centrepiece of a growing flying circus, had to be wound up. The aircraft was restored by BAC, but only to static exhibition standards, and it ended up going to the RAF Museum rather sooner than intended. Both the Vimy and its predecessor, the Gun-Bus, are now on display at Hendon.

The whole project was a magnificent achievement, and showed exactly what could be done by a well co-ordinated bunch of amateurs, especially when they had the backing of a large company. They had also completed the task just in time. A subsequent attempt to build a flying Vimy, to re-enact Ross and Keith Smith's pioneering flight from England to Australia, encountered different obstacles. Some constructional changes were made in the interests of safety (replacing wood with metal in the rear fuselage frame, the engine mountings and the interplane struts), in view of the distance of the flight, but there was no longer any hope of finding Rolls-Royce Eagles in a Dutch pumping station. The intention to use replicas of the original four-blade propellers, just like the Brooklands Vimy, ruled out the use of any modern aero-engine, which would have had to be geared down considerably. Even the 454cu in Chevrolet V8 automobile engines that were selected required a specially designed reduction gear, which ended up costing more than the engines.

New airworthiness requirements meant that the airframe had to be redrawn and re-stressed using a computer-aided design system. The 4,000-page document that resulted only served to show the quality of the job that the original Vickers' engineers had done in their first place, with their wooden slide rules and well-sharpened pencils. The crowded skies of 1995 also required a comprehensive fit of modern radio and navigation equipment, which would have been the main advantage the Smith brothers would have enjoyed if they had found themselves at the controls of the Californian Vimy.

A million pounds were spent on the 1995 replica, eclipsing the spending on the 1969 aircraft, not to mention the 1919 original. It went on to cover itself with glory on the flight to Australia, with only one engine failure over Indonesia, causing a moment of panic and a forced landing. With new BMW engines, the replica later re-created the flight of the Vimy 'Silver Queen' from England to South Africa, and racked up many hundreds of hours' flying time, many of them over England, a consolation for the Brooklands team, whose 1969 aircraft managed less than twelve.

The Black Country Aircraft Collection

FOLLOWING an early interest in aircraft preservation, I was a member of the Midland Air Museum for over twenty-two years, but I was unable to contribute to their efforts directly, and my membership eventually lapsed. Later, researching the history of Boulton Paul Aircraft for a book, I made the decision to form the Boulton Paul Association. At long last, I found myself indulging in hands-on aircraft restoration, despite having little or no practical skill.

After seven years' working on the restoration of the cockpit of Balliol WN149, which involved a large amount of corroded metal, a growing hatred for split pins, the donation of much blood to the cause, and the complete absence of wood, I acquired my own project – two halves of the fuselage of the anonymous Slingsby Cadet TX.1 – for the princely sum of £100. This was all wood and no metal (plus fabric, although there was not much of that to be seen), and I began on a new learning curve.

The restoration of the Cadet taught me one thing above all others – there is no point in simply dreaming about aircraft restoration year after year. For a minimal outlay I was restoring a genuine Second World War aircraft, and regretting all the previous opportunities to acquire aircraft that I had turned down over the years – the Typhoon cockpit in the Brownhills scrapyard back in the 1960s; the Horsa fuselages that were scrapped in nearby Albrighton in the early 1970s; the Miles Messenger, which was the last aircraft at Wolverhampton Airport. They had all been on offer for next to nothing; why had I not snapped them up?

During the restoration of the Cadet, I experienced a marvellous sense of freedom. When I decided to paint it as PD685, the Cadet used by No.43 ATC Gliding School at Walsall Airport during the war, I did not have to persuade a committee. I just did it. When I decided to install an instrument panel as fitted to post-war Cadet TX.2s, because it looked bare without one, I did not have anyone carping about a lack of authenticity, because wartime TX.1s had no instruments. (Their height and speed were controlled by the instructor on the winch, and a bar across the cockpit, which prevented the control column being pulled back too far.)

The Cadet was restored in my mother's double garage in Telford. According to the next edition of *Wrecks and Relics*, my Canberra cockpit and Antonov fuselage were also moving in there. They never did, but the suspicion that I was planning such a move might have created a serious family rift.

Buying a Canberra cockpit introduced me to a third, very different type of aircraft restoration, the one in which most amateurs are involved. The Balliol had been the restoration of a corroded mess, the Cadet as much like furniture-making as aircraft restoration, while the Canberra introduced me to the world of bits and pieces accumulation. Its restoration will involve little more than a strip-down and re-paint, but the major preoccupation is the tracking down and acquisition of the missing instruments and pieces of equipment. The world of the aerojumble – buying and selling, and swapping aircraft parts – became very important to me. (Incidentally, aerojumbles can make the world seem a strange place. At one Whitwick Aeromart I had some Russian electrical/radio boxes that I had salvaged from the rear fuselage of my Antonov AN-2 before it went for scrap. I did not really expect to sell them – I did not even know what they were – but someone was indeed prepared to pay good money for them.)

The Canberra also taught me that, if you choose a common aircraft to restore and preserve, you will be in direct competition with many others for the parts you require. However, you will also become a member of a select group of similarly afflicted individuals who will often pool knowledge and resources. For the Balliol, I was the only one looking for parts (of which there were very few available) and the only one buying, so anyone who had Balliol parts for sale knew where to go.

The Antonov is a different proposition. Finding genuine Russian parts is impossible, so starting with an almost complete airframe is important. Only the smashed canopy, broken by the scrapman's dreaded hydraulic grab, not by the aircraft's landing accident, has to be replaced. Unless another British AN-2 crash-lands without damage to the canopy, holiday in Eastern Europe seems to be the likely solution. Once I had joined the rear of the cabin to the front fuselage, the advantage of restoring a small airliner in the open air became clear. I put two small benches inside it, and on rainy days I could work in the dry, the aircraft becoming its own workshop. I would recommend an AN-2 workshop to anyone. The AN-2 also has its own air compressor (for blowing up its own tyres), but running pneumatic tools off a 1,000hp engine might be a bit too much.

Talk of scrapping the second Balliol cockpit owned by the Boulton Paul Association, WN534, led to me taking it on as another personal project. Since it was my own project I could plan to restore it just as a cockpit; I had wanted to do this with the first Balliol, WN149, but was overruled by a committee anxious to include it as the core of a full-scale model. Assessing WN534, I decided to make an advantage of the fact that one canopy rail had been scavenged for '149, and to restore '534 with one cockpit side missing, so that wheelchair access could be arranged, a rare facility in one- or two-seat aircraft. I also plan not to repair holes cut in the fuselage sides by the scrapman but to leave them, tidied up and covered with perspex, so that all the equipment and systems inside the cockpit can be seen, illuminated by spotlights. To this end, I shall be able to install pneumatic equipment from the lower fuselage of '149, which I had already restored, but which was not re-fitted because no one would ever see it, all fuselage panels having been repaired and re-attached.

I learned a huge amount in restoring the first aircraft, so the learning curve for subsequent aircraft has flattened out considerably. From the outset I dismantle the aircraft to its smallest components, and restore them immediately, to be loosely assembled alongside '534. Too much of '149 was dismantled and put aside to restore at some later date, with the risk of parts going missing every time the workshop was re-arranged, and of my forgetting where they should fit.

Once the Cadet fuselage was finished, I began to look for a new wooden-aircraft project. The acquisition of a couple of Miles Martinet canopies, and then a control grip, led me to consider building a Martinet cockpit from scratch. A convenient pattern aircraft was provided by the Museum of Berkshire Aviation's Martinet project at Woodley. Restoring the canopies and building a blind flying panel from scratch set the project under way, and the aircraft immediately acquired an identity, RG907, a Martinet that had been at Boulton Paul for winch trials in the late 1940s.

Having more than one project on the go at the same time is not difficult, and actually increases efficiency. At the Boulton Paul Heritage Project, I intend to work on the Antonov until it is ready for public viewing, and will then switch to stripping and re-painting the Canberra. Tracking down, collecting and installing parts for the Canberra, and all the other projects, is an intermittent activity that takes little actual time. Work on the Balliol mostly takes place in my workshop at home, as by far the greatest amount of time is spent dismantling pieces and stripping them down to bare metal before re-assembling them. All that needs to be done at Boulton Paul is to separate a piece from the airframe, and then fit the restored piece once it is complete.

The five cockpits that form the Black Country Aircraft Collection – Cadet, Canberra, Antonov, Balliol and Martinet – have recently been joined by a sixth. Having made two blind flying panels for the Martinet, in case one turned out a disaster, I decided to make the second one the first item in an accumulation of parts for a Defiant cockpit. Thinking ahead to the need to make a curved windscreen resulted in the Defiant cockpit getting an identity, that of the prototype K8310, which began with a two-piece windscreen with flat panels that was much easier to reproduce. Pilots' objections to the central pillar in this arrangement led to a switch to the one-piece windscreen.

The restoration/construction of the six cockpits should take me at least ten to twelve years, taking me past retiring age, when I will hopefully have even more spare time – provided of course that I have not been cured of this insanity by then.

Index